W9-BWF-619

DISCARDED

SISTERHOOD OF SPIES

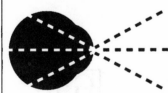

This Large Print Book carries the
Seal of Approval of N.A.V.H.

SISTERHOOD OF SPIES
The Women of the OSS

Elizabeth P. McIntosh

G.K. Hall & Co. • Thorndike, Maine

Published in 2000 by arrangement with Naval Institute Press.

G.K. Hall Large Print American History Series.

The text of this Large Print edition is unabridged.
Other aspects of the book may vary from the original edition.

Set in 16 pt. Plantin.

Printed in the United States on permanent paper.

Library of Congress Cataloging-in-Publication Data

McIntosh, Elizabeth P., 1915–
    Sisterhood of spies : the women of the OSS / Elizabeth P.
McIntosh.
       p.   cm.
    Originally published: Annapolis, Md. : Naval Institute Press,
1998.
    Includes bibliographical references.
    ISBN 0-7838-9155-5 (lg. print : hc : alk. paper)
    1. United States. Office of Strategic Services — History.
2. World War, 1939–1945 — Personal narratives, American.
3. Women spies — United States — Biography.   I. Title.
D810.S7 M375 2000
940.54′8673—dc21

00-044852

To the Sisterhood of Spies, those dedicated women who served their country in the Office of Strategic Services during World War II, and who passed on their trade craft together with a sense of direction in the shadow world of intelligence to their sisters in to-day's Central Intelligence Agency.

Contents

Preface

Sisterhood of Spies is based primarily on some 120 interviews with men and women who served in the Office of Strategic Services and the Central Intelligence Agency, and also with writers, scholars, and historians. Meetings or exchanges of material took place from California to Florida, from Thailand to Slovakia, from the United Kingdom to France.

To further substantiate the information in this book, the following archival sources were utilized: the National Archives and Records Administration (NARA) in Washington, D.C., and College Park, Maryland; the Library of Congress, Washington, D.C.; the Seeley G. Mudd Library, Princeton, New Jersey; the Eisenhower Library, Abilene, Kansas; the Archives Center, Churchill College, Cambridge, England; and the U.S. Military History Institute, Carlisle, Pennsylvania.

The following are among those OSS veterans, friends, and colleagues who helped collect photos from wartime albums, or translated French, Chinese, and German documents, or honed "anecdotage" stories into accurate archival accounts, or put into focus time-blurred memories of a long-ago war: Sylvia Ripley Addison, Elizabeth Blake, David S. Bruce, Laura Catling, Julia Child, the late William Colby,

Joseph E. Coolidge, the late Charles E. Cuningham, Thibaut de St. Phalle, Rene Defourneaux, Sir Douglas Dodds-Parker, David Donovan, Charles Fenn, Rosemary and Alexandra Gaiduk, Mark Gatlin, the late Albert Gleim, Mollie and John Hammerlund, Bernice Hanson, Marjorie Holms, Timothy J. Horan, the late Lawrence Houston, Catherine Huntington, Geoffrey M. T. Jones, Lucy Kirk, Suzanne Wheeler Klein, the late Robert Koke, Patricia Lane, James J. Leff, Shirley Long, Linda McCarthy, Larry McDonald, Charles Maechline Jr., Lani Elizabeth Makholm, Guy Martin, Christof Mauche, Marian Mayo, Margaret Patti, Barbara Podoski, Robert Powell, Edwin Putzell, Marguerite Rawdon-Smith, E. Bruce Reynolds, Marcia Ristaino, Kathlin and Ferol Smith, Pauline Spofford, Eleanor Summers, Carlton and Patricia Swift, John Taylor, Sedgwick Tourison, Laura Tuckerman Trieste, Bernard van Leer, John Winant, Marshall Windmiller, Mary V. Yates, and Maochun Yu.

An especial tribute goes to my husband, Frederick B. McIntosh, a former fighter pilot who in his later years has taken off into the new skies of cyberspace and transcribed my typewritten manuscript into computer-perfect copy.

In writing my first book about OSS, *Undercover Girl*, published in 1947, I was particularly fortunate to have Maj. Gen. William J. Donovan assist me. By that time OSS had been disbanded by President Harry S. Truman, and Donovan had returned to civilian life and his law firm, then located at 2 Wall Street, New York City. I had married a member of his firm, Richard Heppner, and we saw a great deal of Donovan and his family in New York and Virginia. In 1958 my husband and I spent several months with Donovan in Hong Kong, where they tried a case involving ownership of an air fleet.

Since no censorship had yet been invoked on OSS material, Donovan himself offered to read my manuscript as I was writing it, suggesting sources for further information and, in the process, establishing a basic friendship that lasted until his death. One of the treasured yet sorrowful memories I hold today of the general was a visit I made to see him at the Walter Reed Army Hospital, where he was to spend his last year before his death in 1959. Sitting up in his hospital bed, he held out his hand to me. His once wonderful mind was not connecting with the world around him, but there was something reassuring about his bright Irish smile and the blue eyes that seemed to be searching for reality. Behind him was a life of great courage, brilliant ideas that formed the new concept of central intelligence, and a worldwide network of devoted friends and family.

Introduction

Sometimes a bright light will flash across the dark corridors of memory, focusing on long-forgotten scenes from younger years. It happened to me recently on three memorable occasions.

The first flashback happened one warm spring day in 1994. I was standing in front of a white-columned building on a bluff overlooking the Potomac River in Washington, D.C. A ceremony was being held at a government facility, cumbersomely known for fifty years as the E Street Complex, a plot of land deeded in 1664 by England to a colonist, John Longworth. It had been wartime headquarters of the Office of Strategic Services (OSS), America's first central intelligence agency. Until that morning in 1994, the site had been used for covert operations by the successor to OSS, the Central Intelligence Agency (CIA).

An agency color guard lowered the flag in front of the Administration Building, folded it ceremoniously, and presented it to the CIA director, R. James Woolsey. He briefly noted "the tremendous debt of gratitude owed to the dedication, persistence, and sacrifice of women and men who had passed through these buildings." He then handed the flag to me. I was honored to accept it in the name of our late OSS leader,

Maj. Gen. William J. Donovan, and some 21,642 men and women with whom I had served in OSS during World War II.

That flag conjured up memories of a half a century before, of the shadowy figures of young men and women who had volunteered for duty behind enemy lines. They reported here, to our once secret headquarters building, which now stood empty, the handsome moldings and hardwood floors covered with dust and plywood.

In the southeast corner on the first floor was Room 122. This was General Donovan's command post, unmarked today as it had been during the war for security reasons. Up the steps of this now silent building I could see the older, more senior personnel hurrying to Room 122 for briefings. Here decisions were made by a blue-eyed Irishman, holder of the Medal of Honor for service during World War I, leaning over a large mahogany desk littered with top-secret documents. From this office were issued orders that sent OSS men and women to secret training camps where they learned to forge documents, dissemble, kill. Ensuing orders put them "on alert," that tense period when they must report to ports of embarkation for uncertain voyages to war.

During World War II, I had served in the hills of western China, one of the hundreds of OSS women stationed abroad from London to Chungking. A far greater number of women spent the war years in the United States working in support of our overseas operations, from cartography to cryptography, from filing reports to mailing out paychecks. While many regarded their work as routine and yearned to be involved in the exciting operations described in the cables and memos crossing their desks, they accepted their assignments as being equally important in the broad scheme of things.

We were so very young in those days, fighting for freedom and justice as we understood it, our way of life imperiled by the Axis enemy. Many of us were just out of college or had been lured away from careers to serve our country. We passed from that easygoing civilian life to military jurisdiction under the Joint Chiefs of Staff, to which OSS reported. I can still remember my first brush with rigid authority when a scowling sergeant, all spit and polish, ushered me into the fingerprinting room where I became another number on the military roster. I can see the wartime posters on the wall now: a large, almost pulsating ear reminding us that the enemy was listening; a dead soldier reminding us that someone had talked.

Even in those parlous days it was not easy to quash my inborn irreverence for the military. I saw this same disdain for discipline in the young OSS men, similarly just out of college, just into uniform. Instead of a crisp salute there was a casual gesture. Instead of "Colonel Little, sir," there was that friendly sergeant just out of

Harvard calling him Herb. Their uniforms were never starched but hung over their relaxed young bodies like comfortable lounge suits.

My overseas indoctrination continued over the weeks, at headquarters and at special training schools in Washington, Maryland, and Virginia. As law-abiding citizens we were authorized to contact, manipulate, and organize resistance groups, engage in espionage, initiate rumors, forge documents, dynamite rail bridges, and infiltrate enemy lines. The only crime we could commit was to get caught, to "blow our cover."

Although operations were compartmentalized, we crossed the lines at lunchtime and compared notes with our sister spies, chatting in line at the cafeteria, sharing rationed food and unrationed coffee. We envied those lucky girls who had already received orders — to London, Algiers, Bern, Istanbul, New Delhi, K'un-ming. Back in often crowded offices we waited for our own assignments, wrote reports, mastered cryptography, initiated propaganda supposedly originating from enemy sources, and learned to forge documents and double-talk our way out of classroom-rigged emergencies.

Most of us, men and women, were an undisciplined collection of volunteers selected almost at random, for many reasons, and for many objectives. Eventually, as the war progressed and our missions became more stabilized, OSS emerged as an essential arm of military planning in war zones. OSS personnel died fighting behind the lines from France to China. Some OSS women lived perilously in occupied areas, organizing guerrilla groups, unmasking traitors, subverting the morale of the enemy, or arranging safety nets for downed Allied fliers.

OSS veterans paid tribute to one of these heroic women in a second memorable event in the summer of 1994. I was part of this delegation, observing the fiftieth anniversary of the Slovak uprising against Germany in the village of Banská Bystrica. Ceremonies were led by our American ambassador to the United Nations (now Secretary of State), Czech-born Madeleine Korbel Albright. She noted that untrained Czech and Slovak partisans fought six Nazi divisions but were eventually forced to flee into the Tatra Mountains. Ninety Slovak villages were burned, and thousands of people were murdered. Among those casualties were members of an OSS Special Operations team. Twelve were captured in a hunting lodge; only two escaped to safety, led across winter mountains by a young Slovak schoolteacher, Maria Gulovich. She was with us that day in 1994.

Leaning against the door of the rebuilt rustic lodge, she recalled the yells of the German soldiers as they neared their quarry, and the voices too of her own townspeople, traitors, shouting in Slovak, leading the Germans to the OSS team. Gulovich and two other team members had just left the area for reconnaissance, but from their vantage point they could see their teammates, bound and under guard, leaving the lodge as the Nazis set fire to the building. As she finished her tragic story, high in the mountains drenched in sunshine against a backdrop of fir trees, across the stillness a young Slovak soldier sounded taps.

The summer of 1994 held one final flashback for me when America observed the fiftieth anniversary of D-Day. On that very special Memorial Day I had the honor to introduce President William J. Clinton at Arlington National Cemetery services, where he placed a wreath at the Tomb of the Unknowns. Around us, under Virginia's sloping hills, were buried the men and women who had fought for their country since the Civil War, their graves marked by row upon row of square granite stones.

Some fifteen OSS women veterans were with me that summer morning, and I spoke for all of them when I said that our wartime experience was one we would never forget. Beneath the bright sun I could again see the shadows of friends long gone: General Donovan, lying next to his wife, Ruth; OSS comrades, resting nearby in their final underground; my own husband, Col. Richard P. Heppner, who headed OSS in China, buried beside his best friend, Russell B. Livermore, an OSS colonel who fought with the resistance in Italy. Beyond another hill are the ashes of Capt. William Magistretti, the man responsible for the surrender of hundreds of Japanese in Burma. There are many more. The names, the faces, are blurred with time, but not those memories of half a century ago.

I hope this book can recapture and document for the reader that exciting period in our history when women served as a true Sisterhood of Spies on the battlegrounds of World War II.

PROLOGUE

"Wild Bill" Donovan
and the Origins of OSS

When they presented their laminated photo badges to guards at the OSS Administration Building in Washington, D.C., women clerks, secretaries as well as administrative assistants, the planning staff, and overseas liaison officers were admitted into a restricted part of that wartime intelligence organization.

They were all aware of the unmarked room on the south side of the building on the first floor where they might occasionally catch a glimpse of Maj. Gen. William J. Donovan. Usually he was in starched army uniform, flanked by aides. Sometimes he wore a well-cut Savile Row suit, befitting a Wall Street lawyer, swinging his leather briefcase as he strode briskly to his office. He was a handsome man in his late fifties with a sturdy soldier's build and great personal magnetism. Bruce Barton, one of Donovan's colleagues, once described him to Donovan's law partner, Edwin Putzell, as "a rosy-cheeked, smiling gentleman with a voice as soft as the leaf of a shamrock, a shining light in his blue Irish eyes, and a punch in each hand like the kick of an army mule."

To OSS personnel who signed an oath of secrecy when they were recruited to work in this shadow organization, Donovan was an inspiring yet unorthodox leader, a Republican with direct access to the Democratic president, Franklin D. Roosevelt; a man who had developed rapport with British intelligence and who eventually won grudging respect from the American military despite his unpredictable methods of operating.

Donovan began his military career in 1916 long before most of his OSS colleagues were out of elementary school. He commanded the New York National Guard on the Mexican border, hunting down the wily revolutionary Pancho Villa. It was Donovan's first brush with irregular warfare; he applied these basic tactics some twenty-seven years later when his OSS commandos slipped behind enemy lines in France. The members of his elite New York Guard, nicknamed the Silk Stocking Brigade, were whipped into shape by their unrelenting commander. They struggled on ten-mile forced marches with full field equipment, under scorching Texas skies, in desert heat. It was here, his friends of that era believe, that Donovan earned his nickname, Wild Bill.

When the Guards came home to New York to face the growing threat of World War I, they were combat-ready for more deadly conflict overseas. The Fighting Sixty-ninth Regiment, "New York's Finest," sailed for France with Donovan in 1917 to face some of the bloodiest battles in history. Most of his men were Irish; many had been with him on the Mexican border.

Memories of that war are described in Donovan's diaries, scrawled in pencil, now stored with many of his papers at the U.S. Military History Institute in Carlisle, Pennsylvania. Some excerpts were written under bombardment in trenches, others in hospital wards where he convalesced from leg wounds received in battle:

MARCH 7, 1918: Terrific bombardment by torpedoes. Twenty-two men buried in dugout. I spent most of the night there. "E" Company badly disorganized, caught in heavy shellfire and two gas alarms. I hit a man in the jaw to quiet him and the others. It worked. . . .

MARCH 25, 1918: Talked with our chaplain, Father Francis Duffy, this afternoon on death. He believes it to be an ingression. He felt our time is more than likely to come here. Both of us agreed. He also said that if I live, I will go far.

And finally, there was a poem he wrote on 4 April 1918 to his wife, Ruth Rumsey Donovan, in Buffalo, New York. She was the patrician daughter of one of Buffalo's leading families, mother of their two children, David and Patricia:

To My Wife

Little you'd care what I laid at your feet,
*   Ribbon or crest or shawl.*
What if I bring you nothing, sweet?
*   Nor maybe come home at all?*
Ah, but you'll know, brave heart, you'll know,
*   Two things I'll have kept to send:*
Mine honor, for which you bade me go,
*   And my love — my love to the end.*

Donovan did come home to Ruth, proudly marching up Fifth Avenue at the head of the Fighting Sixty-ninth, with Father Duffy beside him. Of the 3,507 men of the Sixty-ninth who went to France, only 1,400 returned. As they passed the reviewing stand, the band played a newly orchestrated march, "The Sixty-ninth Comes Back." It was written by Sgt. Maj. Joyce Kilmer, the American poet who died under fire, following Donovan into action at Meurcy Farm in France, near the Ourcq River.

For his heroic wartime leadership, the then Colonel Donovan became the most decorated soldier in this country's history. France gave him the Croix de Guerre with Palm and Silver Star and made him a Knight of the Legion of Honor. Italy bestowed upon him the *Croci di Guerra*. The ribbons he wore on his uniform represented America's highest awards: the Medal of Honor, Distinguished Service Cross, Distinguished Service Medal, and Purple Heart with Clusters. Later he was to receive the National Security Medal. Donovan placed his Medal of Honor in the Sixty-ninth Regiment Armory in New York City "in memory of fallen comrades to whom it belongs."

At thirty-seven, Donovan returned to Buffalo to practice law with the firm of O'Brien, Donovan, Goodyear, and Hellings. He had taken his law degree at Columbia University, where he was a star football player during his undergraduate years. The Donovan family lived in a comfortable Federal-style mansion on Ferry Street, with stables, grounds, and gardens. As always, he traveled more than he stayed home, with his antennae sharply tuned to world affairs, both in government and in business. But there was time between these trips to be with his children. His son David recalls that his father was a stern disciplinarian, but he also remembers the happy, quiet Sunday afternoons they spent walking the sandlots of Hayward and Elk Streets in Buffalo where boys played baseball, or along the waterfront where his father knew everyone they met.[1]

The Donovan family had settled in Buffalo

21

before the Civil War. The general's father, an Irish immigrant, Timothy Donovan, worked on the Erie and Lakawanna Railroad. The general believed that the Donovan house had been part of America's first organized underground operation, the slave route to freedom in the North. There were ten children in the Donovan family, only three of whom survived: Timothy, William, and Vincent.

William Donovan left Buffalo in 1924 when he was appointed an assistant attorney general in Washington. Here the family moved to a fourteen-room Georgetown house, once owned by columnist Walter Lippmann. Both senior Donovans were avid equestrians, and they later purchased a five-hundred-acre farm in Berryville, Virginia, deep in horse country. Here Ruth Donovan rode with the local hunt and is remembered galloping across the Virginia countryside during the war years on her magnificent bay, G. I. Joe. When William's law practice finally took him to New York City, the Donovans purchased an apartment at Beekman Place on Manhattan's East Side.[1]

The Donovan children grew up in the heady atmosphere of Washington and New York City, where their father had established his law firm on Wall Street. The children followed different roads in their development. Blue-eyed, vivacious Patricia was closer to her father. Thomas J. McFadden, a personal friend of the family and a partner in the Donovan firm, told me that Patricia and her father were alike in their great vitality and love of excitement.[2]

A yellowed newspaper clipping at the Carlisle archives reads, "There is a little girl who will be proud to hear the story of her father's heroism in World War One when she is older. She is little Patricia Donovan, Major Donovan's infant daughter, who was christened by Father Duffy from a helmet-font when the regiment was training at Fort Mills. She was called 'daughter of the regiment.' " Patricia's untimely death in an automobile accident at age twenty-two was one of the tragedies of Donovan's life. His hair turned gray almost overnight. Patricia had been on her way to resume studies at George Washington University on 8 April 1940 when she lost control of her car and was killed near Fredericksburg, Virginia.

David was closer to his mother. He never had a desire to study law or to join OSS. At heart he was a farmer. His second love was the sea. He joined the navy during the war and participated in the invasion of Sicily, where his father came aboard his ship as an observer. He was also part of the D-Day armada at Omaha beach and later took part in Pacific operations. After the war he came home to the Berryville farm to live.

In the years just before America entered the war, the general spent little time with his family. His own lucrative law practice took him abroad, and so did global travel at the behest of President Franklin Delano Roosevelt, an assignment in which Donovan acted as the president's own private unofficial intelligence agent. McFadden once noted that Donovan's travels were also a boon to FDR's personal hobby: Donovan obtained postage stamps in faraway places for the president's collection, including a rare Himmler stamp from the Reich.

In July 1940 the president sent Donovan to London to study the effectiveness of German fifth-column subversion of Western Europe and to observe how the British were facing the threat of a German invasion of their homeland. Europe from the North Sea to the Russian frontier was under the Nazi flag. Donovan was one of the first Americans to report back to Roosevelt that Britain could withstand a Nazi blitzkrieg only if strengthened with vitally needed resources and materiel from the United States.

Aware of Donovan's activities, officials of the British Secret Intelligence Service (SIS) invited him to review their system later in 1940. The British SIS counterintelligence files had been built on a vast collection of information on persons and organizations of every nationality that had come to the notice of authorities since the turn of the century. Of special value were the current files on German and also Communist Party agents, for which there was no comparable information base in the United States.

This early and full cooperation between the highly experienced British organizations and Donovan not only saved the OSS immeasurable trial-and-error periods in its development but was also probably one of the forces responsible for its survival.

On 18 June 1941, six months before Pearl Harbor, Roosevelt summoned Donovan to the White House to discuss the formation of America's first national intelligence-gathering agency. Both men felt that the United States would soon be drawn into World War II, and a unified wartime intelligence system serving both military and government requirements was imperative.

The outcome of this discussion a month later was the establishment of the Coordinator of Information (COI), the first U.S.-organized venture into the combined fields of espionage, subversion, propaganda, and related activities under a single, centralized intelligence agency. After a yearlong tumultuous trial period of intergovernmental turf struggles, mainly in the field of overt propaganda, COI operations were transferred to the Office of War Information, and the OSS functions were set up under the Joint Chiefs of Staff in June 1942.

President Roosevelt himself had authorized the establishment of the Office of Strategic Services in a military order signed 13 June 1942.[3] This newly formed service was authorized to collect and analyze strategic intelligence and to plan and operate special services: "All measures will be taken to enforce our will upon the enemy by means other than military action, as may be applied in support of actual or planned military operations; or in furtherance of the war effort; unorthodox warfare, guerrilla activities behind enemy lines; contact with resistance groups; subversion, sabotage and unorthodox or 'black' psychological warfare."

The OSS now faced the urgent need immediately to increase its facilities and personnel. Detractors at the time sneered at the composition of the agency as it developed, dubbing it "Oh So Social" because of the number of wealthy Ivy Leaguers among the early recruits. However, the need was urgent, and Donovan was forced to build his organization from scratch, with little time for tight security checks of incoming personnel.

Donovan began by engaging people whose loyalty was unquestionable: close friends, business clients, club members, professors from elite colleges, linguists, established writers. This nucleus of early spies-to-be was generally drawn from the upper social strata. They in turn recruited friends of similar backgrounds, and thus the elitist tone of OSS was established. For example, the top-secret Communications Branch in OSS (Commo) was set up by several Dartmouth College graduates. As a result, most of the early Commo operatives were hired directly from among this college's alumni, and they formed a tightly knit unit. Eventually they grudgingly admitted outsiders only if they would learn to sing all the stanzas of "Eleazer Wheelock," a Dartmouth song extolling the virtues of the college founder.

In the initial planning of his unorthodox agency, Donovan often journeyed back in history for inspiration. There was no blueprint in existence for constructing an Office of Strategic Services. One of the junior lawyers in the Donovan law firm, Richard Heppner, spent hours at bookstores and libraries for his boss obtaining material that would tell of earlier intelligence efforts.

Years later he told me that the general was particularly intrigued by John S. Mosby's *War Reminiscences.* In this book the Confederate partisan leader described operations in northern Virginia during the Civil War. Mosby routed Union cavalry, destroyed communications, and appropriated supplies. Beloved by his fellow Virginians, Mosby was also protected by them, and he eluded capture until the day the South surrendered. Donovan applied the essence of this modus operandi later in the war when OSS Special Operations (SO) groups were infiltrated into Italy and France to work with the local partisans. Heppner, later head of OSS in China, used these same tactics behind Japanese lines, where OSS teams operated with Chinese allies.[4]

Donovan's research dipped even further back

into history when he became fascinated by the arcane rites of the Delphic Oracle of ancient Greece, in which he saw the basic techniques of modern espionage applied. Donovan believed that the Temple of Apollo at Delphi on the slopes of Mount Parnassus, where the Oracle was located, was actually a center for intelligence operations. In those ancient times Delphi was a neutral Swiss-type area in the otherwise fragmented sociopolitical structure of Greece. Tribes from all over the Hellenic peninsula traveled to Delphi to hear Pythian priestesses on golden thrones intoning, in frenzied trances, messages from the Oracle, which were translated by priests. The Oracle answered all questions: public, private, religious, political. But to Donovan this was also a forum where secret messages could be sent through conniving priests; disinformation could be circulated and political power established. During the war, OSS secret radio stations, rumor mills, and false newspapers carried out this concept on a much broader basis. Deep in the heart of occupied China, twentieth-century OSS operators substituted a Buddhist monastery for the Temple of Apollo. Here at the base of two colossal golden Buddhas was hidden a Type B MKII radio transmitting information over a five-hundred-mile radius to OSS headquarters in K'un-ming.

As the war progressed, Donovan managed to

arouse resentment at the State Department and the Pentagon. Roosevelt continued to instruct him to deal directly with top foreign officials, including heads of state, rather than go through Washington's official channels. Roosevelt's death in April 1945 started a savage struggle for the control of America's postwar intelligence system. It ended in January 1946 with the establishment of an interim agency under President Harry Truman: the Central Intelligence Group (CIG).

In July 1947 the National Security Act was passed by Congress, and on 18 September, two years after OSS was dissolved, the Central Intelligence Agency took over the duties of CIG. The most important function of this new agency and its director was the coordination of the total intelligence effort of the United States. Donovan returned to his law practice in New York City, although he had hoped to become director of CIA in its early bumpy years. For political reasons "younger men" were selected, but the energetic general continued to lead an exciting quasi-political life for many years.

It was in early 1950, four months before the June outbreak of the Korean War, that General Donovan went to Hong Kong as counsel for the newly formed firm Civil Air Transport Inc. His job: to arrange the legal details of the transfer of seventy-three aircraft based at Kai Tak Airport, Hong Kong. These planes had just been purchased from the Chinese National-ist government by Gen. Claire Chennault and American businessman Whiting Willauer. However, the newly formed Chinese commu-nist government also claimed ownership. A legal battle for possession of the aircraft started in Hong Kong and finally went to the highest British courts in London before the planes were turned over to the American firm.

All the time he was in Hong Kong, Donovan battled with British intransigence and the Chi-nese determination to obtain the planes as le-gitimate property of the communists. The gen-eral was supplied with up-to-date intelligence from China by Jesuit priests who slipped regu-larly into Hong Kong from the mainland. He was forewarned that the Chinese communists would eventually enter the Korean War. When Donovan won the final court battle in London, he thereby denied the communists an air fleet that would have been used against the United Nations in that conflict.

In 1953, when he was named ambassador to Thailand, Donovan undertook an important mission for President Dwight D. Eisenhower. The new ambassador's initial task was to evac-uate Chinese Nationalist troops from Thailand to Taiwan. These men had earlier retreated into Thailand when the communists took over China. By relocating them, he was able to remove any pretext for a Chinese invasion of Thailand. Establishing amnesty centers, Donovan — accompanied by State Department representative Kenneth Landon and a small detachment of U.S. Marines — hiked along jungle trails in northern Thailand to these centers and was able to arrange for some four thousand Chinese to be flown to Taiwan.

As reported in *Newsweek* magazine on 26 July 1954, "Donovan could take credit for another achievement: the creation of an anti-communist bastion in Thailand and the welding of a first class fighting force in a nation known more for its peacefulness than bellicosity. Donovan stopped a communist infiltration in Thailand. He created an atmosphere of trust towards the United States and began operations to bolster Laos and Cambodia. Despite his 70 years, he moved about the country constantly, getting to know the people."[5]

One of Donovan's last contributions to Thailand's development was to involve the United States in redirecting the Mekong River across the Khorat plateau and building dams, navigation systems, power plants, and irrigation networks. The work was done, in part, by the Army Corps of Engineers, which arrived in Thailand to build the great dam that stands today as a tribute to William Donovan. Eisenhower awarded him the National Security Medal for his service.

After Thailand, Donovan had only a few years left before he was afflicted with arteriosclerosis and his remarkable brain began to atrophy. He died in the Pershing Suite of Walter Reed Hospital on 8 February 1959 and was buried with full military honors at Arlington National Cemetery. His brother, the Reverend Vincent C. Donovan, officiated. Donovan's obituary in the *New York Times* of 10 February 1959 read, "He was a living symbol of what we think of as plain, simple, unadulterated courage. No one will remember whether he was right or wrong, wise or mistaken. No one can forget that he was always brave. We need that legacy."

The memories of their wartime experiences, and of the man who led them, are recalled whenever veterans of the OSS meet. There is a special camaraderie that has united the men and women who served with Donovan. Their ranks today are rapidly thinning, but memories survive. In the course of writing this book I have interviewed more than one hundred women OSS veterans. Their story has never been told completely until now.

Looking back in time, most of us agreed that we learned to apply our knowledge, skills, and enthusiasm to a career never taught before in schools; and more important, we believed in our mission and in the man who led us through those long-ago war years.

CHAPTER 1

Invisible
Apron Strings

General Donovan once summarized his concept of the role of women in OSS:

> The great majority of women who worked for America's first organized and integrated intelligence agency, spent their war years behind desks and filing cases in Washington, *invisible apron strings* of an organization which touched every theater of the war.
>
> They were the ones at home who patiently filed secret reports, encoded and decoded messages, answered telephones, mailed checks and kept the records. But these were the necessary tasks without the faithful performance of which an organization of some 21,000 people, with civil and military personnel, could not be maintained. Upon their performance depended the security of the organization.
>
> There were some, however, who had important administrative positions and others

33

with regional and linguistic knowledge of great value in research, whose special skills were employed in exact and painstaking work such as map making and cryptography.

Only a small percentage of the women ever went overseas, and a still smaller percentage was assigned to actual operations behind enemy lines.[1]

These ladies were the "glamour girls" OSS veterans remember when they recall that time in their lives when "the whole country was full of confidence, competence, daring, and *joie de vivre*," as *New York Times* columnist Russell Baker once described these war years to me.

When the general and his staff created the early structure of OSS, they organized it into seven principal working branches, all of which employed women either in support functions or in operations.

The first branch to be organized in COI, the Coordinator of Information, and later transferred to OSS was *Research and Analysis* (R&A). Here was collected and analyzed all overt and covert material for use in planning subversive operations. R&A libraries also maintained a vast collection of books, biographies, and geographical studies that might supply background material in research.

Another important branch was *Secret Intelli-*

gence (SI), tasked with obtaining covert information, primarily through secret means, usually through agents in the field.

Special Operations (SO) was a clandestine branch that organized and executed physical subversion including sabotage, fifth-column activities, and guerrilla warfare.

A similar action branch, the *Operational Group* (OG), was composed of highly trained foreign-language-speaking soldiers skilled in sabotage and use of small arms. They were usually paratroopers.

The *Maritime Unit* (MU) supplied resistance groups that executed maritime sabotage through devices such as explosive limpets attached by divers to enemy shipping.

The *Counterintelligence Branch* (X-2) worked closely at the outset with British intelligence and protected American espionage interests. It surveyed, controlled, and manipulated enemy intelligence operations. In addition, X-2 was responsible for handling information and operations derived from British penetration of the German Enigma machine cipher system, which laid open the Nazi military, naval, air, and secret intelligence communications to Allied agents. The code name of this top-secret activity was Ultra.

There was also *Morale Operations* (MO), which today is often called disinformation. Wartime MO was "black" propaganda, as distinguished from "white" or official news provided by the Office of War Information, now the Voice of America. MO was subversive, its sources disguised and its product disowned by our government if an operation backfired. "Persuasion, penetration and intimidation are the modern counterparts of sapping in the siege warfare of former days" — that was how General Donovan once described MO to me. I was assigned to MO, partly because of my knowledge of the Japanese language, but mostly because of my newspaper experience. After spending three years in MO disguising the truth, slanting stories, and developing rumors, I had great difficulty writing a straight news story once the war was over.

All these operations were supported by a secret communications center located in the basement of the Washington OSS Administration Building. This area was out of bounds to most of OSS, but it was a clacking, noisy home to the men and women who spent six-hour shifts sending and receiving coded messages to and from OSS detachments as far away as the China coast. To these operators General Donovan was 109, his code number known around the world at all OSS "commo" stations.

Few women took part in the activities of SO, OG, or MU, although some women did attend OSS parachute schools commanded by Col. Lucius O. Rucker, a veteran of 119 jumps himself. He trained thirty-eight hundred men, including Americans, Chinese, Thai, British, and

French, and thirty-eight women. In the more than twenty thousand jumps that he supervised, only fifty trainees refused when the time came to jump. Not one of those was a woman. The only complaint the women had was the extensive bruises they sustained when the parachute harnesses snapped roughly against their breasts in jumping.

In the early days of OSS one indispensable woman, Lucy McGuire, was responsible for organizing headquarters offices and responding to the needs of OSS branches abroad. McGuire, secretary to both Donovan and his executive officer, Col. Otto C. Doering, helped create the first OSS administrative office. She once told me that it was set up in a haphazard fashion similar to the general's law firm in New York, with no organizational charts, no maps on the wall, and no central personnel file. To McGuire, those were challenging days. Couriers arrived at headquarters with bags of mail from all over the world. McGuire and her associates sifted through them and made certain the material was stamped and routed to the correct offices or individuals.

Another stellar player was Margaret Griggs, who also began as Donovan's secretary and by war's end was managing OSS Secret Intelligence files. Known to all as Maggie, she once recalled to me a bit of sage advice from her boss: "It's OK to stumble, as long as you fall forward."[2] Griggs also helped recruit women for OSS, following the general's rule of thumb that "the right type of office worker was a cross between a Smith College graduate, a Powers model, and a Katie Gibbs secretary." The "right types" were often difficult to snare because of the high-priority recruiting programs of the newly established women's branches of the armed forces. The army WACs, navy WAVEs, and Marines offered couturier-designed uniforms and high adventure for those young American women who could qualify.

One of Griggs's problems was that she couldn't tell OSS recruits what kind of work they would be doing. "We cautiously advertised in newspapers and magazines," she recalled.

Much of the work required the knowledge of a European, Arabic or Asian language. We also looked for women familiar with a foreign country who had resided overseas or attended schools abroad. These area experts usually were unfamiliar with office routines. I eventually hired civil service workers, and later, women in the military services who could cope with the typewriter and take dictation. Those with area skills were eventually transferred to operational desks or were sent overseas in responsible jobs. I recall, during those early days, meeting Maggie at a ten o'clock coffee break in the cafeteria in a state of unusual perturbation: "The Message Center wants a girl math shark," she groaned. "Research and Analysis wants an expert on Kachins and their tribal life styles; a colonel in Africa wired for a combination secretary-seamstress to sew agents' clothing so they'll look 'of the country' and not off a Brooks Brothers rack. Visual Presentation wants an artist for our London war room. Cartography wants a girl with steady hands to retrace lines on captured maps. And MO just called in for a lady VariTyper. What, may I ask, is a VariTyper?"[3]

The OSS Administration Building also became the home, as the organization grew, for voluminous files on operations, personnel, and war plans. Marian O'Donnell, a personal friend of Donovan, was in charge of his executive files. Before they went overseas, among other headquarters office workers were Julia McWilliams, who as Julia Child later learned to cook, and Aline Griffith, who after an exciting tour of duty in Madrid married a Spanish nobleman and became the well-known author Countess Aline Romanones.

The atmosphere at headquarters was relaxed but stimulating. Caroline Copeland Bland joined OSS when it was less than two months old and consisted of approximately one hundred persons. She worked with the Schools and Training Branch and eventually was sent to

Cairo and later Italy as an SI administrative assistant. "In the intervening years," she told me later, "I have forgotten the details of that tremendous experience, just as I was supposed to do. We were not allowed to keep diaries. Practically no one remembers now what a tremendous job Donovan accomplished in creating OSS. There was no precedent and no time for perfect organization. The job *had* to be done and all individuals involved, however successful they may have been in previous pursuits, were novices at this. It was very challenging."

Vivacious, blonde Irene Nelson was a front-office girl with a different job. Twenty-three years old, just married, she came in as secretary to Edwin J. Putzell Jr., a Donovan law partner and administrative assistant. She recalls those early days when the office was always buzzing with activity: "There was a special electric charge in the air whenever General Donovan came into our office."

Nelson had just been graduated from Simmons College in Boston, and her husband had been assigned to army intelligence at Arlington Hall near Washington. Since his unit was engaged in breaking the Japanese codes, neither of them could tell the other much about their day at the office: "I couldn't tell him when I came home that I had just typed up travel orders for Sterling Hayden, that handsome Hollywood hunk. He sat right there beside me while I was typing them. Sterling said he loved to sail and that he had left Hollywood because he wanted to serve his country. I cut the orders that sent him to England for commando training with the Argyll and Sutherland high-landers."

During jump training, Hayden tore a carti-lage in his knee and injured his spine. He was washed out of commando school but later went to Cairo for OSS where his special maritime know-how proved useful with MU. He helped organize a splinter fleet of fishing schooners and caiques to run the German blockade along the Dalmatian coast, and to deliver arms to the Yugoslav underground.

"And, of course," Nelson recalls, "there was another famous man I couldn't mention to my husband, but I got around that by telling him I had cut travel orders for Sean Aloysius O'Feeney. Just mentioned it over dinner. Didn't impress my husband, but it might have if I had told him that O'Feeney was the real name of the famous Hollywood director John Ford, in charge of the OSS field photo unit."

One of Ford's favorite actors, John Wayne, applied for a job with OSS but was not hired. Nelson remembers him vividly: "I couldn't be-lieve he was sitting there, right next to me at my desk." Wayne's application for a job stated that he was an actor and a very good horseback rider, and that his nickname was Duke. For some reason he didn't qualify for undercover work.

Security was fairly loose in those early days until an episode occurred featuring another administrative secretary, Louise Bushnell: "I was handling the general's appointments after working hours. A guard came in and said that there was a man with a gun, loose in the building and looking for Donovan. The guard told me to hide the general."

It took quick thinking, but Bushnell came through. "Down the hall was the ladies' room, and since all the clerks had gone home I took the general into the bathroom and sent him into the last stall. I told him to crouch on the seat with his feet up and not to move until I returned."

Bushnell said it was the longest twenty-one minutes of her life. The guard finally returned to say the coast was clear; they had captured the deranged intruder. She raced back to the ladies' room and got the general down from his uncomfortable perch. He grunted and told her, "I'm going to ask one thing of you. Don't ever tell anyone what just happened to me." When Bushnell finally told the story, long after Donovan had died, she referred to it as Operation Johnny on the Pot.

The war had transformed Washington almost overnight from a sleepy government town into a crowded, frantic metropolis. Nothing was more difficult than finding adequate housing. Owners of private homes were pressured to rent out extra rooms, and they in turn often charged exorbitant prices for spaces little larger than broom closets. Houseboat colonies sprang up along the Potomac River. The OSS Office of Personnel faced the same problem as other government agencies: where to house incoming bodies from all over the world?

Wanda Di Giacomo started her OSS career in Personnel, tasked with finding living quarters for the growing OSS contingent anyplace in the District of Columbia or in nearby communities in Virginia or Maryland. "It was especially hard when action shifted from Europe to the Far East and OSS people were swarming back from Italy, France, England, looking for temporary accommodations," she told me. Yet another problem was financial. Di Giacomo said that some of the wealthier women who came to work for OSS didn't have to worry about money. They could afford apartments at good hotels such as Wardman Park or the Sheraton, but girls living on a clerk's salary had trouble making ends meet from paycheck to paycheck.

Di Giacomo was later transferred from Personnel to Covert Operations at a training area over a converted warehouse in Roslyn, Virginia. "After my work in Personnel, this was the pits," she recalled wryly. "Bathroom facilities were terrible. I had to share them with men. And what a collection! The place was always full of agents: Chinese, Arabs, French, even Germans, coming and going. And no one ever used their right names."

Here agents were taught basic trade craft: how to make surreptitious entries, blow safes, and steam letters open, according to Di Giacomo. "Many of the so-called teachers were actually safecrackers and other questionable types, but they really knew their business. Some of them had jail terms behind them before OSS picked them up." Di Giacomo admitted that she picked up a few tricks from these instructors, and after all these years she can still steam open a letter. "But it's not the same as in wartime," she grinned. "And besides, it would set a bad example for my grandchildren."

In those days women were usually referred to as "girls," both by men and by themselves. In spite of his busy schedule, gregarious General Donovan always found time to talk to employees. A telephone operator in the Administration Building recalls that he often stuck his head into their office to reassure the operators, "Without you girls, what would I do?"

Once the general picked up a couple of young OSS women who had been lunching at the nearby Watergate Inn, noted for its delicious hot popovers. He too had been eating at this popular Pennsylvania Dutch OSS hangout on the Potomac River. The girls had just started walking back to the office when his staff car idled by and the general opened the door. Elizabeth Sipe and Anne Boyd still remember the incident: "He was absolutely charming. We rode back to the office in style, but there was no one around to notice us driving up in the general's limo. That was one operation we didn't keep secret!"

Later in the war the general gave another OSS girl a ride all the way from Washington to K'un-ming, China, aboard his special plane. Twenty-two-year-old Virginia Rathbun had finished a tour of duty in Cairo, had returned for reassignment in Washington, and was cleared, with orders, to depart for China. There was space on Donovan's plane for one more passenger.

Rathbun was told to have her passport stamped not only for the China theater but also for Burma, India, and the European and Mediterranean theaters of operations. "General Donovan was very busy on that trip," Rathbun recalled. "We landed in London for two days of business. The general set up his offices at Claridge's Hotel, where he met with a constant flow of people, including Lord Louis Mountbatten and his wife, Edwina, who came over for afternoon tea." Rathbun remembered the trip with nostalgia: "It was a great adventure for me, especially since I met my husband-to-be in K'un-ming. He was Gilbert Stuart, a handsome Australian soldier of fortune, fighting with the Chinese commandos." Hers was one of the scores of wartime romances that were sparked in OSS detachments around the world.

Meanwhile, the war was being fought on all fronts. OSS was expanding its operations: infiltration behind the lines in France, black propaganda campaigns against the Nazi's Third Reich, intelligence collection worldwide. New OSS offices were established in London, New York City, San Francisco, Los Angeles, Seattle, and later Honolulu. In Hollywood there were training areas for radio monitoring and photography. At Catalina Island, off the California coast, MU units learned underwater-demolition techniques. In Washington, temporary buildings sprouted along the south side of the Reflecting Pool below the Lincoln Memorial. Safe houses and training areas were assigned throughout Washington, Maryland, and Virginia, including the Congressional Country Club, where agents handled live explosives using the newest OSS demolition devices to blow up the fairways.

One of the earliest and most effective programs Donovan recommended was the intelligence penetration of North Africa. He presented his plan to President Roosevelt on 10 October 1941, two months before Pearl Harbor, when America still had access to the area through business interests, Axis armies were pushing toward Egypt, and British defenses were weakening.

Eventually North Africa became the testing grounds for OSS. Initiated in January 1942, the first large-scale operation involved placing undercover agents to gather intelligence, prepare sabotage units in the face of a possible German invasion, and prevail upon military groups in North Africa, such as the Vichy French, to support an Allied invasion, code-named Torch.

Landing operations in North African coastal areas began on 8 November 1942. Some 107,000 Allied troops went ashore over a stretch of almost two hundred miles while seven Luftwaffe squadrons fruitlessly circled the Mediterranean, three hundred miles east, to bomb a "Malta-bound" convoy. This costly error by the Nazis was the result of a large-scale deception plan initiated by OSS operators.

OSS supplied the invasion fleet with detailed information, up until H-Hour and beyond, as to what to expect at each landing site, working from OSS maps and diagrams of port locations and facilities. The whereabouts of the Vichy French warships in the Mediterranean was also an important factor. These support operations, developed during the planning of Torch, established the value of OSS in future military maneuvers. It had all started when ten American agents under State Department cover began "working" North African facilities. Col. William Eddy, a highly decorated intelligence officer during World War I, was the eventual leader of this special group.

Donovan, in Washington, had been in constant touch with his North African team and had masterminded the planning of this intelligence penetration so vital to Operation Torch. One of his assistants on this project was Eloise Randolph Page, a debutante from Charleston, South Carolina, who started her career with OSS as executive secretary to the general. Page recalled that as the months dragged on and the invasion date drew closer, she became more involved in the actual implementation. "I remember, somewhat proudly," she told me, "how some of these plans originated in the general's office, and that I not only typed them but discussed them with him as we worked late into the night to meet the deadline."

But there was one important requirement levied on the OSS that neither Page nor the women working with her at headquarters at that time could fulfill. British and American military intelligence requested that if at all possible, the French naval codes, held at the French embassy in Washington, be obtained before Operation Torch was launched.

This mission was accomplished by an American woman whose zest for adventure had led her to work as a spy for the British prior to American involvement in World War II. Fortunately, she was available for this OSS assignment while retaining her ties to the British Security Coordination in New York City. Her code name was Cynthia, and she was assigned to work with another OSS recruit, Col. Ellery C. Huntington. Their mission: obtain and copy the French naval codes without blowing their cover.

CHAPTER 2

Code-Room
Mata Hari

When he applied for a job in January 1942,
forty-eight-year-old Ellery C. Huntington Jr.
hoped for an overseas assignment, possibly behind enemy lines. His credentials were impeccable. He had seen service in France during World
War I. He had played football against Eisenhower as a star quarterback at Colgate and knew
him personally. He had taken his law degree at
Harvard and was a highly respected New York
attorney specializing in corporate law. He had
traveled extensively and knew French, Italian,
Spanish, and some German. He spoke with a
soft Tennessee accent.

A squash-playing friend of General Donovan,
Huntington was immediately accepted for duty.
After his security clearance, he was promoted
to the rank of colonel by the War Department.
He was named chief of the newly established
Security Branch on 8 May 1942 and under-
went a crash course in "spymanship" at a
training camp in Virginia.

His first assignment came as something of a shock to this erstwhile defender of the law. Colonel Huntington was ordered to work on an illegal break-in of the Vichy French embassy in Washington to steal French naval code books from a safe in a locked and guarded room. His team would include an OSS safecracker known only as the Georgia Cracker and a French embassy attaché who had been seduced by a female agent, code name Cynthia, working for both British and American intelligence. Plans called for the code books to be removed to a safe room at the Wardman Park Hotel, photocopied, and returned within four hours to the chancery without incurring the suspicion of the embassy staff, the night watchman, or his alert guard dog. In addition, the new security chief was to avoid at all costs an FBI surveillance team that had the embassy and the female spy under watch for alleged pro-Nazi activities. Huntington was also given an alias for contacting Cynthia: Mr. Hunter.

It was not until General Donovan briefed him on the true purpose of this mission that Huntington could approach the assignment with enthusiasm. The naval codes that Cynthia would obtain from the embassy had been requested by both the American and British high commands and were considered essential to the upcoming invasion of North Africa, Operation Torch. William Stephenson's British Security Coordination (BSC) in New York and General

Donovan's office were instructed to cooperate in this venture, and Cynthia would be the key to its success. Eventually Huntington himself would be part of the OSS preinvasion infiltration of North Africa.

At a meeting with BSC officials on 10 March 1942 it was determined to schedule the embassy break-in for mid-June. Huntington would have the entire month of May to organize his team. His first step was to establish contact with the mysterious Mata Hari upon whom the BSC placed such reliance. He was impressed with her record: earlier she had helped obtain German and Italian codes, and she had also developed an intimate relationship with one Charles Emanuel Brousse at the French embassy. With his connivance she had supplied BSC and COI/OSS with a steady stream of diplomatic cable traffic between Vichy France and the Washington embassy.

Travel orders were issued for Colonel Huntington, "within a radius of 500 miles from Washington, D.C. for the purpose of performing official business." In late March 1942 he traveled up to New York City and went directly to the Ritz Carlton Hotel. He was pleasantly surprised when he knocked on the door of a suite in the hotel. The woman who answered was tall and slim with bright auburn hair, a cleft chin, and large, deep green eyes. Her voice was throaty, almost sensuous, but there was a lilt in her greeting. Stylishly dressed, poised, and elegant, this was Cynthia.

According to the information supplied to Huntington by BSC, Cynthia had been working for Stephenson since 1940. Born Amy Elizabeth Thorpe on 22 November 1910 in Minneapolis, Minnesota, she was the daughter of George Thorpe, a much-decorated former Marine Corps officer. Her mother had graduated with honors from the University of Michigan, then studied at the Sorbonne in Paris, the University of Munich, and later Columbia University. She was, as her daughter once wrote in her diary, "a passionate believer in the discipline of good manners and the rituals of society."[1]

Amy Thorpe inherited her father's love of adventure and her mother's inquisitive, bright mind. She studied in France and later in private schools in the United States, made her debut in Washington, and spent summers at Newport, Rhode Island. It was during this frivolous period in her life that she met Arthur Joseph Pack, a commercial secretary at the British embassy. They were married in April 1930. They had two children, Anthony and Denise, neither of whom lived much of the time with their family. Their mother opted for boarding schools and foster homes for these siblings who did not fit into her exotic mode of life.

Cynthia and her husband traveled to European and South American posts, where she conducted a series of foreign intrigues with assorted admirers. She once wrote in her diary, "I love to love with all my heart, only I have to appear cool. Life is but a stage on which to play. One's role is to pretend, and always to hide one's true feelings." When Huntington met Cynthia, her marriage to Joseph Pack was dissolving in divorce. Her amorous relationship with Brousse would culminate after the war in her marriage to the Frenchman who had dared so much for her during his tour of duty in Washington.

Debonair, balding Colonel Huntington, with a pronounced nose and blue-gray eyes, immediately bonded with Cynthia. They became a smooth working team. She respected his confident approach to problems and enjoyed — unusual for her — a father-daughter relationship with him. Their friendship lasted well after the war with exchanges of letters, mostly written by Cynthia, full of gossip, good humor, and information. She was a worldly woman who knew how to communicate.

The colonel and the spy got down to business almost immediately. In her suite, Cynthia dutifully identified herself as working for Mr. John Highroad, whom Huntington knew perfectly well as a senior BSC officer, John Pepper. He introduced himself as Mr. Hunter and outlined his plan for supporting her mission. Cynthia had already been briefed by Mr. Highroad on the urgent need to obtain the codes. Cynthia had assured him that she and Charles Brousse could handle the problem. However, in her diary Cynthia admitted to being worried about her ability to handle it: "I was apprehensive about what I had promised. I worried that I had led my chiefs into placing too much confidence in my capabilities."

Huntington's boss, General Donovan, was also concerned. If the operation failed, it could cause an international incident of major proportions. A presidential directive gave OSS limited power for subversive activities against neutral countries within the Western Hemisphere. "An embassy is a foreign territory," Donald Downes, an OSS officer later assigned to Huntington, cautioned Donovan. "Entering a foreign embassy clandestinely and borrowing code books is full of great risk for everyone concerned."[2]

There was also top-level concern about Huntington's ability as an untested though possibly overzealous neophyte agent. Donovan's aide, Col. Edward G. Buxton, warned that the general "had his hands full reacting, not always positively, to Ellery Huntington's schemes."[3]

It was also in mid-April of that year, as plans for the embassy break-in proceeded, that the political scene in France changed radically. The venerable Marshal Pétain was replaced as head of the Vichy government in France by pro-Nazi Pierre Laval. As Laval announced over French radio, "My return to power is significant to everyone. For a long time I have always maintained that reconciliation between France and Germany is essential for the peace of Europe." Shortly afterward, five members of the Washington French embassy staff resigned on the grounds that they could no longer support Laval's policy. Vichy France had now become a tool of the Nazi regime.

In this climate of indecision and disenchantment, Huntington and Cynthia began to make concrete plans for their part in the acquisition of the codes. As head of the OSS security office, Huntington had access to other sections within his organization dealing with undercover work, specifically the Special Operations Branch headed by Donald Downes, organized "to meet any situation that might arise." Huntington's own office was equipped with necessary wiretapping devices, special-purpose cameras, and, most important, an expert safecracker whose skill with locks and combinations had led him to one unlucky caper, and from there to a Georgia prison. He was one of many former convicts released from prisons and employed by OSS after agreeing to accept dangerous wartime assignments. To consolidate the operation, Cynthia had taken an apartment at the Wardman Park Hotel. It was here that her lover Brousse lived with his wife, and where the OSS security team moved to set up their photographic equipment.

After her New York meeting with Huntington, Cynthia flew back to Washington and was scarcely prepared for the swiftness with which her controller acted. She had hardly unpacked when she heard a knock at her door. She opened it warily to see a man in work clothes carrying a "large pump-like device."[4]

"I'm the exterminator," he barked loudly and pushed his way into her suite.

For a brief moment, Cynthia panicked. Had the Nazis or the Vichy French finally caught up with her? How had she blown her cover? Inside the room, as she closed the door, the man winked at her: "I'm from the OSS," he said sotto voce. "I'm checking your room for 'bugs.' "

Under cover as a pest-control worker, he logically could have been hired by the management to exterminate the cockroaches and rodents that infested old hotels such as the Wardman Park. Cynthia watched as he systematically searched under wall panels, floorboards, and phone outlets for bugs of another variety. Once he had ascertained that Cynthia's suite was free of electronic devices, he returned to the OSS safe room in the hotel with his report.

Cynthia and her OSS case officer held many careful planning sessions working from a ground plan of the French chancery provided by Brousse. The safe containing the codes was in the naval attaché's office; somehow Cynthia must arrange to break into the safe, remove two bulky code books the size of large family Bibles, get them to the OSS photo team at Wardman Park, and have them returned within a few hours!

At this point Huntington was introduced to Brousse. The Frenchman was fifty years old, a handsome, robust man with a twinkle in his eye. Several times divorced, he was currently married to an American woman of some wealth, the former Catherine Calhoun Graves, great-great-granddaughter of U.S. vice president John C. Calhoun.

Cynthia's assessment of Catherine Brousse allayed Huntington's fears about possible repercussions from a jealous wife: "She is not possessive nor spirited and is mentally and physically a doll type, absolutely guileless and rather helpless as a result of delicate health. She is not interested in her husband emotionally, but is dependent upon him and his judgment. She is not female, but feminine."[5]

Cynthia's affair with Brousse had begun in May 1941, when she was asked by BSC to infiltrate the Vichy French embassy in Washington and establish a relationship with either the ambassador, Gaston Henry-Haye; his counselor, George Bertrand-Vigné; or Brousse, then an aide to the ambassador. Posing as a freelance writer, she was able to obtain a two-hour interview with the ambassador and also to meet Brousse, who was immediately attracted to this

58

American woman. She spoke French like a native and seemed more interested in him than in the ambassador. He sent her a bouquet of roses the next day, leading to a second meeting at her Georgetown home where they made love that afternoon. From that day on, Brousse became more and more passionately involved with Cynthia, and she became his case officer as well as his mistress.

Brousse had started work at the embassy in 1940. He was from Perpignan in the Pyrénées-Orientales, near the Spanish border. He was a bombardier with the French air force during World War I, and at the start of World War II he worked with Anglo-French air intelligence until France collapsed. Before leaving France he was president and co-owner of a leading regional newspaper string in the Perpignan region.

Cynthia appealed to her lover's anti-Vichy sentiments and was soon receiving daily resumés of embassy cable traffic. Eventually, when the delicate job of breaking into the code room began to take shape, it was up to Cynthia to convince Brousse that he would be acting as a loyal Frenchman, fighting Hitler through Allied channels. Brousse at this point did not know that Cynthia was also working for the British. Like so many of his countrymen, he felt that England had betrayed France, first by retreating in the face of the German invasion of his homeland, and more specifically by destroying French warships at Mers el-Kébir near Oran, North Africa, to prevent the warships from falling under German or Italian control.

It was vital that Brousse join the team as a witting and willing agent. After urgent sessions with her case officers in New York and Washington as the time grew shorter, Cynthia called her lover and asked him to meet her at her apartment. She came right to the point: "I must have the naval ciphers!"

Brousse looked at her in disbelief. "It's impossible. I am not authorized to enter the code room."

"Please, Charles, please. This is the way we shall handle it."

Brousse finally succumbed to the plan as she outlined it to him, partly because he was already so deeply involved in the conspiracy, partly because of his infatuation with this beautiful and bewitching woman.

The next night Brousse put Cynthia's plan into motion. He casually walked along with the night guard of the embassy as he was making his rounds. He confided that he had a problem. There was this girl he was seeing, without, of course, the knowledge of his wife. Because of his position at the embassy, it would be risky to take her to a hotel room; his wife might discover his infidelity. It was difficult to get away from home unless he was working at the office. He would like to "work late" some evenings, and if his wife telephoned the office, he would be able to answer the phone. Brousse begged the guard to help him, slipping him a generous bribe when the man hesitated.

The ploy worked, and for the next few weeks in early June the security guard stayed conveniently out of sight while Brousse and his "girlfriend" spent several late-night hours together on a comfortable sofa in one of the two ground-floor salons at the chancery or in Brousse's office. When they left after each assignation, there was the usual friendly handshake with the guard, a pat on the head for his dog. The guard respected Brousse's position at the embassy, but he also seemed to get vicarious enjoyment from *les amourettes* of a fellow countryman and a very beautiful woman.

On the night of 19 June 1942 the plan for the break-in of the chancery was activated. By then both Cynthia and Brousse trusted the night guard, who had respectfully ignored their midnight trysts. Cynthia had some reservations about the alert guard dog, which had become accustomed to them but not to any other intruders.

They drove up to the embassy building with the Georgia Cracker hidden in the back seat of the car, which they parked across the street. They appeared at the entrance to the embassy in gala spirits, arm in arm, with two bottles of champagne. They explained to the guard that they were celebrating the anniversary of the day they had met and wanted him to join them in a friendly toast to their happiness. The wine was passed around several times. The second glass the guard received contained a dose of Nembutal, which Cynthia had been given by her BSC case officer. As planned, the guard went to sleep very quickly, and Brousse slipped a stronger dose into the dog's drinking water.

Soon they were able to let the Georgia Cracker in the front entrance of the embassy, past the sleeping guard and his equally laid-out dog. They led the Cracker to the locked code-room door, which he quickly opened. Once inside, the safecracker went to work.

As Brousse later wrote, "After many weeks of careful preparation under the supervision of Mr. Hunter we have on 19 June entered the naval room of the Embassy in most dangerous conditions at 1 A.M. with a specialist in safes brought from New York by the American service. After many hours of work, he found the secret of the safe."[6]

Unfortunately, it was nearly four o'clock in the morning when the Georgia Cracker was able to open the safe to reveal the large code books. Cynthia was torn. There were the books, but it was too late to remove them, take them to the hotel for photo reproduction, and return them; by that time, cleaning crews would be arriving and the embassy would be opening for business. Cynthia longingly eyed the two big black books but allowed the Cracker to close and lock the safe. He wrote down the combination for her — "4 left 5; 3 right 20; 2 left 95; 1 right 2; stop" — and the three left the embassy as the guard dog was just beginning to twitch. The quick-acting, short-lived barbiturate would leave no traces, and the guard would feel only a slight hangover.

Encouraged by the initial venture, both BSC and OSS handlers agreed that Cynthia and Brousse should make another attempt to obtain the code books on 21 June. Unfortunately the Cracker would not be available, but Cynthia would attempt to open the safe with the combination now in their hands. A hesitant Brousse agreed but refused to drug the guard a second time.

The pair arrived around midnight and spent an hour laughing and smoking in the salon. After they heard the guard start on his tour of the grounds, Cynthia slipped into the code room. She nervously began to twirl the safe's dial the way the Cracker had instructed, but nothing happened. She recalled his testy remarks about the safe: it was too old, it was not well lubricated. Brousse tried to read the numbers to her so she could concentrate, but still the safe would not open. It was nearly two o'clock before Brousse insisted that they give up for the night. They left the embassy and notified the OSS photographer parked across the dark street that the job was off.

It was after three in the morning when they reached the hotel and reported their failure to both Huntington and BSC's Mr. Highroad, who ordered Cynthia to immediately catch an early flight to New York. He met her at the airport and escorted her to a deserted stretch of beach on Long Island, where to her surprise the Georgia Cracker was waiting in a paneled truck. In a back seat he had installed a safe similar in design and age to the one at the French embassy. Sitting on makeshift seats facing the safe, the ex-con and Cynthia began a three-hour lesson in the secrets of safecracking. The Cracker not only made Cynthia memorize the combination but instructed her in the "feel" of a safe mechanism: hesitate between each turn of the dial; listen as the tumblers drop into place before going on to the next sequence. She finally passed his rigorous course to his satisfaction.

Exhausted, Cynthia flew back on the afternoon plane to meet Brousse and Huntington. It was agreed that there would be one final attempt to obtain the code books. In spite of her excellent tutelage in safecracking, Cynthia insisted that the Cracker be available as backup. They could help him enter the code room through a low window. It was also arranged that he would park across the street from the embassy and wait for an all-clear flashlight signal from Cynthia.

Brousse had earlier told the guard that he and his *amour* would spend a last night together; his wife was getting suspicious of his

64

long nights away from home. Brousse and his lady walked from the hotel to the chancery on Wyoming Avenue. It was a soft June night, and there was not much traffic in wartime Washington at that hour.

As they neared the chancery, they noticed two strange cars parked on the opposite side of the street with occupants in each car. Cynthia surmised that they were probably the FBI agents who had been randomly tailing her since February 1941 on suspicion of espionage.[7] Later she learned that a nosy hotel clerk had reported her to the bureau as a "trashy" woman who met strange foreigners in her rooms. She was not reassured by the presence of the cars, and her nervousness increased when they reached the embassy compound and there was no guard in sight. Brousse opened the door with his own key.

As they started their usual routine of smoking, laughing, and making low, intimate conversation on the couch in the salon, Cynthia became tense and uneasy. She strained to hear some sound that would indicate that the guard and his dog were on duty. After half an hour more of disquieting silence, Cynthia acted upon a sudden impulse. She sat up on the couch and began quickly to disrobe. When Brousse started to protest, she commanded him in a whisper, "Get undressed, quickly."

Cynthia's instincts were right on target. While Brousse was still reluctantly undressing, the door behind them opened without warning. A blinding flashlight beam swept across the room. The light caught Cynthia as she stood up, nude except for a string of lustrous pearls. She played the part to perfection, hiding her nakedness with both hands, mouth agape. The flashlight beamed over Brousse, half undressed on the couch. There was a throaty whispered "Merde" from an embarrassed guard, who stumbled out of the door with muttered apologies. This action on the part of the guard convinced both of them that the watchman had beaten a hasty retreat to allow them their last night together.

Shortly after the guard disappeared, they heard two cars driving away from the embassy. After a ten-minute wait, Cynthia picked the code-room door lock as the Cracker had instructed her, ran to the window, opened it, and signaled the Cracker, who was crouching below on the ground. He was inside in minutes and quickly knelt by the safe. He verified their hunch that the guard had gone out and talked with the occupants of the cars, and that they had driven away.

The Cracker swiftly opened the safe. They removed the two dark-colored code books, which they handed down to him as he climbed through the window. They heard him running toward the street and a waiting car. He was on his way to the Wardman Park Hotel, and their mission had been half accomplished.

It was a long, tense wait for Brousse and Cynthia. As he wrote later, "I do not wish to underline what could have been the consequences, outside the physical danger from the armed guard, if we had been caught."[8]

They waited in darkness, Cynthia sometimes slinking over to the code-room window to watch for the Cracker. Their nerves on edge, they smoked one cigarette after another, anxiously watching the doors, not daring to dress until they had heard from their teammate. Their deadline had been 4 A.M., and it was now almost 4:30. Had something gone wrong? Had the FBI picked up the Cracker? With his past record, they could easily incarcerate him. Would the guard return?

Finally, at about 4:40, Cynthia heard a movement under the window: the Cracker was back with the books. Swiftly he climbed through the window with an agility he had not lost since his early days as a second-story man. The books were replaced, the safe locks back in the position they had found them. Fingerprints were wiped clean, and the Cracker was out the window and gone. Brousse and Cynthia dressed quickly and left the embassy arm in arm. They arrived at Apartment 215B at the Wardman Park Hotel and entered a busy room filled with photo equipment, two cameramen, Huntington, and, most important, photographs of the code pages spread out to dry on several tables.

Huntington congratulated them both. Brousse left almost immediately to change his clothes and return to his office to make certain that everything there was in order. Cynthia, weary and spent, crept into her own flat for a well-earned sleep. In the weeks ahead she was transferred to OSS from BSC for more Washington-based operations, but with Donovan's approval she continued to collaborate with the British BSC until the war's end.

The precious ciphers were sent to London within forty-eight hours of the theft. OSS agents were the main beneficiaries of the codes, using them prior to and during the North African landings. Colonel Huntington was one of those OSS men for whom the Vichy codes proved invaluable in their undercover work with agents in North Africa before the landings.

Some twenty years later Ellery Huntington and his wife, Kitty, visited the Charles Brousses in France. Huntington had met attractive Helen Catherine DuBois in Algiers when she was secretary to the OSS intelligence chief there. They were married in 1946 and lived in New York and Washington until Huntington's death in 1987.

In an interview with Kitty Huntington I learned that she and her husband had been traveling in Europe in the early 1960s when Ellery said he would like to look up his charming colleague from OSS days, who was living with her husband in a tenth-century hilltop fortress near Perpignan in the Pyrenees. "I remember when we arrived at Perpignan, the only town near the Brousses' château, we were met by Brousse himself," Kitty Huntington recalled. "He took us to lunch in town because they could not afford servants at that period in their marriage. He had renovated Château Castellnou for his wife at great expense, and I gathered they were short of funds."

Brousse drove the Huntingtons up the mountainous road to the magnificent château with crenelated walls and large, spacious gardens. Mrs. Huntington had never met Cynthia, as her husband often referred to her, but she had been impressed by his tales of her beauty and charm. She continued: "Mrs. Brousse greeted us at the entryway, surrounded by three black and brown dogs with curly tails and sharp muzzles. She was talking to them the same way she did to us, as if they understood every word she said."

Mrs. Huntington was not prepared for the person who reached out unsteadily and shook her hand. By then Cynthia had been suffering several years with cancer. She welcomed Ellery especially effusively and showed them into the drawing room for tea.

"She was not the same woman Ellery had told me about," Kitty Huntington recalled somewhat sadly. "In her many letters to my husband she always wrote vivaciously, with good humor. These letters somehow reflected her great zest for living. Standing before us now was almost a shadow of this other person. I felt then that she would not spend much time at Castellnou."

While they were having tea in the lovely room overlooking the mountains, Kitty Huntington noticed a portrait of a beautiful woman, tall and slim, wearing a white gown, long gloves, and a tiara over short reddish blonde curls. "The woman in the portrait was so beautiful that I spontaneously picked it up and asked Mrs. Brousse who it was. She looked at me for a short time in silence, then smiled. She said it was she, then Elizabeth Thorpe Pack, when she had been presented to the king of England at a court levee in 1933."

Cynthia died a few months later, on 1 December 1963, and was buried in a park at Château Castellnou where she and Charles Brousse had lived during the happy years after the war.

CHAPTER 3

The Girls of R&A

The shadow world of spies and dark intrigue was a small albeit exciting part of OSS, but the Research and Analysis Branch (R&A) was the heartbeat of that organization. This branch produced economic, social, political, and military studies of all the strategic areas where OSS and Allied military operations were conducted. In R&A, Donovan created a corps of carefully selected and trained academicians with a knowledge of languages and research techniques. With no historical precedent, he raised from scratch an army of analysts with the same level of expertise as their counterparts in the intelligence services of Britain.

William L. Langer, a Harvard historian, headed R&A for four years. He built up his staff from leading academicians who in turn drafted their own students, assistants, and protégés, resulting in a fine pool of younger talent. As the war progressed, R&A also employed refugees who brought linguistic fluency, area knowledge, and cultural and political sensitivity to the branch. By war's end, R&A had grown into a professional corps of analysts respected for their intellectual credentials and for the modern scholarship methods they applied to the analysis of intelligence data. Under orders from Langer, R&A could not recommend or determine the strategy or tactical decisions of the war.

Some of the women of R&A are very much alive today, with memories that span half a century. Many served their wartime careers with OSS in Washington; several hundred were sent overseas. A few rose to relatively high positions, such as Dr. Cora DuBois, who became head of R&A Ceylon. In Chungking, Agnes Greene, who grew up in China and spoke the language, established the important Reports Section and was responsible for the collection of the R&A intelligence so vital to field operations. These were the exceptions. Many women with doctorates, former professors and even college department heads, found themselves working for younger men who generally lacked their experience and equivalent academic credentials.

One-time OSS-er Patricia Barnett, a Vassar graduate, was assigned to Southeast Asia in OSS after a short stint with the Institute of Pacific Relations in New York City.

"Some of the requirements they levied on me were mind-boggling at a time when our research files filled only one and a half drawers in a safe," Barnett recalled. "For example: in one day I would be asked to identify bombing targets in Southeast Asia; produce a plan to weaken the Japanese economy on the home front; assess political changes the Japanese occupation army had made in Indonesia! More often, we spent days poring through masses of material, to find one clue that would tell us, for example, that the enemy's war machine was short of tungsten, vital to armament production."

Barnett continued: "In order to identify potential bombing targets in Southeast Asia, for example, I had to know what the Japanese were obtaining from these areas, such as metals, food, or fuel. Then I would try to determine where these supplies were located. As time went by, we built up an incredible filing system, but in the beginning we relied on our imagination, overt material, and the area knowledge of people who had been there." Also on Barnett's wish list in the Far East: information on arsenals, munition dumps, auto and truck repair shops, airplane assembly plants, cement and chemical works, rice mills, and lumber, rubber, coal, phosphate, zinc, tin, salt, and alcohol plants.

One way to obtain such information was suggested in a cable Barnett sent to DuBois in Ceylon in December 1944:

Attached are two outlines of information

we desire on industrial plants in Thailand and Indo China, prepared with close co-operation by the London office. We don't want you to do a major research job on these topics, because we know your staff limitations. We want to supply you with questions in case your people happen to meet a business man from Thailand over tea, or share an aperitif with a Frenchman from Indo China. We need details of plant layouts, number of buildings, construction, size, capacity, and bomb damage. Finally, what are the Japanese using the plants for now?[1]

An important R&A priority was to obtain aerial photos and maps of potential and designated targets in Japan itself for U.S. bombing missions. Japanese war industries were primary targets. The prewar maps of Tokyo that were available usually showed unidentified buildings. However, R&A contacted a British businessman in London who had worked as an insurance underwriter in Japan. He had kept street maps showing important buildings in Tokyo that also identified these structures as government or business establishments, factories, and residences. Another source of information became available toward the end of the war when the Allies overran German intelligence offices in France and found cabinets full of material on the locations of Japanese industrial facilities.

One a legendary source of photographic intelligence on Tokyo was baseball catcher Moe Berg, who played for the Washington Senators before he was recruited for OSS. Shortly before the war, Berg had made a trip to Japan with an All-Star American baseball team. In addition to being a great catcher, Berg was also a superb linguist, a Princeton graduate, and a better-than-average photographer. During his tour in Japan with the All-Stars, Berg picked up a fair fluency in Japanese and was idolized there by baseball fans. He was allowed to travel freely throughout the country and took scores of pictures of the city from rooftops. These were supposedly utilized in the Doolittle raids on Japan.

Combining these sources with many others, R&A came up with a package that won a commendation from the Joint Chiefs of Staff.

In every government office worth its salt there is an administration officer who coordinates. In the case of R&A Far East there was Bernice Hanson, who was on the Far East outpost desk, and who coordinated correspondence from overseas personnel in India, Ceylon, Burma, and China. She was also responsible for getting people out to the field. Dr. Cora DuBois was one of the first women she placed in Ceylon.[2]

By November 1944, R&A outposts had been established in London, Algiers, Cairo, Caserta,

Paris, Stockholm, New Delhi, Bari, Honolulu, Chungking, Bucharest, Istanbul, Rome, Lisbon, Kandy, and Bern. These stations not only relayed material back to headquarters but also performed the functions of an R&A branch for local consumers.

It was through Bernice Hanson's office that all the "bodies" required for the Far East R&A sections were filtered. Her qualifications were excellent: married to foreign correspondent Haldore Hanson, she was with Yale-in-China, Shansi Province, when the Japanese invaded. Eventually she returned to the United States with her husband and took her degree at the University of Chicago. When the Pearl Harbor attack launched this country into war, Hanson came to work for OSS through the auspices of Harvard's John Fairbank, the noted China scholar.

The R&A staff in Washington was fortunate in having an Indonesia expert who spoke the language, had lived there before the war studying island dance forms, and had been on a first-name basis with Indonesian leaders. She was the late Clare Holt, born in Latvia, a vibrant woman interested in everyone, who made herself and her background knowledge available to the entire staff. She also lectured at OSS training seminars. Under her direction R&A prepared a valuable study of the economic and political changes made by the Japanese during their occupation of Malaysia, and predicted the decline of Dutch influence in the region.

Another productive member of the Far East staff of R&A was Dr. Evelyn Colbert, who had been working on her Ph.D. at Columbia when her husband was called to government service in Washington. "My thesis was 'The Doctrine of Retaliation in International Law,'" Colbert recalled. "So when Dr. Charles Burton Fahs, a professor at Columbia then serving in OSS, suggested that I join that super-hush-hush organization, I was assigned to Japan." Colbert admitted that Japan wasn't exactly her field of interest, but she learned quickly:

What made my work so enjoyable, was that it was so heavily populated by academics with no political axes to grind, people who were really tops in their fields. But even then, the chief of the branch, Edward A. Krack Jr., was of little help in our studies. He was an expert on the Sung Empire in China. Fahs was the only old Japan hand. In addition to Fahs, we had an itinerant guru who had spent many years in Japan. He visited us from Harvard three times each week to review our work. He was Dr. Serge Elyseef, who was also loaned to Morale Operations and any other area in need of his help. We depended upon a Nisei, Dr. Chitose Yanaga, who consulted with us on Japanese problems and helped straighten out some misconceptions about that country. He was a political analyst and director of the Oriental Language Unit in the Library of Congress.

As the war progressed and the workload increased, Fahs gathered his Japan staff together once a week at the home of Mrs. Robert Reischauer, widow of a famous Japanese scholar (the brother of a later ambassador to Japan, Edwin Reischauer). These meetings were invaluable in assessing and analyzing the problems of a military takeover of the government with the eventual surrender of Japan.

"So I became an expert on the Japanese police system, their water supply and sewer networks, local and national Japanese government organization," Colbert said with a shrug. "Some of our most violent arguments had to do with the Japanese emperor. Younger liberals were in favor of cutting off his royal head. But the more conservative in our shop won out. It was decided that all things being equal, the emperor was a stabilizing influence in Japan, and we felt that he shouldn't be loosed from his moorings."

A conciliatory decision was finally reached by R&A, which in essence allowed the emperor to continue his traditional representation of the Japanese.

Personnel assigned to R&A offices to service

OSS European stations discovered that only a trickle of material was reaching the United States from Axis countries. To solve this problem, President Roosevelt approved the establishment of an interdepartmental committee (IDC) composed of several branches of government, including OSS, to collect overt material abroad. The committee chose Switzerland, Sweden, and Portugal as target countries through which to obtain this information.

As the European war progressed, the Stockholm office proved to be one of the most productive. The IDC representative there, Dr. Adele J. Kibre, worked with all OSS units, assuring the flow of Axis material through London to Washington. By 1943 some twenty thousand pages of material a week were going from her office to Washington.

Impressive results were obtained from this massive accumulation of material: details of the total reorganization of German armament and munitions industries in November–December 1942; first confirmation of German submarine oil tankers; first photographs and intelligence on Nazi tankers refueling at sea; details of recruitment, uniforms, and insignia of Russian volunteer units in the German army.

One of the R&A women who participated in this form of analysis was the late Mary Painter, an American economist who was an innovator in the use of statistical techniques during the war. In OSS she pioneered the use of original methods for analyzing Nazi military capabilities. She devised a statistical model for estimating the size of the German submarine fleet in the North Atlantic. Military confirmation after the war showed her work to be startlingly accurate.

Painter's sister, Mrs. Charles Morse, saved some of her wartime letters written from Washington. In one dated 10 May 1942 she described her work: "Our agency does things that the Joint Chiefs of Staff want, and when they don't make specific requests, OSS does things it thinks JCS might want." In another letter, dated 27 September 1942, she reported that she had been transferred to the R&A International Trade and Shipping Section: "My boss is Henry E. Brodie, who is nice and amusing. He's very intelligent, which is more than I can say for some of my former bosses in government service. Brodie and I are working on a startling (at least we are going to make it startling) report on blockade running in the Mediterranean and the Bay of Biscay."

Painter continued: "I can't tell you much more about what I'm doing, except that we deal with both neutral and enemy countries. The boss is under the illusion that I am a very good mathematician. I work out formulae and curves, not only for him but for other sections. I'm glad I started reviewing calculus. It's a great help in this work."

In a letter to her family in Minnesota later

that year Painter reported, "Having just finished a memorandum on drug companies in Cuba, i.e., certain pro-German drug firms, I shall relax. I spent yesterday in the Commerce Department going through the new files on these companies. Quite interesting!"

Many of Mary Painter's letters to her family reflect the hectic life of wartime Washington. She came to Washington after graduating from Swarthmore College in 1942 and went to work first with the Board of Economic Warfare, then OSS. Life was not simple:

Last night we were caught in the blackout. I was downtown in front of the Willard Hotel waiting for Barbara Hauer, who works in our office. We were going to Brodie's house before the blackout started. Everyone had been warned about it, and consequently, Washington was prepared. As Barbara noticed, every whore in the city seemed to be hastily gathering for business in front of the Willard. After an embarrassing wait we flagged down a taxi to take us to Brodie's, arriving just as the town blacked out. In the pitch darkness we couldn't locate Brodie's house until an air raid warden guided us to it.

Painter was scheduled to go to London for OSS, but her work in Washington was considered too important. Later she did go overseas

81

to Paris, as part of the first group of economists who set up headquarters for the Marshall Plan, and was in charge of analyzing the French and German economies at the U.S. mission to NATO. After returning to the United States to work for a time at Columbia University, she went back to Paris to join the Organization of Economic Cooperation and Development.

At that time she met her future husband, one of France's outstanding cooks, George Garin. When she retired as an economist, Mary Painter Garin became, in the best tradition of restaurateurs' wives, *la patronne* of Chez Garin on the Left Bank, presiding over the cash register.

Many R&A assignments were far from dull statistical research. Jane Clark was assigned the job of tracing the movements of a famous Nazi commando of the Waffen-SS, Maj. Otto Skorzeny. "The Skorzeny story read like a spy novel," she recalled. "I was fresh out of Barnard when I came to work for OSS and R&A. I had been raised on war stories by my father, Clinton Clark, who served with his old Buffalo, New York, friend Bill Donovan on the Mexican border. But Skorzeny was awesome!"

Clark said that the picture of a burly thirty-five-year-old Skorzeny took shape over several months in intelligence reports sifting through R&A from station agents, although much more of the story came out at the Nuremberg trials, where Skorzeny's commando activities were under investigation as war crimes. General Donovan himself, armed with R&A reports, interrogated that German OSS counterpart during these trials. Clark described Skorzeny as a big hulk of a man, a Viennese adventurer, over six feet tall with a dueling scar across his left cheek. Although an officer in Himmler's SS storm troopers, he was known as Hitler's Commando, having established the *Führer's* first organized commando unit.

Clark picked up Skorzeny's involvement with Mussolini at the point where the Italian government had deposed il Duce (12 May 1943) and was holding him prisoner in an area thought to be inaccessible to the Nazis, in the Gran Sasso d'Italia, high in the Abruzzi mountains east of Rome. The site was impregnable from the ground, a ski resort situated on a narrow ledge in a veritable eagle's aerie. The only approach was by funicular, both ends guarded by *carabinieri.*

Hitler personally ordered Skorzeny to rescue Mussolini, fearing that the rebellious Italian government would make a separate peace agreement with the Allies. The commando elected to use gliders for the initial assault, despite the dangerous approaches and terrain. One glider team in camouflage clothing landed at the base of the funicular at midafternoon, 12 September 1943, and overpowered the guards; the troops in the other two gliders, led by

Skorzeny, secured the hotel area and cleared a makeshift runway in the rocky meadow near the hotel for the rescue aircraft to land. Being a pilot, Skorzeny had selected the reliable high-wing utility Fieseler Storch airplane, because of its fine record in reconnaissance and mountain rescue work.

"There was just one little bit of planning that went awry," Clark said with a smile. "We picked it up later in agent dispatches. Skorzeny had not counted on rescuing a much-over-weight il Duce. Mussolini, garbed in a heavy black overcoat, was stuffed aboard the small plane. Together with Skorzeny and the pilot, his added weight, plus the effect of the high altitude on the available short runway, created questionable takeoff conditions."

The commandos had cleared a two-hundred-yard downhill runway. At the end was a three-thousand-foot drop into the valley, and an undesirable tail wind. Mussolini, a pilot also, gripped the cabin braces on the side of the fuselage as the pilot revved the engine to full power and released the brakes. The plane slowly began to move over the bumpy ground toward the alpine precipice. Lacking adequate flying speed, the skillful pilot guided the aircraft over the valley edge and in a near-stalled condition was able to dive the Storch toward the valley floor, gain safe flying speed, and fly on to a Nazi-held airfield near Rome. From here Mussolini was flown to safety in Vienna, later to Berlin. The plane believed to be the one used in that rescue is now a prized exhibit at the Smithsonian's Paul Garber Facility at Silver Hill, Maryland.[3]

Skorzeny surfaced again in Clark's OSS traffic in 1945 during the Battle of the Bulge, when the Allies were taken completely by surprise by that unexpected and powerful Nazi counteroffensive. It took days for the Allies to pull back from the massive attack, regroup, and prepare their ultimately successful onslaught. There was a great deal of confusion during this cold winter period, heightened by clever German use of psychological warfare. Here again Skorzeny was in command, personally ordered by Hitler to head an infiltration effort, code-named Operation Greif.

"This time," Clark continued, "Skorzeny recruited English-speaking German soldiers, dressed them in American uniforms, and sent them forward, ahead of the German army. Their mission: to assassinate Eisenhower, Bradley, and Patton. So thorough was Skorzeny's deception that his men wore American paratroop or airman uniforms, complete with correct insignia, with some even driving jeeps!" Alerted by security forces, American troops developed a series of test questions to be used to identify any suspicious soldiers at the fluid and undefined front line: "Who is Betty Grable? Where is the Grand Canyon? What position did Lou Gehrig play?" One U.S. Army captain,

Knox Peet, while on supervisory guard duty, shot and killed an advancing soldier in an American uniform. Captain Peet said there was something about the way the man walked. There is an almost unnoticeable slouch about American GIs, but this one coming toward him walked stiff and erect. Peet's instincts were correct: the man was an infiltrator.[4]

Years later Clark finally saw Skorzeny in Madrid, where he lived on Calle de Alcala. Clark's fiancé, Edward Ericksson, then with Time-Life, was having a birthday luncheon at Madrid's trendy Horchers Restaurant on the Calle Alfonso XII. The owner, Otto Horcher, had been host to many Nazi visitors. For Clark the encounter was startling. There at the next table sat the legendary Nazi whose exploits had taken up so much of her time and so many of the files in her OSS safe. He was tall, scarred, arrogant, and free.

CHAPTER 4

Coordinating Secret Intelligence

Most women assigned to the OSS intelligence division usually spent their careers analyzing and cataloging incoming intelligence material and forwarding it to the proper desks. Secret Intelligence (SI) was directly involved in espionage activities, and its agents abroad were on-the-spot gatherers of information from within neutral or enemy territories.

Jean Wallace Douglas, assigned to SI operations in Washington for the European theater, remembers pouches coming in from overseas, dirty and dusty in cumbersome duffel bags. Her job was to sort through the material and mark it for distribution to the proper branches.

Douglas, daughter of Vice President Henry A. Wallace, who also served under Roosevelt in several cabinet positions, lived with her family in an annex of Wardman Park Hotel in Washington. This area was also the temporary home of members of the Supreme Court, the cabinet, and the Dwight D. Eisenhowers. Douglas walked to work with her father from their apartment, she to her office near the Reflecting Pool, he to the White House. "It gave us exercise and a chance to think," she recalled.

Douglas also recalled that there were certain words in the incoming intelligence cables that required an immediate routing to either President Roosevelt or General Donovan. One such phrase was "heavy water." It piqued her curiosity to the extent that she ignored OSS rules and asked her father about it one night after work. Vice President Wallace looked his daughter straight in the eye and said simply, "Yes, it is important!" He would not discuss it further with her, and she knew from the tone of his voice that it was a closed issue. She never brought it up again with him or with her colleagues; one of the basic rules in OSS was never to mention anything that was classified, not even to the vice president.

A great deal of intelligence material came from underground agents, mainly from France, later from Germany, Douglas recalled. Once she found Mussolini's pistol and holster in a pouch from Italy. She wasn't certain how to route it, so she sent it to General Donovan. She often wondered what happened to it: "It was so beautiful and shiny."

Douglas came to OSS shortly after her graduation from Connecticut College, New London, and after a brief stint with Nelson

Rockefeller's American Affairs Office. She did not go overseas during the war, opting for marriage with Leslie Douglas, then serving in the navy. Today they live in a quiet Washington neighborhood. Leslie Douglas is active in investment banking, and his wife shares her father's love of ecology and agriculture. The vice president was famous for hybrid corn development; his daughter experiments with strawberries.

SI cable traffic to and from the field was usually impersonal. Julia Cuniberti's job was to set up files, route them as they came into Washington SI headquarters, and forget anything she read.

Cuniberti was on the Italian desk. She spoke the language; she knew the country and the people. Her family came to the United States from Italy in 1930 and settled in Chicago, where her father became an attorney after taking his law degree at the University of Chicago. Later, as an officer with the International Exchange Bank, he returned to Italy and the family settled for three years in Bologna, close to relatives. While there, Mr. Cuniberti bought a villa in Pavulo in the Apennines, a hunting lodge that had once been part of their family estate dating back to the 1700s.

After attending schools in Italy, Julia Cuniberti returned to the United States with her family. She had just been graduated from

Vassar when war broke out. Her area knowledge and fluency in Italian, French, and German attracted talent scouts from OSS. She was assigned to SI and was soon awash in the tons of material coming from OSS posts in and surrounding Italy. As the Allies came to occupy more and more of that country, capturing Rome in June 1944, she also began receiving messages from the Italian partisans, sabotaging the Nazi war machine as it pushed northward into the Apennines.

Cuniberti could picture the area vividly. To escape the war that had ravaged southern Italy, her uncle, his wife, two maiden aunts, and four children had moved to Pavulo. It was a beautiful turreted rococo lodge, made of carved bricks with stucco overlay painted a deep pink. Built in the same period as George Washington's Mount Vernon, it was called La Bella Palazzina. In her mind's eye she could see the kitchen with its enormous fireplace, its copper pots for boiling water over a charcoal stove, its vaulted ceilings darkly beautiful from wood smoke. There was a music room where the family gathered and one of her aunts played the piano. Murals decorated the grand staircase; paintings of the four seasons adorned the ceilings. At the top of the stairs was a huge armoire with carved wooden doors from an ancient monastery. Outside in the fields were sheep, cows, chickens, rabbits, and pigs, tended by a tenant farmer. Formal gardens surrounded the lodge itself, which was on a slope on one of the highest peaks in the Apennines. As far as Cuniberti knew, her Italian family was safe in this hideaway, braving the severe winters but supposedly far from the fighting.

One day, as she was plotting the course of the war raging in Italy in mid-1944, with Mussolini's puppet government in exile in the northern mountains and the Nazis fighting delaying action against the Allies, she logged in a cable from OSS field headquarters, sourced to partisans outside Pavulo. The cable stated that Germans had moved into Pavulo and established headquarters at La Bella Palazzina. They had fortified the hunting lodge and moved the Italian family living there to the attic. Nazis were using the building as an observation post. The partisans were calling for an Allied air strike against this fortress, giving its exact location by triangulation from prominent landmarks.

"You can imagine my reaction," Cuniberti recounted. "I couldn't notify my uncle and aunts and cousins. I could only pray!" The Allies bombed the Palazzina two times, and narrowly missed. Partisans holding a nearby hilltop cabled the results of the raids. These cables too were received in Washington by the woman whose helpless family was huddled in the dark, cold attic of the Palazzina.

The Germans held out for a year and a half in the area before finally surrendering. It wasn't till the fall of 1945 that Cuniberti received a letter through the Red Cross telling her that her family had survived the Nazi occupation of their home in Pavulo and were safe in Bologna. They wrote that they had been given kitchen privileges, although they were forced to occupy cramped quarters in the attic, unmercifully cold during the winter. They had also been able to plant a garden and use farm animals for sustenance.

Cuniberti learned later that the German officers who occupied their home were of World War I vintage, and they tended to respect the tenants of the lodge, although they never learned that it was owned by an American. But the soldiers under them were young teenagers who lacked the Wehrmacht discipline. "Sometimes, when they were sent to other duty posts, they tried to steal some of our family treasures," Cuniberti said. "One of my aunts, who was very feisty, reported it to the commanding officer, and the valuables were returned."

Before the war was over Cuniberti had been posted to the OSS station in London, where she arrived in May 1945 shortly before V-E Day and was almost crushed in the crowds surging around the Parliament buildings to catch a glimpse of Churchill. She was squashed against iron railings, but she did see the prime minister holding up his hand, making his famous V for Victory sign. From London she went to Wiesbaden, again to set up SI files in

OSS offices, this time located in a champagne factory. She recalled that the wine fumes were heady and permeated the work areas. After a final tour in Bern, Cuniberti left OSS and studied art for two years at the Corcoran Gallery in Washington. She later attended the Academy of Fine Arts in Florence before settling in Washington, where she is a freelance graphics artist.

The ceremony held at the Dutch embassy in September 1948 was small but impressive. Jeanne Van Den Bosch Begg stood with her husband as Ambassador E. Nivan Kleffens read the citation:

> As Deputy Liaison Officer of the Office of Strategic Services and later as Chief of the Low Countries dissemination and research division of this same organization, Mrs. John Murray Begg was instrumental in many projects and activities concerning the work of the Netherlands Resistance Movement.
>
> Due to her intimate knowledge of the Netherlands and her great devotion to the task, Mrs. Begg materially contributed to the Netherlands' cause during World War II.
>
> In recognition of these outstanding services, Her Majesty the Queen has decided to issue the following decree:
>
> We, Wilhelmina, by the Grace of God,

Queen of the Netherlands, Princess of Orange-Nassau, on recommendation of our minister for foreign affairs of April 9, 1948, have approved and ordered to appoint a Knight of the Order of Orange-Nassau, Mrs. John Murray Begg.[1]

Jeanne Begg is the only OSS woman serving in Washington to have been so honored by the Dutch after the war. Daughter of a retired Dutch naval officer who settled in the United States, Begg had a European education. She attended schools in Spain, France, and Holland and took her master's degree at Oxford. She spoke Spanish, French, Dutch, German, Italian, and English with a British accent. In her younger days, growing up in Holland, she had been a friend of Queen Wilhelmina's daughter Juliana and had attended parties near the royal castle. In an area of many picturesque lakes, they could water-ski and then go to the castle for supper. "It was most informal," she recalled. "We were just kids having a good time."

Begg's first job after her family came to the United States was with Hearst's *New York Daily Mirror*. She was one of the first women feature writers and the first Hearst reporter trained to take her own news photographs. She remembers an interview she had with violinist Yehudi Menuhin, when she was just learning to use her Speed Graphic camera. Unable to adjust the flood lamps properly, she had to enlist Menuhin's help.

The war ended her newspaper career. Begg joined the Red Cross in Washington as a public-relations writer. She recalls an incident when dignified, very regal Queen Wilhelmina was visiting Washington. The entire Red Cross contingent eagerly crowded the building to meet her. Begg was in an upstairs office, barely able to see out the window, when her name was called on the loudspeaker; the queen, whose husband was a friend of Begg's father, had personally asked to meet her.

Shortly after the war began, Jeanne met and married John Begg, a State Department official, who later joined the U.S. Information Service. At about the same time she was also recruited by OSS and was assigned to the North African desk as a reports officer. Begg was taught to examine raw intelligence from the field and write reports for the Joint Chiefs of Staff, OSS branches, the State Department, and occasionally other government agencies involved in the area or action. "We would receive bits of paper," she recalled, "often dirty and torn, sent direct from agents in North Africa, dealing with events there, or from Italy or France. They had been collected by OSS agents, shipped out clandestinely, and pouched to Washington headquarters."

Begg's next assignment was the Spanish desk. By then she was hankering, like so many other

OSS women, to get an overseas post, but her boss intervened. He told her she had such a wonderful marriage and was so essential in her job that he wouldn't approve a transfer. He said that too many marriages were broken up when women went abroad during wartime.

The OSS Spanish desk dealt with both the Franco and the anti-Franco factions still active in Spain. Franco had assumed power after the civil war in Spain ended in 1939 with the defeat of the Loyalists and the Popular Front. Franco had been aided by fascist Italy and Nazi Germany. The Loyalists were supported by the Soviet Union, and by volunteers from all over Europe, including the Abraham Lincoln Brigade, composed of several hundred American liberals. Spain was neutral during the war, but no one could be certain whether Franco might cast his lot with the Nazis and allow them to cross neutral Spain to take Gibraltar and block the eventual Allied attack on North Africa. This situation was of particular interest to the American leftists.

Begg remembered an unusually intelligent woman named Helen Tenney who had been very active in leftist Spanish organizations during the civil war and had worked in New York for the OSS Foreign Nationalities Branch recruiting and training emigrants of many nationalities who had come to the United States. Tenney, a highly qualified researcher with fluent Spanish, was later assigned to work in

Begg's hush-hush Spanish division.

At the time, Begg did not know that Tenney had been placed in her branch by the Communist Party. Subsequent investigation revealed that Tenney had collected highly classified material, which she carried up to New York every two weeks when she visited her mother there. Her contact was Elizabeth Bentley, a communist undercover agent who was later exposed by the FBI. "I remember Tenney as a very hardworking woman," Begg said. "But she was like an old maid, with no life of her own. An excellent researcher who kept to herself, she always wanted to work late and close the office. I never allowed her to do so, as I was careful always to close it myself." The last Begg heard of Tenney was when she read in a newspaper article several years later that one of Elizabeth Bentley's cohorts had been uncovered. Tenney had stood in the middle of a street in New York City screaming, "I'm a spy! I'm a spy!" She had been taken to the Bellevue psychopathic ward. Apparently the strain of spying had been too much for her.

Begg assumed that much of the material OSS was receiving from Franco sources was being channeled directly to Soviet spies in New York and back to communist cells in Spain. In those days, with the USSR an ally against Hitler, known communists were permitted to work for OSS. The only person Begg ever spotted as suspicious was a young German who had been drafted into the U.S. Army and who strutted through the corridors of their building like a storm trooper. He would kick open a door instead of opening it; in her office he was intransigent and cocky. She decided to report him one day when she was walking behind him to the cafeteria and heard him whistling the *Horst Wessel* song. The junior *Führer* was quickly reassigned.

Begg's final wartime assignment was staff liaison with the Dutch military mission in Washington, located on Massachusetts Avenue. She had an office next to Whitney Shepardson, OSS SI chief, which she papered from wall to wall with maps of Western Europe, tracking the Allies as they advanced toward Holland.

OSS SI activities in Holland were limited. In accordance with a verbal understanding reached with the British Secret Intelligence Service in 1942, no penetration of OSS SI into Holland or Belgium could be mounted before the entry of Allied troops into the lowlands. Missions were then planned to enter Holland immediately after liberation to develop a close working relationship with Dutch intelligence services for joint agent operations against retreating German forces.

This agreement stemmed in part from the fact that the British had developed considerable skepticism about the viability of their own network in Holland. Subsequent exposure of a German operation revealed that most of the

Dutch and British representatives of the Special Operations Executive had been apprehended by German security police upon arrival in Holland. These agents were forced or persuaded to collaborate in a gigantic deception, code-named North Pole, based on a spurious underground organization that was officially exposed only in the early winter of 1944. The success of this German operation undermined confidence in Dutch liaison with British and U.S. intelligence agencies and created a crisis in England at the cabinet level. Eventually, as North Pole was assessed and Allied assets were reevaluated, there began to be close cooperation in London between the intelligence services and Prince Bernhard, leader of the Dutch resistance movement.

The process of building resistance forces and coordinating them with London operations continued. Queen Wilhelmina's government-in-exile gathered together three main resistance organizations under the command of Prince Bernhard. "The prince, who was Juliana's husband, was a bon vivant, given to extramarital activity, but he got the job done," Begg remembered. After D-Day the resistance in Holland swelled by thousands of recruits; new communication nets were established, agents were infiltrated, and soon London was pinpointing targets for sabotage action. One Dutch woman radio agent with OSS, dropped behind German lines with her companion, tried to thumb a ride from a passing lorry full of Nazi troops re-treating from France. The truck stopped to pick them up, and during the loading process the agent's radio fell onto the ground. She and her companion were shot on the spot.

As the volume of intelligence data increased, OSS headquarters analyzed the contents and forwarded it to the Dutch and other clients in Washington. Jeanne Begg visited the Dutch mission once each week. She still remembers her very first encounter with the head of the mission. He met her outside his office in the waiting room, uncertain as to how to deal with a woman. He asked her, in front of his office staff, what she had to tell him. "I was shy, only about twenty-six years old, but I had been trained in security regulations," she recalled. "I insisted on going into his private office before I would say a word. After that, we got along beautifully. In fact, after the war when I visited the Netherlands, his military unit put on a review at the Dutch war college, just for me."

One of the highlights of Begg's work with the Dutch military mission was her meeting with General Eisenhower at an official dinner party at the Dutch embassy, given by Dutch general Van Tryk. "I was the only one there under fifty," she recalled.

After dinner, General Eisenhower sat with me and was most attentive, asking what I did. I told him I was with OSS, SI Reports

Section, on the Dutch desk.

I had followed the Arnhem fighting closely in September 1944 and had been puzzled by reports of the Ninth German Parachute Division. We had located one part of the division near Arnhem, and then we received reports of another unidentified Nazi parachute division with different shoulder patches turning up in a different battle zone. We had no record of these new patches, and it puzzled me.

As we talked, I ventured to tell Eisenhower how concerned I was about the unidentified German parachute patches. I told him my theory: the paratroopers were from the same unit but had pinned new identification patches on half the division to make it look as if there were more German soldiers in the field than there actually were. The general smiled at me and nodded. "Right on," he told me.

Today Begg is following a new career, breeding thoroughbred horses. After being widowed, she married a longtime friend, Harold C. B. Claggett Jr. They live at Roedown Farm in Davidsonville, Maryland.

The work Jeanne Begg did, together with other SI women in Washington, formed a solid basis for overseas planning and penetrations of enemy-held territory.

CHAPTER 5

Black Propaganda, Coast to Coast

Morale Operations (MO), the production and dissemination of slanted covert propaganda, originated in OSS establishments in Washington, New York, and San Francisco. This material was further tailored in the field to specific targets. Several women administrators worked in MO at Washington headquarters, where OSS also had its training grounds for psychological-warfare support personnel who were eventually dispatched to OSS stations around the world.

Far East MO activities began in mid-1943, after India opened up. The Washington manager for Far East MO was Jane Smith-Hutton, daughter of an army officer, wife of a naval commander. She added a bit of spit and polish, and also order, to an otherwise laid-back group of ex-newspaper reporters, artists, cartoonists, and radio announcers. These psy-warriors were learning their trade in the sprawling offices at Que Building at Twenty-third and Constitution

Avenue, NW, and would be stationed overseas at the end of a training period that lasted from three months to a year.

Their destinations were Sri Lanka, Myanmar, Thailand, Vietnam, and the People's Republic of China — translated into the country names of fifty years ago, Ceylon, Burma, Siam, French Indochina, and China. In the world atlas, only India has remained constant, albeit divided and no longer part of the British empire.

A great deal of the training took place at the Congressional Country Club near Washington, where experts lectured on MO-related subjects. Smith-Hutton spoke on Japanese psychology, social structure, vulnerabilities, and group cleavages.

She knew her subject well. She had spent twelve years in Japan, spoke the language, and had been interned in Tokyo at the beginning of the war. As part of training, Smith-Hutton asked the students to write leaflets targeted against Japanese soldiers in the field. These leaflets were then translated by Japanese-American Nisei and given to a small group of Japanese prisoners of war (POWs) working for the MO branch in a restricted area, Collingwood, located in rural Virginia.[1] The candid critiques of these POWs helped improve MO production in Asia as the war progressed.

Smith-Hutton summed up a class exercise in

a report she has kept with her records: "The POW reactions to MO class leaflets seem to be that the majority of Japanese soldiers would not understand them. There are a lot of Japanese soldiers who can't even write their own names. The class was admonished not to write in formal idiom because the soldiers will resent these leaflets, and they also won't be able to understand them. Make them short. Use simplified calligraphy."

Slogans were also part of training. A Japanese prisoner told Smith-Hutton that such punch lines as "Down with the military clique" or "Attack your commanding officers now" would never fly; they were on a par with that famous Japanese banzai charge against American GIs that was reported from the Pacific, "Down with Babe Ruth!" The MO class was told by the POWs that the average Japanese soldier would never entertain the idea of killing his commanding officer. His training and discipline precluded him from acting independently. His fear of the consequences, in case of failure, would far outweigh his personal desires.

The MO advanced training courses boasted many outstanding women lecturers in addition to Smith-Hutton. Anthropologist Margaret Mead, whose husband, Gregory Bateson, was serving in Ceylon with MO, spoke to the students on working relations with Allied personnel, particularly the British. Dr. Ina Telberg, with a doctorate in Asian studies, discussed Japanese secret societies, military ideology, and MO target planning. Telberg was later assigned to MO Calcutta as a desk chief. After the war Dr. Telberg, who spoke fluent Russian, became an instantaneous translator at the United Nations.

Another lecturer was Edith Sebald, herself Japanese, who spoke on Japanese behavior and personality, pointing out psychological vulnerabilities. She returned to Japan after the war, where her husband was State Department adviser to Gen. Douglas MacArthur.

There were also other area experts: Dr. Clare Holt lectured MO operators destined for Southeast Asia on the politics and social structure of the Dutch East Indies. Lucy Starling, a missionary from Siam with an overwhelming but unfulfilled desire to parachute back to her parish in Chiengmai, discussed targets in Siam. The late Mildred Turner, an expert on French Indochina, spoke to the classes about MO projects aimed mainly at capitalizing on native superstitions.

Smith-Hutton also was liaison officer with MO's Project Marigold, located in midtown New York City, where Capt. Max Kleiman and a group of seven Nisei operated a print shop on the seventh floor of a busy office building. She remembered that Marigold consisted of a series of smaller offices abutting a large conference room where she worked with the Japanese personnel producing leaflets and eventually newspapers. The operation was conducted with a high degree of security, and none of the personnel was allowed to visit the main OSS office at 630 Fifth Avenue. In May 1945 the project was terminated and the personnel released for operational missions in the Far East.

Some of these Marigold agents were transferred to an MO radio station with a 50,000-watt transmitter at 432 Post Street in San Francisco, which had become operative in April 1945. The personnel also included three prisoners of war who were quartered in the studio. The production unit prepared scripts for "black radio" transmission and also supported the OSS black radio operating in Saipan the last month of the war.

Twenty-one programs in all were beamed from the "Voice of the People," all heavily jammed by Tokyo. One woman announcer, Dorothy Ogata, wrote and delivered her own programs. She had the ability to put real drama into her voice as she read "letters" from the front and other emotionally charged scripts. Another capable writer in the department was Mitsui Iwamatsu, whose matronly voice was a direct contrast to Ogata's, but equally effective. She gave the woman's point of view, reading "letters" from wives whose husbands were fighting on faraway fronts. The tone was inevitably defeatist, stressing the advantage of a cessation of hostilities and expressing hope for the Japan of the future.

Smith-Hutton did not have contact with the San Francisco operation. Her main job was transmitting Washington headquarters and Marigold material to the field. "I always felt that women made excellent MO operators," she told me later. "MO challenged me to use my imagination when working on enemy targets. It was a process of mixing detailed truth with believable lies." Since she had been in Japan until she was repatriated, Smith-Hutton knew the people and modern language usages better than most Nisei who worked in the MO shop, most of whom had never been to Japan.

Smith-Hutton was recruited almost before she disembarked from the repatriation ship *Gripsholm*, which brought the Smith-Hutton family home from Japan. She was contacted in New York by an MO officer, Edmund Taylor, a former newsman with CBS who had covered the fall of France. Taylor had written the basic book on psychological warfare, *The Strategy of Terror*. This book played an important part in awakening America to the power of the morale operations so skillfully used by the Nazis during their invasion of France. Nazi propagandists preceded their armies, spreading rumors, forging documents, and faking newspaper stories that proclaimed widespread German victories and the inevitable fall of the Allied powers.

One of Smith-Hutton's contributions to the MO programs in the Far East was her weekly Rumor Mill session with the staff. Here she helped dream up rumors to be sent to OSS stations in Burma, Ceylon, China, and later Thailand. Once accused of having a mean streak in her nature for her ability to develop devastating rumors, she explained, "The more you like people, and I do like the Japanese, the more you can hurt them because you know their weaknesses."

Some of the rumors generated in her sessions were used in China when the Allies were planning an invasion of Canton, which was aborted after the atom bomb was dropped on Hiroshima. In a massive disinformation campaign, Smith-Hutton's colleagues in K'un-ming circulated her rumors that the Allies were planning to attack Hong Kong. They also managed to disrupt Chinese puppet relations with the Japanese by announcing alleged plans by the Japanese military to impress Chinese pilots into kamikaze suicide squadrons.

Smith-Hutton remained in Washington for the entire war. After a busy day at the office, she would share her life with a young daughter born before the war and a husband who listened with incredulity to some of the ideas his wife was concocting at that strange OSS office of lax discipline and mad ideas. At war's end, the Smith-Huttons were posted to Paris. Henri Smith-Hutton was much in demand; he spoke not only French but also Japanese, Russian, German, and Spanish. OSS's David Bruce was ambassador at the time.

After a busy life abroad, the Smith-Huttons came home to Palo Alto, California, to retire. Following her husband's death, Jane Smith-Hutton returned to live in Washington, with a summer home in the mountains of North Carolina near another MO conspirator, Leo Crowley, a one-time Honolulu gossip columnist and her loyal supporter and colleague.

Morale Operations was also very effective in the European and North African theaters. Operators, mostly men, were trained in Washington and dispatched to the field. The Joint Chiefs of Staff charged the branch with "the execution of all forms of morale subversion by divers means including false rumors, freedom stations, false leaflets, false documents, the organization and support of fifth column activities by trained personnel and supplies and the use of agents for the purpose of creating confusion, division and undermining the morale of the enemy."[2]

Another woman helped to coordinate MO projects from Washington for Europe and the Mediterranean. She was blonde, chic Kay Halle, who wore two *chapeaux:* development of themes for MO and correlating MO subversion programs as they were perpetrated in Europe and Africa.[3]

Halle, familiarly known as Mata Halle, was related to a wealthy department-store family in Cleveland and had been a radio broadcaster for a Cleveland station. She recalled that, like everyone else who was caught up in the early excitement of the war, "we felt a strong sense of mission — a fire in our belly!" She worked in a plush, carpeted war room with large maps on three walls showing MO spheres of subversive influence, outposts, and stations joined by a colorful overlay of yarn that reached from France to the China coast.

As in the Far East, rumors were one of the main outputs of European MO, in this case rumors based on such themes as splitting the Italian-German alliance. An example of a successful rumor: Mussolini had applied to Switzerland for asylum in case of an Allied invasion of Italy and was turned down. The rumor reached not only Italian troops defending their homeland but even the American minister in Bern, who cautiously warned State Department sources that "this information be given careful protection."[4] There were many cases of clever MO disinformation being picked up in France by OSS Secret Intelligence agents and relayed to Washington, where it was accepted as basic intelligence until checked at headquarters with MO production.

Overall worldwide propaganda campaigns were also planned in Washington at weekly meetings of the Psychological Warfare Board, composed of representatives from the State Department, the U.S. Navy and Army, OSS, and the Office of War Information. Halle and

Smith-Hutton attended these meetings. The purpose was to coordinate propaganda themes, both black and white, with overall objectives in support of the Allied war effort. Weekly MO directives on the meetings were issued to field stations for this purpose.

One of the most effective MO operations against the Germans in Europe was the Musac project, which started in July 1944.[5] Based on the concept of the potency of music in propaganda efforts, this program was run jointly by the British Political Warfare Executive and MO London, with support from MO New York. The Washington liaison officer was a woman, Rhoda K. Hirsch. The program was called "Soldatensender West" and was broadcast from England to Germany and German-occupied areas in Western Europe. The Wehrmacht was the primary target.

"Soldatensender West" was aired from 8 P.M. until 8 A.M., supposedly from German stations relaying news and music to the front, and was transmitted on a dozen medium- and short-wave frequencies. The British produced the slanted news, while the Americans provided the entertainment features that during the last year of the war commanded a steadily growing audience of German troops. This fact was attested to by hundreds of prisoners of war who were interrogated. American music eventually became the mainstay of "Soldatensender West."

German lyrics were written for songs by Gershwin, Rodgers and Hart, Cole Porter, Jerome Kern, and Irving Berlin. The lyricist was an OSS agent, Lothar Metzl, who had formerly produced songs for Austrian theaters. Kurt Weill, German-born composer of such works as the *Threepenny Opera*, orchestrated and arranged the songs to suit the German mood and temperament. His wife, singer Lotte Lenya, recorded many of these songs, together with such stars as Marlene Dietrich, her daughter, Maria, Greta Keller, Jarmilla Novotna, and Greta Steuckgold of the New York Metropolitan Opera. Dietrich was the only performer aware of the OSS connection. The use of these songs by OSS constituted a violation of American copyright laws, a fact that OSS lawyers were greatly concerned about, but the MO New York office was finally given a green light, and most of the artists, with the exception of Dietrich, were not told the real purpose of the operation. Dietrich herself was cautioned to be most discreet in connection with the copyrights.

A dummy corporation was set up through the J. Walter Thompson advertising agency to handle negotiations with the Musicians Union, hiring an orchestra, and renting rehearsal and recording studios. Nine MO operatives, eleven German or Central European–born vocal artists, and a fifteen-piece orchestra were assembled. Between July 1944 and April 1945 the company produced 312 recordings on sixteen-inch Vynolite discs, which were played over "Soldatensender West" eight times a week. Many of the songs had no propaganda content but were intended solely to attract and hold listeners for the news segments. Others had a nostalgic appeal designed to promote war-weariness and defection. Still others were hard-hitting satirical songs attacking Nazi leaders or relating to the discomforts and disillusionment of war. In addition to straight musical programs, there were also fifteen-minute variety shows in the best tradition of the political cabaret so popular in Europe.

At the time Musac went into production, Marlene Dietrich was already a front-line hit with the Allied soldiers. She appeared before the troops, often under fire, bringing them entertainment and a touch of glamour. Lothar Metzl contacted her somewhere in France, and she agreed to participate in Musac. She came to London in the autumn of 1944 to make a series of recordings. Some of the songs she sang are still alive today: "I'll Get By," "My Heart Stood Still," "I Couldn't Sleep a Wink Last Night." By far the most popular effort was "Lili Marlene," that song the soldiers of all armies were humming by war's end. Lili was "the enemy alien who cannot be interned," as writer John Steinbeck described this plaintive ballad of a soldier who had left his girl and knew someone else had replaced him. His fear of dying brings back memories of how he first saw her, "underneath the lamplight," their two shadows melting into one as her lips reached up to his.[6]

There was a haunting, nostalgic allure to Dietrich's singing. The undertones of deep sadness even touched the romantic Irish in General Donovan, who wrote to her, "I am personally deeply grateful to you for your generosity in making these recordings for us." Several years later Dietrich wrote to the general, asking him to help her get a release for her OSS album. In almost schoolgirl handwriting she explained, "I hold the original cuttings of my recordings made in 1944 and I signed a letter that I would not use them commercially. I would be grateful if you would help me to get a release so that Columbia Records, where I am now recording, can bring them out. As ever yours."[7] The general, after prolonged legal proceedings that involved Lawrence Houston, general counsel for the Central Intelligence Agency at that time, and a West Coast law firm representing the recording company, was able to get a release for the songs that once were beamed to war-locked Germany. In 1951 the records were released in the United States, where "Lili Marlene" still evoked wartime memories for many veterans who had first heard the haunting song at front-line USO shows or on the Armed Forces Network.

After the war Dietrich was awarded the

Medal of Freedom, the highest civilian honor the United States bestows; France named her a Knight of the Legion of Honor, and Belgium made her a Knight of the Order of Leopold. She died at the age of ninety in Paris.

Kay Halle was aware of the extremely sensitive Musac project, even though it was tightly compartmented within the secret New York studio. At the end of the war she debriefed MO personnel as they filed in from field stations across the world. She interviewed them and assessed the achievements of MO within their theater.[8] Her reports were later integrated into CIA planning, and MO did indeed have a part in the new world of subversive mind twisting now known as disinformation.

One of the best examples of the effectiveness of MO in the field was Operation Sauerkraut, in which a young WAC private stationed in Rome was able to induce the surrender of some six hundred Czechs impressed into Nazi service. Barbara Lauwers became an OSS legend in the years after she served with an MO unit working with German prisoners of war in Italy.

CHAPTER 6

Operation Sauerkraut

She hesitantly opened the door of her small apartment in northwest Washington, D.C. The robust, red-cheeked man standing there smiled, knelt suddenly on one knee, and murmured, "Zuzka, *mon ange!*" Then he kissed her outstretched hand.

She had been looking forward to this unbelievable reunion for months, ever since receiving a query from one Will Williams, asking if she was that "lovely Czechoslovak girl nicknamed Zuzka, the OSS WAC from the 2677th Regiment in Bari, Rome, Caserta, and Siena, Italy, during 1944–45." He had traced her through the OSS Veterans Office in New York City.

The story of their exciting wartime adventures unfolded as these OSS veterans relived the events in a series of interviews with me. They had met fifty years before in 1944 at a German prisoner-of-war camp in Averso, Italy. She had introduced herself as Barbara

Lauwers, stiffly correct in her WAC uniform, speaking flawless German. He was one of eighteen prisoners of war she was interviewing: a twenty-four-year-old Berliner, then called Willi Haseneier, captured 4 June 1944 in Rome.

Now she put her arms around him. "It's been a hell of a long time since we met at Camp 326," she smiled. "And I see you have changed your name. Can't blame you. Doesn't Haseneier mean rabbit eggs?"

Williams had indeed changed his name after the war. "I worked as an artist and public-relations executive," he explained. "That name the family glued on me for almost twenty-six years had to go!"

Inside the apartment, they traveled back in time. Lauwers had spread out her wartime memorabilia on the small dining-room table. "Just think, Willi," she reminisced, "if those German officers hadn't tried to assassinate Hitler back in 1944, we probably would never have met." These two veterans had once played vital roles in Operation Sauerkraut, an innovative Morale Operations (MO) program that had capitalized on the attempted assassination of Hitler.

Operation Sauerkraut had been initiated after the midday explosion of a bomb in a briefcase in Hitler's East Prussia headquarters on 20 July 1944.[1] The bomb had been planted by Count Klaus von Stauffenberg, who represented a substantial clique of disaffected army officers. The count and his accomplices were shot that day; a vengeful Hitler ordered thousands more executed in the weeks that followed.

Sauerkraut was set up a few hours after the assassination attempt, which provided an unusual psychological opportunity to attack the morale of the German army, if news could be circulated without delay. The object was to undermine the will of enemy troops to fight by citing growing discord among the top German military. The operation would be implemented by passing agents directly through front lines to distribute freshly conceived rumors, leaflets, fake orders, and "official" proclamations. The need for instant replay suggested to MO planners the use of a small group of carefully screened German prisoners.

Lauwers was a private in the Women's Army Corps, assigned to the Rome OSS station at the time; she was a Czechoslovak by birth with a law degree from Masaryk University, Brno, fluent in English, German, Czech, Slovak, and French. At midnight on 21 July 1944, she and Maj. William T. Dewart Jr. departed Rome for a prisoner-of-war compound at Averso, near Naples. They went by way of Caserta, where they obtained the necessary permission for the operation from Col. Edward Glavin, OSS head in Italy. They also requisitioned a truck to transport the prisoners they selected from Averso to Rome.

As Lauwers and Dewart were driving through the night along the seacoast, work was progressing at MO headquarters, OSS Rome, preparing for production of newspapers, documents, and leaflets. A special "order of the day," purporting to come from Field Marshal Walther von Brauchitsch, was also forged. It proclaimed that the field marshal had taken control of the German army and that the revolt against Hitler was continuing. Meanwhile, another MO officer, Edmund Lindner, was dispatched to Siena to requisition German weapons, uniforms, insignia, credentials, and "pocket detritus" as part of the cover for the prisoners who would infiltrate the front lines near a point on the Arno River.

Lauwers spent the entire day of 22 July interviewing German prisoners. She finally selected sixteen who met her rigid demands. Some of Lauwers's comments as submitted in her report to MO headquarters, Rome:

Hans Tappert: Former naval officer from Brussels; intelligent, tries to create impression he is interested in revenge.

Karl Heiderich: Nineteen years old; lived in Canada; returned to Germany and sent to Russian front. A Boy Scout type; thinks it's all fun!

Ernst Fichter: Comes from Innsbruck, auto

119

mechanic, inducted in 1942 and sent to the Russian front; later turned himself in to Italian partisans. Eager beaver. Definitely good.

As Lauwers recollected in her reminiscences with me, most of the prisoners she interrogated were young men. Some were dissidents who had seen the carnage on the Russian front where the Nazi war machine had been routed; others were from forced-labor battalions, critical of the Reich. Many were deserters. A university student told her that he had seen too many cruelties committed against civilian populations; he had once witnessed the burning of an entire village where three hundred innocent people perished. He was a Christian and could not condone such atrocities. A young carpenter from a Slovenian farm had been forced into the German labor corps; when Lauwers spoke to him in Czech, he burst into tears. Another, a Bavarian forester, had spoken up against the Reich after a drinking binge near Nice and had been arrested; he jumped off the train taking him back to Germany and surrendered to Italian partisans.

Once Lauwers made her selections, the prisoners were issued American army fatigue coveralls and ordered into the truck, bound for further indoctrination in the environs of Rome. Two members of the military police rode with the prisoners. Lauwers and Dewart followed in their jeep. "The journey took us through desolate, uninhabited country," Lauwers explained to me. "If the prisoners had wanted to escape, they could have easily overcome their guards and disappeared into the foothills. But they all sat stolidly in the open truck, some of them even singing."

The prisoners were billeted outside Rome in a tile-roofed two-story villa hidden by trees and stone walls. Here they worked with Lauwers, memorizing their cover stories. She created a new identity for each man based upon intelligence reports sent to her by OSS Research and Analysis teams. OSS order-of-battle staff updated important details for uniform insignia, pointing out, for example, that a German division had changed its shoulder patch from a single small red diamond to one red diamond within a larger one; such information was vital to the cover preparations. A prisoner with an Austrian accent had a cover story tailored to his background. His own name and his family names were all changed. Former occupations were woven as closely as possible into a new identity, and the cover story was drilled into the men's subconscious. They would be awakened in the middle of the night and asked their new name and rank.

One of these men was Will Williams (then called Willi Haseneier). An artist and a graduate of Düsseldorf Art Academy, he had spent the first six months of his army career in Kiel doing a sculpture of Adm. Erich Raeder before starting basic training. His military service was marred by his inability to take orders; he was eventually transferred to a motion-picture company, and he later specialized in troop entertainment.

Lauwers soon detected Williams's ability to draw and to counterfeit signatures, and he proved a great help in forging credentials. He had a difficult time with Field Marshal Albert Kesselring's signature. "As supreme commander in Italy, I guess Albert felt he had to put a lot of flourishes on his signature," Williams told me. "But since I would be using his name on one of my own false credentials, I was very careful. It worked out, because I later learned that Kesselring was forced to deny authorship of an 'official' proclamation bearing his well-forged name."

Less than four days after Operation Sauerkraut was conceived, the first teams of German prisoners were ready to infiltrate the front lines. They would be put through in two waves, the first at midnight, the second at dawn. They would be led across no man's land by OSS officers to a point on the Arno River where they would then be told to go on alone, crossing the river and penetrating as far as they could. They were ordered to nail leaflets and proclamations on trees, leave them in buildings and on trucks, scatter them in the streets of the small Italian towns occupied by Germans. If challenged, they were soldiers trying to find their respective units; they had been on special assignment and were rejoining their group; they were returning from leave, and their unit had been transferred.

They were all equipped with forged identity papers and passes, Beretta pistols, German rifles with forty rounds of ammunition each, compasses, Italian or Swiss watches, and three thousand pieces of MO material. They also carried between 2,300 and 7,000 Italian lira of all denominations. They wore German steel helmets and uniforms and carried field equipment, first-aid kits, and one vital bartering item: Italian cigarettes.

Williams told me, in reviewing those days of long ago, that he wasn't too keen on going behind the lines: "I remember a black cat ran across our path en route to the river. It seemed like an omen, but everything worked out fine. Lauwers's cover story held up. I was with the Twenty-fifth Pioneer Battalion, lowest of the low; we shoveled trenches and planted mines and didn't know how to salute properly."

When Williams was accosted by a sentry as he shambled into a small town, he played out the part: "Password? What password? Has it changed again? I've been digging trenches all day." When the sentry hesitated, Williams pulled out a package of cigarettes and offered him one, which he accepted greedily. "I just trudged past him, grateful he hadn't looked into my knapsack, which was full of MO material. I got rid of it as soon as I could."

Williams penetrated about two miles behind the lines. Once he watched a patrol of eight SS men picking up some of the material he had placed in a local market area. "They all read the 'official' proclamation denouncing Hitler's policy of destroying the German Wehrmacht for the sake of the Nazi party," he said. "They discussed it heatedly among themselves and pocketed the material."

Williams returned through the American lines after unloading his weapons, advancing with hands over head and calling out the passwords that got him and the other prisoners back to Rome: "Take me to the commander-in-chief." All sixteen men returned, unharmed. They, like Williams, reported that they had been able to move about freely and had disseminated their propaganda. All along the Italian front, German soldiers were reading documents intended to create the impression that a revolt against the Nazis had begun at home.

Although it was not their primary mission, these agents also brought back valuable intelligence. One prisoner of war, Hans Mauer, penetrated enemy lines north of Siena where he discovered, six miles forward, eighteen German Tiger tanks under camouflage. These were destroyed by Allied bombs. The success of this first mission demonstrated the value of this new technique of infiltrating POW agents back across enemy lines, despite skepticism on the part of some British officials who feared that the prisoners could be easily "doubled."

More than anything else, the success of Operation Sauerkraut showed that such an operation could be carried out consistently and could be expanded. The services of these agents were requested by the Fifth Army Intelligence Branch (G-2). Several holding areas were established in Italy for further training.

Lauwers was assigned to assist Sauerkraut agents in their safe-house villa producing MO material. She worked with an OSS team of twenty-two men including Eugene Warner, the chief of the section; Lt. (JG) Saul Steinberg, the noted artist; Maj. William T. Dewart Jr., publisher of the *New York Sun*; Capt. Temple Fielding; Jan Libich; and Cpl. Egidio Clemente, the man in charge of printing.

Lauwers was the only woman on the staff. She is credited with inventing the "League of Lonely War Women," which was so credible that the *Washington Post* ran a story about it on 10 October 1944. The story, datelined Rome, stated that "German soldiers on leave from the Italian front have only to pin an entwined heart on their lapel during furloughs home to find a girl friend." This information was credited by the *Post* to a captured circular from the Eighth Army front.[2]

The circular had been written by Lauwers and the language carefully honed into soldier vernacular — the German counterparts to American army slang terms like *GI Joe* and *mess hall* — that would be familiar on the German home front. The circular disclosed the existence of the league, whose members were willing to give themselves over to the fulfillment of soldiers' dreams. Its purpose was to make furloughs pleasant and to bolster Germany's birth rate. A button was affixed to the circular. "Take this button and display it visibly," the instructions read. "Soon a member of our League will take charge of you and your front line dreams and longings will find fulfillment. There are members everywhere, since we German women understand our duties toward the defenders of our country. Don't be shy. Your wife, mother, sister or sweetheart is one of us. We think of you and we think of the future of Germany."

In one of our long discussions of wartime episodes, Lauwers recalled one of her own assignments while working with the German prisoners: "I remember sitting in our jeep next to a driver, and waiting for some of the prisoners to emerge from a Roman dwelling following an 'afternoon of a fawn' with the local *putanazzas*. It was my chore to pay for their well-deserved pleasures after a successful mission across the lines. I often wondered how this expenditure could be explained to the American taxpayer by the OSS disbursing officer!"

A chance remark by a German prisoner jump-started another very successful operation by Lauwers that won her the Bronze Star. She learned that several hundred Czech and Slovak soldiers had been attached to the German army on the Italian front, mainly in the capacity of service troops doing menial tasks. She requested, and received, permission to develop a plan targeted against these soldiers. She prepared two leaflets, one in Czech, the other in Slovak, to be infiltrated across the lines by her German prisoners. The leaflets were produced using the only Czech and Slovak typewriters available, which were in an office in the Vatican. The leaflets read, in part:

Czechoslovak soldiers with the German army! In September, 1938, at the Berlin Sports Palace, Hitler swore before the world that not a single Czechoslovak would serve in the German army. Yet today, our soldiers are being used by the Nazis to service their troops! On the side of the Allies in Italy, behind German lines, fighting underground with Italian partisans are men and women who left their homeland so they could one day return to Czechoslovakia as free people. You men were sent to fight against this underground. You came to this battle ground to protect Germans. The fate of Germany is already sealed. Hitler's armies are falling apart, beaten in Russia, Italy, France, they are now retreating to their own borders.

There is only one command for you, soldiers. Shed this German yoke of shame, cross over to the partisans. Come at once. Only one road leads to the homeland: the road some of your countrymen chose four years ago. Remember President Masaryk's words: "We are fighting for the freedom of Europe and mankind!" Czech and Slovak soldiers: Fulfill your obligations to a land that for 1,000 years has retained its spiritual independence. Come across to us!

The same message was broadcast by the BBC and directed at the Czechoslovak garrisons in northern Italy. The leaflets that Lauwers had written were found in the pockets of more than six hundred Czechoslovak soldiers who crossed the lines.

Private Lauwers, in starched shirt and trim winter uniform, wore her new corporal's stripes for the first time at a ceremony held on 6 April 1945 when she was presented with the Bronze Star for this operation. Behind her stood the MO team with whom she had worked. A spit-and-polish officer read the citation as the cold wind blew across the hills of Rome. He spoke of Barbara L. Lauwers, A-1000765, corporal, Women's Army Corps, and her meritorious achievement in connection with military operations against the enemy in Italy.

For Lauwers it should have been a day of glory. But she described it to me, humorously, as a moment of agony as she waited for the speaker finally to pin that medal on her uniform:

The officer went on interminably, speaking of that effective OSS action aimed against Czechs serving with German units. He droned on and on. I was unable to listen and absorb because suddenly I felt the excruciating need to pee so terribly that I thought I'd faint. It occurred to me that if I should let go, it would run down my legs into my shoes, onto the pale gray concrete of the slight incline where I was facing the Brass. The puddle would proceed, grow, and spill toward the detachment of soldiers behind me.

I started to pray to *all* my saints, not knowing which one could handle such a situation. I prayed that the ceremony would end before I burst. I obviously reached the right saint, and I was spared that final ignominy.

A few weeks after the award ceremony, Lauwers was sent up to Livorno to meet those Czechoslovak troops who had marched to freedom. At the gate she was greeted by their commanding officer, who introduced himself as Major Konvalinka. She was taken for a tour of the premises in an abandoned agricultural compound. The major then commanded his group, "Fall in and present arms."

129

These were the Czechoslovaks who had read her message and obeyed. They were still in German uniforms, but above the Nazi insignia they wore a piece of red, white, and blue ribbon. The major confirmed that more than six hundred had marched across with their own band, which played the Czechoslovak national anthem as they came through the front lines. The war on the Italian front had ended the day they defected, on 29 April 1945.

Immediately after the cessation of hostilities, Will Williams was sent by OSS to the War Crimes Branch in Salzburg, where he made posters to be used at the Nuremberg trials depicting the most wanted Nazi war criminals. Later he went to Hollywood, where he worked for another OSS alumnus, director John Ford.

Lauwers herself went home to visit Brno after the war, where she had been born Bozena Hauserova. She had transferred from OSS in Italy to civilian status with the Office of War Information (OWI), where her multilingual talents were in great demand and where she was given the assimilated rank of first lieutenant. One of her jobs was to help revive the famous Salzburg Musical Festival. There she managed to wangle a seven-day pass and transportation. She was also issued a pair of silver bars and an American flag patch that strengthened her identity in the Soviet zone beyond Plzeň. Her trilingual pass was in English, Czech, and Russian.

Out of Plzeň the landscape looked starkly different, Lauwers recalled. She had left her home in 1939 as the bride of an American executive with Bata Enterprises. Now, in this postwar world, communities were deserted, shutters closed. There was no sign of life, either human or animal. East of Prague the roads were in almost total disrepair. After an overnight stop, her jeep finally lurched into familiar territory.

"On that road to my home, I suddenly came to life. I asked the driver to please turn right, pass the church, over the railroad tracks, go slowly up the hill towards a beautiful linden tree. And there, walking down the road, with a jug in her hand, was my mother!" Lauwers yelled at the driver to step on the brakes; she bolted out of the jeep. "Mother, mother! My whole insides screamed after her. She turned around, dropped the jug, ran a few yards and fell into my arms. The scene was replayed when I met my father. They all had thought I was dead. The reunion with my siblings was less dramatic. But they enjoyed walking me around the town. The American uniform was definitely an attraction in the sea of Russian red stars."

Returning to Salzburg, Lauwers was given a choice: two more years with the OWI unit in Austria, or immediate repatriation to the United States. She opted for repatriation.

Lauwers's ship put in at the Boston port of

debarkation. No one met her; her husband had divorced her during the war. She worked at a number of jobs: selling hats, working as a dental assistant, broadcasting briefly for the Voice of America, working as a "girl Friday" at the National Academy of Sciences in Washington. She finally found permanent employment with the Library of Congress, where she met her second husband, Joseph Junosza Podoski. He was a Polish aristocrat who also worked at the library as a research analyst. He died in 1984, after thirty years of marriage. She returned his ashes to Polish soil as he had requested.

OSS loomed up once more in Barbara Lauwers Podoski's life. The Veterans of Strategic Services, composed of men and women who had served OSS all over the world during World War II, met for a commemorative banquet in Washington in 1991. Podoski was a guest at my table, which included another OSS veteran from the Far East, Joseph R. Coolidge of Boston, a recent widower.

In September 1945 Coolidge had been the first American wounded in Vietnam. He had been returning from Da Lat on official business when his team was ambushed by hostile Annamites in Thu Duc, a Saigon suburb. Shotgun pellets tore through his body and ruptured his aorta. Ironically, he was rescued and taken to the hospital by a group of Japanese soldiers who broke up the ambush. Coolidge still has seventy-five bird-shot pellets in his chest to remind him that he became the first American to receive the Purple Heart on that first day of the Vietnam conflict.

Between Barbara Podoski and Joseph Coolidge that night a magical friendship was born and continues. He gave her a wedding band, which she wears as a token of their special relationship, which "only death can part."

As Joseph Coolidge says, more tenderly, "I can but stand in astonished ecstasy. To crib from Shakespeare, 'Time does not wither nor custom stale' the infinite miracle of us. It looks as if the first seventy-five years of our separate lives were simply preparation for these golden moments we now know."

Today they divide their time between Squam Lake, New Hampshire, on Golden Pond where Coolidge lives, and Podoski's Washington apartment.

As early as February 1942, several years before OSS agents such as Barbara Lauwers Podoski went into action in the war zones of Europe, support for important covert operations was being developed in New York City. This metropolis offered a variety of opportunities: access to foreign nationals arriving from abroad; liaison with foreign and neutral agencies; the establishment of cover organizations. Women recruited from all over the world were involved in these OSS activities.

CHAPTER 7

Underground in
New York City

There was no name on the door of the suite of offices on the twenty-fifth floor at 630 Fifth Avenue, New York City — only the number 3663. Inside, a blue-uniformed guard checked badges that stated the names and addresses of employees. An OSS regulation required that these badges be worn around the neck on a cord during business hours and carefully guarded at all times.

The mystery office had quietly opened for business in February 1942, when OSS was still COI, the Coordinator of Information. (OSS was created on 13 June 1942.) It was under cover, and its mission was to obtain intelligence, recruit agents, and maintain liaison with foreign government representatives in New York, primarily the British.[1]

In the early days there was a hot line between this office and Washington headquarters. Elinore Grecey Weis manned this phone. She often put calls through to General Donovan in Washington and to Allen Welsh Dulles, the first director of the New York establishment. Occasionally she would catch a glimpse of the general himself, slipping into 3663 on secret matters.

Another tenant at 630 Fifth was the United Kingdom Commercial Corporation, the cover name for the British Security Coordination, headed by Britain's master spy, Sir William Stephenson. "He was a clever, hard eyed Canadian," Dulles wrote of Sir William. "He had much to teach me and I picked his brains."[2] In the months ahead, further cooperation between OSS and BSC was maintained at the top-secret Camp X, 250 acres on the north shore of Lake Ontario in Oshawa, where more than five hundred Allied men and women received training in clandestine operations and unconventional warfare.

As OSS work expanded in New York City, more offices were set up, and eventually the agency became overt. A pictorial records center was established at 1600 Broadway to catalogue and assess photo material from abroad. Morale Operations was hidden off Times Square in midtown Manhattan. Research and Analysis took separate offices at 55 West Fifty-third Street. Other branches leased hotel rooms, safe houses, and studios for recruitment, classified conferences, and black-radio production.

Weis recalled a very structured regimen:

We worked from nine in the morning often until eleven at night, sometimes for four-teen consecutive days before we had duty lay-offs. I was just twenty-three at the time. New York was very exciting during those war years. Emigrés were pouring in from Europe, and Mr. Dulles was developing a staff of experts on foreign affairs who interviewed refugees, built up data banks on personalities, industry, and political developments.

Quite often the girls in the office were too busy to go out for lunch, and we shared milk, crackers, and candy bars. We were lucky to have a co-worker named Charlotte Gristede who thoughtfully brought us goodies many mornings from one of her family's stores.[3]

Allen Dulles remained in New York until November 1942, when he was appointed "assistant to the American minister" in Switzerland. He left for Bern to organize undercover OSS activities. Replacing him as head of the New York offices was his Princeton associate, John G. Hughes, who in later years served as U.S. ambassador to NATO.

As a base for penetration of enemy intelligence services, X-2, the OSS Counter-intelligence Branch, required a vast amount of background material. Quite a few women were employed by X-2 in New York for the massive filing effort, including Marya Mannes and her assistant, Patricia Warner Fowler. Mannes was in the process of divorcing her naval-aviator husband, then in the Pacific. Fowler, at twenty-two, was a recent widow whose husband had been killed in the Pacific. Both women were left with young sons to raise.

Remembered today as a talented writer, Mannes was the niece of Walter Damrosch, the one-time New York Philharmonic conductor. Mannes's father, David, was an accomplished violinist who with his pianist wife ran the Mannes Music School in New York. Fowler recalls her vividly: "She was my first boss in X-2, a writer-artist who was model-beautiful, wrapped in an aura of mystery, especially when it came to outlining my duties."[4] Fowler explained:

Marya Mannes would come into my office with a mound of cards. She'd say something like, "Pick out enemy agents from these Iberian references. Sort of divide them into 'friendlies' and 'unfriendlies' just for starters, and we'll go on from there, I hope." It was difficult to know how to begin. It took some time before it dawned on me that none of us in the lower ranks of the early OSS hierarchy was supposed to be clear about anything, except the smallest part of the puzzle.

Fowler was eventually transferred to London

and then on to X-2 Madrid. The hardest decision she had to make when she was assigned overseas was to leave her small son: "Knowing what I do now as a psychotherapist," she said, "I never would have left my child, Robin, even for a day. But during one bleak and endless night I made the decision that he would be better off in the care of a cheerful nurse and a devoted circle of grandparents than he would be with a grieving mother who had a passionate belief in the cause her husband had died for in the South Pacific."

Like Fowler, Mannes could not deny her desire to serve her country. In her book *Out of My Times* she wrote that after reading the endless stream of reports from occupied countries and Germany, and after detailed exposure to the unparalleled horror of the concentration camps, she was filled with a hatred of the Nazis so intense that she was determined to do anything she could against them, however small. But her decision to leave her son was, like Fowler's, traumatic. She wrote that she came home from overseas to a small boy, "more beautiful than ever, who looked at me as if I were a stranger. No greater reminder of what I had done to him was needed."

Mannes described one of her assignments as "sheer bliss." She was in X-2 intercepts, which involved reading other people's private correspondence: "I could not only read other people's letters, but I was *ordered* to, thus breaking a lifetime of discretion." In this job she was asked to assess the writer, after having been briefed about his or her identity and business, and to determine what each might be up to, and through what business or political connections the subject operated.

Mannes too was being groomed for an X-2 job in Spain and was sent to a large sprawling apartment on the West Side of Manhattan. "Here," she wrote, "about six or eight of us, mostly men, were taught things that enthralled my Mata Hari soul: how to pick locks, how to piece together small bits of paper retrieved from trash, how to break codes, how to take photographs without being noticed. Since I was equally poor at picking locks and breaking codes, I marvel I was not then kicked out of X-2. They asked me instead to go to Spain."

Some of the women employed by the New York office brought to their work a high degree of competence, language ability, and area knowledge. One such person was Miss Bertha Carp, also known as Betty Carp, who came to OSS with a glowing endorsement from Allen Dulles. In an interoffice letter of 27 February 1942 Dulles wrote:

> We are enlisting the services of Miss Bertha Carp, who held, for over twenty years, a highly confidential and important position in the American Embassy in Turkey and

who has just arrived from Istanbul. I have known her personally since 1920 and can absolutely vouch for her. In addition to an extraordinary knowledge of the Near East and all its personalities, she speaks and writes fluently English, French, Iranian, German, Greek and Turkish. She expects to become an American citizen as soon as the law allows. In my future memoranda about her I shall refer to her as BC.

BC was born in Istanbul in 1898, of Austro-Hungarian parents, and when she was sixteen years old went to work for the American embassy there as a switchboard operator. Her warm personality was such that she attracted people at all levels, from shopkeepers and police to American and foreign diplomats; as these officials moved to other stations around the world, they kept in touch with the "little round, vivacious lady" noted for her ability to cut through red tape in a country notorious for bureaucratic quagmires. Dulles was bringing her to New York to help develop Project NET-1, a plan that would use Turkey as a base of operations against enemy-occupied southeastern Europe. The project description stated, "From Istanbul run the only land routes into southeastern Europe and from Izmir small boats can be operated into the Dodecanese and Aegean Islands and to the Greek mainland. The base would recruit and infiltrate agents into these territories for the purpose of organizing subversive operations."[5]

In February 1942 Carp arrived in the United States. Her cover, as arranged by Allen Dulles, was to be a clerk at Sullivan and Cromwell, his law firm in New York City. This rather thin cover story caused one of her State Department colleagues to tease her: "What sort of law are you going to practice?" Carp parried nicely: "I'm only interested in divorce cases of my State Department friends, and I'd like to start with you!"[6]

Carp brought with her a letter of recommendation from the American ambassador to Turkey, John MacMurray, in which he noted her sensitivity and quickness of perception and her resourcefulness in finding practical solutions to almost any problem: "She has deep understanding and tolerance, and love for her fellow humans, of all degrees, as nearly selfless as any man or woman I have ever known."[7]

Before moving to New York to develop Greek agents for Project NET-1, Carp reported to OSS Washington, where she prepared a series of memoranda analyzing political developments in Turkey and also suggesting possible OSS recruits who were already in place in Istanbul. In one of her reports she wrote that the most dangerous enemies in Turkey were the Germans: "The colony is enormous, full of German businessmen, teachers, technicians, bookstores and clubs." She dined with her friend Irene Boyle, secretary to Lord Fairfax, the British ambassador to the United States, and reported, "She told me the British are anything but pleased with Turkey's game. They expected to be treated as allies and yet the Turks are in constant negotiation with Franz Von Papen, the German ambassador. England no longer trusts Turkey." A close friend of Von Papen's told her that "the Ambassador and former German Chancellor insists that as long as he is in Ankara, he can guarantee that there would be no German invasion of Turkey. He stands for peace with Turkey." Her own observations: "The Turkish policy is for Turkey and Turkey only. The specter of famine ridden Greece had a devastating effect upon the Turks, less from pity of the gallant Greek fighters, than from fear that the same fate would befall them. Fear of Russia is also a big factor in Turkey's stand."[8]

Once she was transferred to New York City, Carp began her search for Greeks in the city who could be used in Project NET-1. One of the first places she chose to survey prospects was a dingy little restaurant at 269 West Twenty-fifth Street, the Spartacus Club. Here she found Greek workers and seamen lounging everywhere, talking across tables, arguing with the Greek waiters. When the dainty little lady sat down quietly at a table by herself, they eyed her with suspicion. But as soon as she began to order her food in perfect Greek, the curious men crowded around her, asking where she was from, who she was, where she lived, and what was she doing in a dive like the Spartacus Club. Soon they were begging for the latest news from Turkey, but more important, they wanted to hear about their own homeland, and about the starvation and other wartime atrocities their countrymen were said to be suffering there at the hands of the Italian and German fascists.

Carp kept her audience enthralled with her firsthand knowledge of the situation in that war-devastated area of Greece. Eventually the president of the club, Constantine Contogenia, who also owned a Greek-American newspaper, sat down with her. He explained that the club's main purpose was to support the Russian War Relief. All the members were communists, but he invited Carp to join on the assumption that she was not a fascist and that she sided with the Allied cause. He invited her to become a "great patroness" of the club, sharing the honor with Mrs. Maxim Litvinoff, wife of the Russian ambassador to the United States.

"They all treated me with lavish hospitality," Carp reported to Dulles in a memorandum dated 28 March 1942. "On leaving, they thanked me for preferring their Greek food to that of the Hotel Astoria." This meeting led to many more sessions with her new friends. She attended a Russian War Relief rally, spent many more evenings at the Spartacus Club, and began the assessment of men who would later find themselves working for OSS out of Turkey.[9]

After the war, Carp returned to her old job in Istanbul at the American embassy. General Donovan personally sponsored her application for American citizenship.

When Hughes inherited Dulles's rapidly growing New York operation, another well-qualified woman, Toni Sender, was hired to work in the international labor field, targeted at what she called Germany's "Achilles heel." Sender sought access through labor organizations to the thousands of foreign nationals, including Italians, who had been impressed into work in Nazi factories, virtual slaves in the industrial sectors that supported Hitler's war machine. Later, French prisoners of war and forced laborers were added to this promising OSS target.

A German émigré, Sender became an important member of the OSS Labor Branch in New York. Born 4 December 1888 in Biebrich, Germany, she was named Sidonie Zippora Sender, Toni for short. Her father, Morris Sender, was an Orthodox Jew who presided over the local Jewish community in Biebrich. During World War I Toni worked for the Democratic Socialist Party and also with the Socialist Women International, where she was known as an agitator and "child of the revolution." In 1919 she became editor of the Daily Volksrecht, an ardent advocate of women's rights, calling for "equal pay and equal work." That year Sender was the only woman to be elected to the Frankfurt am Main municipal government. The next year she was elected to the German parliament and assigned to the economic and foreign policy committee. Forced to flee Germany when Hitler came to power, she eventually emigrated to the United States in 1935 and applied for citizenship. In her book *Autobiography of a German Rebel* she wrote, "Thank you, America, for taking me in and for giving me the opportunity to start a new chapter in pursuing those ideals for which the noblest of people have died."

In 1942 Sender and other trade unionists set up the European Labor Research Group, which Sender headed. Housekeeping for this research project was funded by OSS in New York. For the next year she prepared numerous reports based upon her contacts with European labor leaders. In New York her work for OSS was vetted by Gerhard (Gary) Van Arkel, general counsel for the National Labor Relations Board, and by Arthur Goldberg, whose later titles included secretary of labor, associate justice of the Supreme Court, and U.S. ambassador to the United Nations.

In a report to Hughes in January 1943 Sender wrote, "During the last month our labor sources in Europe have sent us valuable information. This memo includes the following: underground movements of workers;

printers, seamen and transport personnel in a number of European countries; names and contact points with labor leaders; resistance movements organized by seamen in Germany, Austria, France, the Netherlands; survey of the labor situation in Germany."[10] Always she stressed the potential strength of the millions forced to work as slave laborers for the Reich who nevertheless remained sympathetic to the Allied effort.

Reporting on her contacts in German industry in the fourth winter of the war, she wrote, "It is a concentration of the entire European production for Germany's war needs. There is almost a complete standstill of civilian production. There are bottlenecks throughout the Reich because of labor shortage and deterioration of plant installations." Sender's contacts once interviewed a German worker who had been able to make a clandestine visit to Switzerland in 1941. He revealed sabotage slowdown tactics at the Hamburg plant where he worked. Here the workforce had built only five submarines between April and December, although the men maintained that they could have easily finished ten in that time. The informant said that the workers went along as slowly as possible, especially the foreign craftsmen, who blamed their poor output on lack of experience and difficulty with the German language.

In the course of her work with OSS, Sender

had contact with some hundred Social Democrats and labor leaders in Sweden, Switzerland, and England, including the exiled Willy Brandt who would become chancellor of Germany in 1969 and a Nobel Peace Prize winner. She reported on specific intelligence:

About 300,000 to 400,000 German-speaking workers from the Sudetenland region have been shifted to the Reich; there are now about 140,000 Czech and 80,000 Slovak workers mostly in central Germany and the Ruhr employed in mining, metal working and textile production. Slovaks are escaping in great numbers, returning to their homeland. Here, at the Skoda munitions works, there are from 25,000 to 60,000 workers, between the ages of 16 and 25, assembled at the factories under general conscription. All boys and girls are ordered to register.

Toni Sender was an energetic, dark-haired rebel who constantly urged her OSS colleagues to develop a positive, aggressive program targeting the slave-labor forces of Europe. She was an admirable and influential asset.

There was another office in the OSS New York complex that was simply marked "United States Government." This was the headquarters at 610 Fifth Avenue of the Biographical

Records Section, one of the earliest Secret Intelligence branches designed to obtain foreign intelligence mainly through interrogating the émigrés swarming into New York from abroad.

Emmy Crisler Rado started work for this section, then called Oral Intelligence, on 23 September 1941. Rado was a dark-haired, attractive Swiss-born OSS analyst married to Alexander Rado, a New York psychologist. (The dangerous Soviet double agent, Sander Rado, the Swiss mapmaker, was no relation, although occasionally there was some confusion of the names in radio traffic.)

At the time Rado was hired, the office had no access to ship manifests. The first refugees interviewed were fearful and jittery. Many expressed fears that the unidentified OSS office was a Gestapo-inspired organization that would report back to Germany. Rado wrote in an office memo, "The attitude of refugees changed as soon as the United States entered the war. They then felt it was our government's right to question them, and they looked for very official titles on our door and letterheads."[11]

It was also difficult, before Pearl Harbor, for Rado's office to establish credibility. Her agency was not known, and its agents were not supposed to say what they were trying to obtain. Rado gave an example: "Sherman Kent's Africa Division wanted road maps of Morocco and Algiers and he could not go to different companies and request them. He asked us for help and I went to the American Automobile Association, of which I was a member. I talked them into lending me maps of North Africa promising to return them immediately. I had to give them the name of a private firm I once worked for, then I had to rush to the firm and explain that I was expecting a package from the AAA!"

Rado recalled that at first the greatest difficulty they had was that OSS branches requested interviews with refugees but did not provide interviewers with specific questions to ask. "Things straightened out eventually, especially when London began to receive our material. They sent definite requirements: What are shoe soles made of in Germany? How was the hemp crop in the south of France?"

Eventually Rado organized a system for interviewing, although she understood that different methods of questioning had to be devised for different people. Her psychologist husband helped in developing these special techniques. Among his suggestions:

— The first interview must not be conducted to elicit information. Establish confidence, find out what interests each subject, and be a good listener. Don't take notes; it intimidates the more fearful ones.

— The second interview should be based upon subtle flattery. Tell the person that what he had to say is of such interest that you would like to take notes. Take them in such a way that the person being interviewed can read them. Even ask the subject to correct what you have written. Interviewing should be done in private. A confidential conversation between two people, especially when trying to get them to divulge military or other secrets, must be conducted behind doors, one on one.

— Finally, interviewing can be a very exacting and tiring job. Customers within OSS branches must establish information priorities and inform interviewers at once of any change in these priorities.

Rado said that she found it useful to speak German to the Germans, French to the French. Most people would open up a little more, even when they also spoke English. "And my Swiss dialect worked wonders with the Swiss émigrés."

The women members of the staff who conducted these interviews were, like Rado, fluent in foreign languages and knowledgeable about international affairs. There was Carry Hepner, born in Germany in 1907, who had studied German literature and history at the University of Berlin. She was employed for twelve years in a publishing house before emigrating to England at the outbreak of war. She worked with refugee groups there until coming to the United States in 1940.

Caroline McMahon, daughter of an army general, spent most of her life abroad and was educated at the Convent de Sacré Coeur in France and in a Quebec convent. She started her career working for the U.S. military attaché in Tokyo, with fourteen years there in army intelligence. She learned the language, studied the phobias and customs of the Japanese, and wrote a bestseller, *Paradox Isle*, before being repatriated on the *Gripsholm* after Pearl Harbor. Fluent in French and German, she had a broad knowledge of Axis politics that was valuable in dealing with German refugees.

Another staffer was Bavarian-born Ann Stewart, who had studied and practiced law in Munich. She was interested in international student organizations and met her English husband in Munich shortly after Hitler came to power. They fled to England, where she worked with refugees until moving in 1940 to New York, where she later joined OSS. Her interviews involved mostly emigrants from southern Germany.

One employee at 630 Fifth Avenue had worked in the Vienna underground movement after Hitler took power. Dr. Marie Deutsch, wife of Dr. Julius Deutsch, former Austrian War Ministry official, was born in Austria in 1884 and studied history and geography at the University of Vienna. Later she became president of the Free Trade Union in that city and was imprisoned when the Nazis marched into

Vienna in 1938. After being released, she emigrated to London and eventually to New York.

Biographical Records interviewers felt that their work was exacting and exhausting, requiring alertness to detail and a quick grasp of psychological subtleties to be successful. Interviewers agreed that the best approach was to let the subject talk about himself as much as he pleased. It made him feel good and loosened his tongue. The nuggets they mined were sometimes important in themselves; more often they became part of a larger jigsaw puzzle. For example:

— *Techniques of deception:* When Allied airplanes were sighted sweeping toward Berlin, all the large factories in that city were alerted. These factories had installations on the grounds that could, if the weather was favorable, generate an artificial fog, which tended to screen familiar Berlin landmarks and factories from the pilots' view.

— *Notes from Berlin:* German soldiers appeared in Berlin wearing Czech uniforms that they had taken after the invasion of Prague in March 1939. They brought fur-lined gloves back to their families after the Norway invasion. Coal deliveries and garbage removal in Berlin were done by Polish prisoners wearing a *P* on their sleeves; no one talked to them. French prisoners worked on farms and were better treated. A camp had been set up for black Africans, who were treated well; after being imbued with Nazi doctrine, they were returned to Africa for propaganda purposes. Thousands of Italians were living in Germany, most of them hairdressers and waiters.

— *About women:* Among the most enthusiastic supporters of Hitler were older women of wealth who did practically nothing but attend teas and social functions. Working women who were avid Nazis were given government positions under the Reich, and even the Gestapo had a woman executive on its staff.

— *Nazi doctors:* The medical profession in Germany was one of the first professional organizations to turn Nazi, and the first to hang out the Nazi flag from its Medical Association Building. The doctors quickly filled the places of dismissed dissidents or Jewish physicians at universities and hospitals. They helped from the beginning by cementing the Nazi ideology and adopting its master-race theory. They were responsible for carrying out "mercy deaths" and finding a rationale to justify that work. (Rado and her section spent five months producing an extensive report on the medical profession, which was passed on to General Donovan in October 1944.)

In the course of their interrogations, the interviewers were also able to obtain documents such as German work papers or travel permits and samples of ersatz goods and clothing that were used later in equipping OSS agents dropped behind the lines in France.

Between June 1943 and June 1944, the Rado team interviewed 2,003 Germans, 977 Italians, 706 Austrians, 164 Belgians, and 252 French. The German files alone contained material on 5,069 key personnel in Germany and comprehensive reports on a variety of Germans: clergy, doctors, journalists, industrialists, and railroad personnel, among others.

In 1944 Rado became interested in the German Confessional Church, the *Bekenntniskirche*. This group represented the mainstream of officially recognized German churches, mainly Catholic and Protestant. Rado's concept of using the church as a positive influence in postwar Germany started with bits and pieces of information gathered during interviews: Bibles were in great demand but were no longer printed because of the paper shortage; Catholic and Protestant magazines were forbidden; there were fewer chaplains in the German army than during World War I.

Rado also talked to an American newspaperman with the Associated Press, Louis P. Lochner, who had lived in Berlin since 1921. On his return to New York he told Rado that the Catholic Church was playing a large part in facing up to the opposition. He had had many conversations with church leaders, and they were developing a broad front against the Nazi regime. Protestant churches were also becoming aware that Christianity in Germany was being undermined by Hitler. Rado began collecting lists of German pastors. By December 1944 she had the names of some three hundred men and women who would be the nuclei for a project she originated, code-named Crown Jewels.[12]

As the result of lengthy interviews with two Lutheran pastors and information collected from other sources, Rado and her associates prepared a memorandum on the importance of the Confessional Church, copies of which went to General Donovan and Allen Dulles. Dulles, whose family had known Rado through the World Council of Churches, wholeheartedly approved the project and urged her to come to Bern, where she could continue to make her contacts. He also felt that her dual citizenship would be useful. Rado agreed enthusiastically, and orders were cut in January 1945 for Bern via London. Her job description: clerk in the American embassy. Later, as Germany began to crumble, Rado was the first OSS woman to enter Berlin with Dulles, providing his team with valuable advice on how to deal with the Germans.

In those early, heady days in Berlin, Rado seemed to dazzle everyone she met. According to an OSS colleague and friend, S. Peter Karlo, she was a marvelous combination of beauty and brains. "And she loved to swim nude in the Danube," he recalled with a smile.[13]

Six months after OSS operations began in New York City, the first overseas station was opened in London, which served not only as a base for clandestine activities in Northern, Central, and Western Europe but also as a collection and dissemination center for intelligence of interest to U.S. and Allied agencies. By mid-1944 this OSS station included more than three thousand men and women serving fourteen branches, with offices located throughout wartime London.

CHAPTER 8

London Station

The London cable from General Donovan came as a complete surprise to the distinguished Foreign Service officer who received it at his Back Bay Boston home in early July 1942. It was a request that Ambassador William Phillips head up an OSS office in London, then in the process of organization.[1]

"I knew nothing about OSS except that it had been created by the President a few months earlier," Phillips wrote in his book *Ventures in Diplomacy.* Cautiously, he contacted President Roosevelt, saying that he would not consider the proposal without presidential approval. He was reassured by Roosevelt's immediate response: "Delighted with idea!"

Phillips's career had already included State Department assignments around the world: first secretary of embassy, London; assistant secretary of state under Woodrow Wilson and Roosevelt; minister plenipotentiary to Holland and Canada; and ambassador to Belgium and Italy. Intrigued by the prospect of an entirely new type of career, Phillips went to Washington, where he met Donovan for the first time at breakfast at the general's Georgetown home. The new recruit was immediately charmed: "He had an in-depth knowledge of world affairs, coupled with an immense vitality and an unwavering conviction that OSS would play an important part in the war."[2]

Later, when he met the personnel at OSS headquarters in Washington, Phillips was "deeply impressed by the fine spirit pervading the entire organization, and by the high types of women and men Donovan had gathered about him." He was also challenged by the arcane nature of the work they were doing, all geared toward supporting the war effort abroad.

On 18 July 1942 William Phillips boarded a Pan American flying boat bound for his new assignment in London. He was accompanied by his special assistant, David Williamson, and by Evangeline Bell, who was his office administrator and secretary. Later she would become the wife of David Bruce, Phillips's successor as chief of the London station.

An embryonic OSS staff, headed by Fisher Howe, met their station chief at Paddington Station, London, and escorted the group to the embassy headquarters that had been set up for their temporary use while OSS offices were being prepared nearby on Grosvenor Street. Here Phillips was briefed on the relationship between OSS and British intelligence. He learned that the newly spawned American spies were considered upstarts by a service that dated back to the sixteenth century, when Queen Elizabeth I had established England's first far-reaching intelligence agency. Her ambassadors abroad were also secret agents, with a supporting attaché system; Jesuit priests spied on political activities within their own church; third countries such as Italy were used to mount subversive action against the queen's archenemy, Spain; disinformation campaigns were developed that kept the Spanish Armada from attacking England for at least a year. Phillips was up against a spy system that had been in place for four centuries!

The British were not his only adversaries. Phillips also had to establish a working relationship with suspicious American military leaders wary of that "fly by night OSS outfit trying to horn in on the war."

In the five months that Phillips headed the station, his diplomatic training, plus a new appreciation for OSS goals, enabled him to lay the groundwork for OSS intelligence operations throughout Europe. At the peak of pre-D-Day activity, in the spring of 1944, London was the largest OSS overseas station, with 3,255 employees. There were 446 women, including American civilians, members of the Women's Army Corps (WAC), and British, French, and Australian employees.

Most of these women were well educated; many had college degrees, a fluency in foreign languages, and area familiarity. Some were dropped behind enemy lines with resistance groups; one was captured by Germans but maintained her cover identity as an interpreter; another was placed surreptitiously at Claridge's Hotel where she and her husband established liaison with exiled King Peter of Yugoslavia. Others developed cover stories for agents going to France. Many spent long, weary hours in the secret cable room, locked away from the sun and fresh air. Still others, in the Research and Analysis Branch (R&A), were learning that the major tool of the intelligence trade was the three-by-five index card, which, when painstakingly pieced together with other bits of intelligence, revealed patterns of enemy actions.

Women assigned to London during this period were instructed to bring warm clothes. No one could count on obtaining a stylish wardrobe in that war-torn city. The Personnel Office also advised them to bring flannel pajamas, pillow slips, blankets, and their own bed sheets. (These cost $12 apiece in London.) The army commissary had basic supplies: razor blades, toilet paper, soap, candy bars, and toothpaste. Liquor was obtainable only "for millionaires and naval officers," according to one source. Laundry and dry cleaning required two weeks, as did shoe repairs. Nylons were scarce, and one woman, prone to colds in the damp London winters, said she "would have killed for a box of Kleenex!"[3]

Civilian women preferred sharing flats with their OSS colleagues, mostly in the Mayfair area of London and within walking distance of the OSS offices, which were clustered about Grosvenor Square. Many of them did their own housekeeping. Other women, assigned to the R&A headquarters at 7 Ryder Street in the Picadilly section, chose flats in Knightsbridge with its proximity to Hyde Park. Ruth Ellen Thomas, now Mrs. Matthew B. McCullough, took a flat that had been evacuated by an English family. She shared the Knightsbridge apartment with two other OSS women, plus a housekeeper. They went to work on bicycles. She remembers that she ate out a lot, as it was difficult to get a variety of groceries with her ration card.

In addition, these women were working under blitz attacks of German V-1 and V-2 bombs launched from across the Channel and raining death and destruction on English targets. The V-1 was a small, pilotless airplane, the buzz bomb or doodlebug. It flew a predetermined course and distance, the forerunner of today's cruise missile. The V-2 was a rocket, flying at great heights, the prototype of the ballistic missile. Its only warning came upon impact, a terrific explosion capable of disintegrating buildings. It could not be heard during flight and was therefore not as psychologically unnerving as the V-1 with its raucous buzzing.

In a report submitted by WAC Katherine Keene it was noted that there was only one month when London experienced no air-raid activity in the two and a half years starting in 1943.[4] A British government announcement made in July 1944 stated that civilian bomb casualties totaled 12,441 killed or missing. Of these, 2,746 were men, 3,876 were women, and 485 were children. At war's end the OSS gave a citation to all women in the London office who had worked throughout these bomb attacks.

The bombings over London are still vivid memories to Alma Mattison, then twenty-four, the only woman secretary in the Communications Branch. "I worked in the Grosvenor Street office," she recalls. "I pulled night duty regularly, which meant patrolling the top floor of the building, often in frigid weather. I would watch fires flare up all over the city, like huge volcanoes. It was heartbreaking to see the destruction. I was once a near victim in Hyde Park. The taxi in which I was riding was nearly hit by a bomb, and I was jolted up and down like a bucking horse from the concussion."

Reports of the buzz-bomb attacks caused more concern in the United States than they did in London. The parents of two women working for the Security Branch cabled the American embassy in London to have their daughters returned to the States. One was Priscilla Johnson, whose father was in the State Department; the other was Mary Norris, who later married James Symington. Both women refused to be sent home. Symington, then twenty-two, said she wanted to stay and defied her parents' wishes. David Bruce, OSS London chief at that time, wrote that he "considered the request disgraceful — as well as placing the girls in an invidious position."[5]

Symington later recalled her London experience as one of the highlights in her life: "Such wonderful memories! We arrived in London from a peaceful United States, just in time for a huge bomb blitz. The buoyant, imperturbable temper of the British during those attacks was terrific. We were so lucky to share this experience with them."

William Phillips was also deeply affected by the devastation. "The scenes were heart rending. And yet, the great church of St. Paul's was still standing with an air of proud defiance, almost unscathed in the center of complete ruin," he wrote.[6]

Phillips left his London post on 28 December 1942. He had been asked to go to India as President Roosevelt's personal representative, with the rank of ambassador, to open up that country to OSS. He was accompanied by Maj. Richard P. Heppner, who later headed the OSS detachments that resulted from this mission in India and Ceylon. Phillips's successor in London in January 1943 was David Kirkpatrick Estes Bruce, forty-four-year-old son-in-law of Andrew Mellon; Bruce was a lawyer, a Virginia legislator, and a man who could occasionally beat General Donovan on the squash courts.

Combining tact with inherent leadership, Bruce continued to work closely with British intelligence and the American military. The British traitor Kim Philby, then high in MI6 (the British Secret Intelligence Service), unkindly characterized Bruce and his staff as a "notably bewildered group whose arrival was a pain in the neck."[7] Yet a year later that "bewildered group" was working on its own, outfitting, documenting, and dispatching agents to the field, eventually to Germany.

The initial WAC contingent destined for OSS London arrived bleary-eyed and cold in late November 1943. The first enlisted women to sail on the liner *Queen Mary*, they had crossed with a record number of troops and had been buzzed by an unidentified airplane. After constant bombing drills, crouching in their bunks in backpacks, overcoats, and steel helmets, they finally reached London by train from Scotland.

One WAC, Katherine Keene, remembers the arrival vividly. "After an all-night train trip in the blackout we arrived in an early-morning fog," she recalled:

The trucks transporting us to our billets got lost. It took almost three hours to get from Victoria Station to Upper Brooks

Street near Marble Arch, where we were quartered.

I looked down the street and saw a leafless tree two blocks away in what I was told was Hyde Park. Then I looked the other way and saw more leafless trees — Grosvenor Square, with a gray elephantine-like barrage balloon sluing about in the slight wind. The sky was gray. The buildings were gray. Then our deep-voiced master sergeant informed us that we were at 49 Upper Brooke Street. My instant reaction was "So what! Why didn't they let Hitler have it?" In front of us were our billets: two London townhouses, five stories high, with newly replaced windows. The old ones had been blown out. Inside it was damp and cold.[8]

This was the inauspicious introduction of sixty-two OSS WACs to their new assignment and their new quarters. They were destined to run into problems with their civilian sisters in OSS, who usually had better salaries but were not, as a general rule, better qualified than the uniformed WACs. Most of the women in the OSS WAC contingent were college trained, and the group had one of the highest average IQ scores of any unit in the WAC. There were three officers included in the group.

From the outset they followed military routine in their barracks. "In that first winter in London we wore overcoats and gloves in our billets," Keene recalled. "We washed ourselves and our clothes in cold water, unless we were one of the lucky ones to get off work early, around 6 P.M. After that the hot water disappeared." Keene recalled that the WACs at first lived out of their barracks bags until their supply officer, Lt. Jane Tanner, was able to discover, in a reverse lend-lease list, that she could order "chests, wood" and "cupboards, wall." When she requisitioned this somewhat battered composition furniture, the WACs had space for clothes and accessories about fourteen inches wide and five and one-half feet high. According to army regulations, their clothes had to be ironed and hung in order of length from left to right. Shoes were lined up in order of height under the bunks, and the blankets had to be placed with the lettering "U.S." in dead center.

They ate in the OSS mess in the basement of one of the office buildings. "Here we descended a circular staircase, into a large room once used by the house servants. We stood in line and the mess personnel splatted food into our divided trays," Keene remembered. "We seemed to have creamed corn — which splashed — at least three times a week. I have not cared for creamed corn or tomatoes stewed in bread since then. But one had to eat everything. If we arrived late, the tables were littered with bread crumbs and splats of food."

Keene remembers a GI who came into London from one of the OSS field stations once a month and always ate with them. He also played the piano in the adjoining lounge, and they liked listening to his music much more than the jazz that usually blasted from the American Force Network during mealtime. The visitor was married and never dated any of the WACs. "He told me he liked visiting our billet," Keene said, "because we were like the women he knew back home, well mannered and not swearing all the time. He particularly liked the male-female mess because he could say, 'Please pass the butter' the way he was brought up, instead of having to say, 'Pass the goddamn grease.' "

According to army regulations, the WACs had to keep their billet spotless. Keene remembers that there were seventy-two white marble steps that were scrubbed daily, plus a large marble foyer. There was a daily inspection, and if a WAC failed to perform her allotted task properly, she was confined to quarters for the weekend.

Keene was in charge of the company's physical training program. By popular request, she devised a nonstrenuous routine "for finger dexterity and ankle mobility." She recalled, "All went well until we had a sudden spot inspection by army headquarters in London. Their report stated that our physical-education program was a farce. The same report also criticized our first sergeant, Amanda Bertha Koester, for saying, 'Hurry up, honeys!' as we assembled in the hall for morning roll call. After praising absolutely nothing, they also reported that our morale was high, which seemed to confound them."

The WACs had been in London for less than a month when the air raids started up again. Three WACs from each billet were placed on fire-guard duty, stationed on the roof to extinguish any incendiary bombs that might hit. "These guards wore steel helmets," Keene explained. "Our helmets seemed very tiny, and our shoulders felt very broad, when shrapnel began falling on the roof." The WACs were generally sequestered within OSS office confines during the day. When they did venture out into the London streets, the harassment they suffered from American soldiers was something Keene still recalls bitterly: "Wherever we went there was a chorus of wolf calls and whistles. It got tiresome. There were also incidents of GIs walking behind us talking in loud voices about our legs, our breasts, and how we would be in bed. More than once they told us that WACs were overseas to sleep with the men — that was their mission!"

Notwithstanding this guttersnipe harassment, Katherine Keene's important mission with OSS was working for R&A at 40 Berkeley Square. "We kept track of production, not just for Germany but for Fortress Europe," she explained.

We soon became much more accurate

than ground intelligence behind enemy lines, which relied primarily on agents counting boxcars to estimate materiel production. We painstakingly traced, through factory markings and serial numbers, the production of airplanes, half-tracks, tanks, self-propelled guns, large ammunition, and vehicles of all sorts. Military intelligence personnel supplied this basic information at our request, and we also visited ammunition and tire dumps in the U.K. At most, there were only a dozen people in the group, and I was the only WAC.

The information we received was used by OSS R&A's Enemy Objective Unit down the hall from our office, which then recommended bombing targets. Walter Rostow was in charge of this group of economists, and Rosalene Honerkamp ran the office for him. We all worked hard to make certain our information was accurate. Every raid based upon our intelligence meant some of our boys in the air corps could be killed.

Keene continued:

I can give one rather grisly example. I worked with tires. I noticed that a small company in Fulda was suddenly making more tires with high mold numbers. Tires are made in molds, and each carried the number of the mold for quality-control purposes. This clearly meant to me that since the Nazis could not afford to lose all their tire production in the bombing of one large tire factory, some of their tire production had apparently been transferred to Fulda. We notified our friends at the end of the hall, and within a week I read in the London papers that Fulda had been bombed because they were making aero tires!

Some years later Keene visited Fulda, where a monument to that raid had been erected in the street square. Here 702 civilians had been killed, suffocated in plaster or crushed by falling beams.

The work that Keene's office accomplished was noted by Albert Speer, Hitler's minister in charge of German industry, who testified at the Nuremburg trials. He said that the Germans never expected their enemies to have the patience to keep track of serial numbers and other markings on German materiel, and thus estimate the output of individual factories. He considered this work an outstanding feat of Allied intelligence!

Keene, after a short tour of duty in Paris and Berlin, returned to the United States in 1945 and she took her degree at Columbia University under the GI Bill of Rights. She returned to her home in Seattle, where she taught school until her retirement. Her specialty: Western civilization.

Many of the WACs serving with Keene won decorations for their work. First Lt. Jane House, goddaughter of Marjorie Merriweather Post Davies, was awarded the Certificate of Merit for her work as supply officer with the Air Operations Section. She was responsible for dispatching supplies to resistance groups and was remembered warmly by one of her OSS colleagues, William Hornaday, as a "grand girl."[9] He saw her occasionally at packing stations outside London where air drops were prepared. House, on occasions, planned an entire supply phase for special operations into Norway or Germany.

A WAC corporal, Ida Lampton, won the Certificate of Merit for her work as a translator and processor of valuable Finnish intelligence.

First Lt. Anne Winslow was awarded the Army Commendation Ribbon for identifying and interrogating German intelligence personnel. She also coordinated activities with the army's Signal Corps, which resulted in the apprehension of Nazis and collaborators after D-Day. Fluent in German, French, and Russian, Winslow was skillful in questioning prisoners. She had a remarkable comprehension of the nuances of the languages, vital to sensitive interrogation.

In another field, Mary Donovan Corvo was assigned the job of writing up citations for men and women who served in the London station.

The OSS WAC unit, augmented by twenty-five more who arrived on D-Day, was given a unit citation in October 1945 for the members' bravery under the constant bombing of London, and for the contribution they made to OSS during the war.

The Research and Analysis Branch in London employed the greatest number of professional women. Of the sixty-six American women in the branch, nine were analysts and five were assistant analysts. They were researchers, economists, geographers, political scientists, and historians, many with a fluency in several languages. Examples include Julia Phelps, a graduate of Radcliffe and Harvard, a professor of fine arts who had traveled in England and on the Continent and spoke German, French, Italian, and Spanish; Jacqueline Hare, a Wellesley graduate who spoke fluent French, Italian, and Spanish and fair Russian; Emmy Lou Williamson, of Mary Baldwin College, Staunton, Virginia, a French major.

The branch was headed by economist Chandler Morse. Agents worked out of 68 Brook Street, across the street from Claridge's Hotel and a block away from the American embassy. The cozy, busy R&A library, located at 29 Grosvenor Street, contained political publications, sociological and psychological books, and stacks of historic-backgrounders in most European languages.

Arthur Schlesinger Jr., a Harvard graduate, later a Pulitzer Prize winner for history, worked in the Political Section of R&A with Harold Deutsch, another historian with degrees from Michigan and Wisconsin. In addition, Ruth Ellen Thomas was assigned to Schlesinger's staff for R&A economic targets in Germany and Italy. Her job was editing the *European Political Review*, which was prescribed reading in the military and the intelligence community.

"I was the youngest member of Schlesinger's staff, and I felt terribly in awe of some of the famous economists and historians who worked in the same office with me," Thomas told me later. "I spent days poring through newspapers, publications, intelligence operations, agent reports, trying to make sense out of what was going on. Men like Arthur Schlesinger had a grasp of the overall picture, but they needed people like me to pull all the details together, following their direction."

Thomas continued her work after D-Day when she was sent first to Paris, then to Biebrich, near Wiesbaden, where she filed documents on German leaders being uncovered by the American military and OSS agents. "It was hectic, but it had its lighter moments," she recalled. "Our headquarters was in a champagne factory, and we could get a glass of bubbly for ten cents. Once General Patton gave a party, and the OSS girls from Biebrich were escorted across the Maine River in tanks." She also remembered dancing with Gen. Omar Bradley to the music of a displaced-persons band.

Secret Intelligence (SI) agents operating out of the London station were seeking information vital in the determination of strategy or the formulation of policy. Lillian Traugott started her SI career in London and became an SI labor desk officer later in a fourteen-month tour of duty in Stockholm. One of her accomplishments was a questionnaire she wrote for her contacts in Stockholm to ascertain what the Nazis did with leaders of German labor unions, district secretaries, and other officials who had disappeared from the workforce after a "cleansing" of German unions.

In a memorandum Traugott noted:

> We have been asked by the War Crimes Commission to cooperate in obtaining evidence against some of the principal Nazi leaders in Germany.
>
> I should like to ask my trusted contacts in Stockholm to determine what happened to labor leaders in Germany after the seizure of three trade union associations in May and June of 1933. The best qualified evidence should be gathered as soon as possible. Find out the nature of the arrest, confinement of leaders, assaults, maltreatment, murders, "suicides after arrest," "killed while trying to escape," etc. Clear evidence will go far in ex-

plaining the guilt of these disappearances.[10]

Neutral Sweden was a favorable vantage point for the penetration of Germany. Traugott was the only American woman OSS agent assigned to work with communist groups in Scandinavia. From Stockholm she recruited several agents whom she succeeded in dispatching to Germany and enemy-controlled areas, resulting in procurement of important intelligence. She was later awarded the Certificate of Merit.

Another SI agent, Sue Gordon Hannifin, joined OSS in 1943 and was assigned to the Grosvenor Square office of Henry Sutton, a former Austrian socialist and trade unionist, a walking encyclopedia about conditions inside Germany. Hannifin worked with him in developing agents to return to Germany for OSS. She recalled his expertise in the German labor movement, and especially his fluency in current European "socio-politicalese," invaluable in dealing with labor refugees from the Continent.[11]

Of all the establishments of OSS throughout London, the building at 14 Ryder Street, just blocks from St. James Square, was one mentioned only in hushed tones. Here OSS and the British MI6 shared offices and collected files on enemy espionage agents and cover organizations. By war's end the OSS collection of cards on three hundred thousand individuals was considered one of the best counterespionage storehouses in the world. OSS, in cooperation with the British and other Allies, contributed to the apprehension of thirteen hundred enemy agents in military zones.

Chief of X-2, the OSS Counterintelligence Branch, was Norman Holmes Pearson, one-time professor of literature at Yale and a Rhodes Scholar at Magdalen College, Oxford. Partially crippled from a childhood disease, Pearson was an indefatigable worker. He moved about London and environs as OSS X-2 liaison with MI6 and Britain's most secret Twenty Club. This "club" consisted of intelligence officials from the British military, MI5, and Home Forces. Charged originally with counterespionage, the Twenty Club coordinated planning on how to redirect disinformation obtained through doubled German agents. In the X-2 office, Pearson often worked until midnight. He utilized his lunch and dinner hours to meet with British, American, and other contacts including members of London's literary set.

Pearson and his small staff arrived in London in April 1943. Two months later he was joined by Grace Tully, who organized the office and kept it in operation until being moved to Spain. Tully had worked with Pearson in the days he sat on the Central Information Division (CID) in R&A and had helped to assemble, assess, and file over two hundred thousand documents. She immediately pitched in at Ryder Street to organize the rapidly growing intelligence files that X-2 was collecting. Later she performed the same task for X-2 in Madrid and Barcelona. On her return to London she was made an X-2 security officer and served as assistant desk chief in charge of Iberian and North African operations. She worked not only in analysis and evaluation of intelligence but in direction and guidance. At war's end she was the recipient of the Certificate of Merit.

There were many outstanding women working for X-2. Catherine Seerley worked as an intelligence analyst on the French desk, directly under Pearson. Helen E. Osmun, who had been special assistant to the chief in Algiers, was transferred to London where she was senior case officer handling all projects affecting the German Abwehr.

Sophie D. Egloff was one of the few OSS women working in the Scandinavian theater, where these northern countries served as a passage for intelligence. Egloff, assistant to the X-2 chief in that area, later served as chief herself. She was in a most unusual position for a woman in that she acted on an equal level with officers of the British and American armies in exercise of operational control and in a liaison capacity. Under her tutelage special X-2 representatives were trained for entry into Denmark and Norway, briefed on objectives that were the results of her estimates. A great deal of interest centered on the production of heavy water in south central Norway.

James Jesus Angleton was one of the more colorful characters in the X-2 offices at Ryder Street. The son of a Mexican War veteran and a beautiful Mexican woman, he was raised in Ohio and then in Italy, where his father was vice president for overseas operations of the National Cash Register Company. He was graduated from Yale and almost immediately signed up with OSS.

In those days, long before he was to become famous as a mole hunter in the Central Intelligence Agency, Angleton was totally committed to the idea of penetrating the enemy by exploiting its own agents. He brought an army cot to his small office where he often slept after working well past midnight. His room, 23B, reeked of tobacco smoke; Angleton was a chain-smoker, an indefatigable searcher, and a theorist enamored with counterintelligence. He also drove his many secretaries close to suicide.

Frances Perdita MacPherson remembers him well, and with guarded frustration even today. "Jim Angleton," she wrote in exasperation:

You must remember we were both in our twenties. This was his first assignment. Temperamental workaholic. Slept in the office most nights. Expected other people to function the same way. Impatient, demand-

178

ing. Brilliant, of course, oh yes. A very small office, claustrophobic. I typed his reports and labored interminably in a card file. Hardly knew what he was talking about, the pressure was so intense and he was always rushing about from one thing to another. I would have become a nervous wreck, eventually. Fate intervened and dispatched him to Italy in 1944. I visualized him in afterlife, perpetually immured with documents, files, and spooky characters. Not too far wrong![12]

Perdita MacPherson had been recruited for OSS by Norman Pearson, a close friend of her mother, the poet Hilda Doolittle. She was educated by tutors and governesses "in a hit-and-miss fashion" with no continuity. Living in Switzerland, she learned French as a child and German soon afterward. She traveled around the Continent and went to work at Bletchley, Britain's cipher-breaking center, when the war began. She remembers Bletchley as a dump: "One of the most hideous baronial halls in England. The grounds were cluttered with Nissen huts and literally thousands of workers. I was at the bottom of the slave ladder, copying stuff, decoding, translating unrelated bits and pieces. Boxes within boxes. Nobody knew what anybody else was doing." Today, whenever she feels depressed, she thinks back on Bletchley, and everything brightens up.

MacPherson was later sent to Germany,

where she was distressed by the bomb ruins, displaced persons, and despair everywhere. "It was the most glamorous life for a girl," she recalls, "if you could call it that. I didn't. Sought after, fought after by hundreds of men! Exhausting." For her work she was awarded the Certificate of Merit upon the recommendation of her boss, Norman Holmes Pearson, on 30 June 1945. After the war she emigrated to New York City, married a literary agent, John Schaffner, and had four children. When her husband died she relocated to East Hampton, where she now lives.

Aimee Russell Corsini also worked for Angleton. She replaced Anne Milliken, who perhaps in desperation was leaving the London office to marry an Italian, Mario Franchetti. When Angleton was transferred to Italy, Corsini went with him. She too complained that he was "pressing more and more work" on her, and she left to marry Cino Corsini, a childhood sweetheart. Angleton told her that Washington would take a dim view of all his secretaries leaving him to marry Italians.[13]

However hard he drove his staff, Angleton was always amiable and interested in the well-being of his overworked secretaries. One secretary compared him with Gregory Peck — a lonely man, stooped, with long hands and fingers. Another compared him fondly to a "little wet dog" in need of comforting. A senior secretary, Grace Dolowitz, was less affected by this shy, preoccupied scholar. She was a valuable translator as well as a secretary and had finished her doctorate on Proust at Bryn Mawr. French material from Bletchley arrived on Angleton's desk untranslated, and Dolowitz proved irreplaceable in handling this material.

Discrimination against women in government service during the war was obvious. The women in X-2, for example, were fully as well educated as the men, they spoke the same number of foreign languages, on average were the same age (early thirties), and most had traveled abroad. But in X-2 they were secretaries, filing clerks, or translators. There was one decoder; two were listed as associate head and administrative assistant. None achieved executive positions in X-2.

However, there were a few OSS women whose jobs defied description. Sylvia Tim Yarrow was one of those who flitted down the back stairs of Claridge's Hotel, a confidante of queens and chauffeur for her pseudo-diplomat husband. And there were others, such as feisty Anne Mary Cairns, who risked their lives driving for the OSS motor pool through bomb raids and blackouts.

CHAPTER 9

From Royal Suites to Back-Street London

Representatives of exiled governments in London offered extremely valuable sources of intelligence to the Allied cause.[1] Local undercover groups in Poland, Holland, France, Czechoslovakia, and Yugoslavia were able to smuggle out to their London agents information that was then made available to both the British and American services.

Of particular interest to General Donovan was the situation in Yugoslavia, where OSS agents had been in contact with the two major guerrilla forces since 1942. Army colonel Draža Mihajlović led the first organized resistance force, the *chetniks*, in support of the exiled ruler, then Prince Peter. Mihajlović was a Royalist, a distinguished career officer, who took his men into the hills of western Serbia, rugged terrain ideal for hit-and-run guerrilla tactics. The second group was organized by Josip Broz, better known as Tito, a communist trained in Moscow whose leadership attracted thousands to his camp. Both factions fought the Nazi occupation of their country, with Tito eventually winning out and establishing a provisional government in 1943. Meanwhile, in London, King Peter continued to press his claim to the throne of Yugoslavia.

In order to monitor the developments affecting King Peter, Donovan undertook a reckless operation. He attached a spy to the court of King Peter and his family in London, where the seventeen-year-old king enjoyed the protection and financial support of the British government and the friendship of his uncle, the king of England. Donovan's move was a clear breach of the Arcadia agreement reached earlier by Roosevelt and Churchill, that their countries would never spy on each other.

The agent Donovan selected for his mission was Bernard Yarrow, an anti-Bolshevik émigré from Russia who spoke Russian, Polish, French, German, and several Balkan dialects. Before emigrating to the United States he had attended the Universities of Cracow, Poland, and Odessa in Russia. He came to New York City in 1922 and three years later was graduated from New York University. In 1928 he earned his law degree from Columbia Law School and was an assistant district attorney under Thomas Dewey. Resigning to join OSS in 1942, Yarrow became a member of the OSS clique of upper-class anti-Bolshevik émigrés that included Ilya Tolstoi and Serge Obolensky.

In London, Yarrow worked smoothly with dethroned families of the European monarchical society who were hoping to reestablish their lost positions by playing one side against another, becoming especially close to King Peter.

There is no written record in the Donovan papers as to who actually authorized the Shepherd project, as it was called.[2] The State Department had declined to accord Yarrow either diplomatic protection or status. The department did list him as special assistant to the American ambassador in London, and to the Yugoslav government. There is also no evidence that the Joint Chiefs of Staff were aware of this project. The probability is that Roosevelt himself sanctioned it verbally. Certainly no one had authorized the role that Sylvia Tim Yarrow was to play as confidant to the royal family of Yugoslavia.

Sylvia was pert and pixyish, an artist of some repute in New York City with a sly sense of humor. She remembers her recruitment, in September 1944, by no less a secret agent than General Donovan himself. "My husband and I had dinner with Bill Donovan at the St. Regis in New York," she recalled with a smile. "Bill told me that there was an unwritten rule that OSS husbands and wives could not serve in the same theater. He was breaking this rule for me." The general explained that she would be working with her husband, Bernard, ensconced in a suite at the elegant Claridge's Hotel in the heart of Mayfair. Her job was to become friendly with Peter, his wife, and his mother-in-law. Bernard would do the rest. Thanks to OSS planning, the royal entourage was conveniently located in another suite at Claridge's directly below the Yarrows'.

Sylvia agreed to Donovan's invitation and was processed into OSS with minimal training in trade craft. She had to remember, in dealing with OSS personnel at the Grosvenor Street office, to refer to her husband by his pseudonym, John Farmer. "It wasn't easy to explain this close 'friend' with whom I was living at Claridge's," she later recalled. Sylvia also managed to learn to type, but her spelling remained hopeless.

Bernard preceded her to London to establish their residence at Claridge's. She was busy at her studio home at 112 East Seventy-fourth Street when his cable arrived asking her to join him. Like many other OSS women, she had to choose between maternal obligations and leaving her three children at home while she went to war. Her answer was immediate: "Thrilled. Will come any time." Bernard returned to New York to brief his wife on her duties in London: cultivate the royals; drive an embassy-furnished car serviced by the OSS motor pool, for use in her work; type all messages from her husband to Donovan and drive him to the OSS Message Center to send reports on to Washington.

Sylvia closed her studio, with half-finished sculptures in marble and stone, said a tearful good-bye to her children and their nanny, and in early 1944 boarded a flying boat for London. Her husband met her and took her to their flat on the fourth floor of Claridge's, complete with fireplace, large living room, bedroom, and office. Below on the third floor was Yugoslavia's new king, the teenaged Peter, who had fled Yugoslavia after the Nazis invaded his country and had set up a government-in-exile in London. Accompanying him was his new wife, Princess Alexandra, and her mother, the domineering Aspasia, widow of King Alexander I of Greece. It did not take the friendly American woman long to establish rapport with the royal family. Her credentials were impeccable: wife of an influential State Department officer, talented sculptor well known in art circles, fluent in French, competent in German.

I spoke with Mrs. Yarrow at her New York City apartment six months before she died on 10 February 1993. It was a beautiful sitting room, with her striking sculptures displayed in alcoves, an autographed photograph of the one-time kings of England and Yugoslavia with their wives, and a portrait of her handsome late husband over the fireplace; Bernard Yarrow had died in 1973.

"I became great friends with Peter and his wife, Sandra." she recalled. "We would go up

186

and down the back stairs to each other's flats. I went everywhere with the queen and her mother. The king was always followed by a guard, assigned by his British hosts, but the ladies were free to travel, shop, go to the theater, despite the bombings. It was helpful, too, that I had an 'embassy' car at my disposal which we used on outings."

Mrs. Yarrow thumbed through a scrapbook. There were photos of her in a pert and stylish hat, coat, and gloves in a London park with the thin-faced young girl queen and her forbidding mother. There was also a picture of Bernard Yarrow and King Peter in front of a light plane. She pointed out that the king always chafed at being a virtual prisoner in England, and so President Roosevelt sent him an airplane as a Christmas present for his very own use. The king was delighted, like the little boy he was. It was not a very substantial plane, but one known as a "bamboo bomber," a utility aircraft made of plywood and linen and generally used for pilot training.

Mrs. Yarrow said that Peter promptly invited her husband to go flying with him to see his uncle, the king of England, who at that time was living outside London in his country estate at Balmoral with the queen and their two little daughters. "I immediately protested that Peter didn't know how to fly the airplane, and I didn't want Bernard to take any undue risks," she recalled with a wry smile. "Later I was as-

187

sured that the cousins, as we euphemistically called our British allies, had assigned an RAF pilot to fly the king's plane. So the boys took off and had a wonderful time."

The king and Yarrow established a very close working relationship, especially during the period when Churchill was trying to pressure the king to accept the title of regent in view of Tito's growing power in Yugoslavia. "Very often, after meeting with Peter, Bernard would dictate a communiqué, which I dutifully typed," Mrs. Yarrow recalled. "The king was always badgering Churchill or the king of England, especially when they were urging him to give up his throne in view of the political situation in his homeland. He fretfully reported back to us everything that was said at these meetings. He would pass copies of notes he had sent to Churchill and the king, stating time and again that they 'must be aware of his responsibilities' and that no one could compel him to sign an agreement he didn't want to sign."

Some of these memoranda are on file at the National Archives in Washington. On 2 January 1945 Peter sent the following note to the king of England:

Dear Uncle Bertie:

First, let me say again on behalf of Sandra and myself, all my good wishes to you and Aunt Elizabeth and the girls for a very happy New Year. I am sending a copy to you of a letter I wrote to Mr. Churchill. Please help him to understand my point of view. I cannot act against my oath to the Constitution. I did not bargain in the dark days of 1941 when I came in on the side of the Allies, unhesitantly. I stood by our traditional friend, Great Britain, and it is only fair that Great Britain should stand by me now. On my side, all my life I will try to be worthy of this friendship and trust.

Love, Peter

In view of the delicate nature of the information Peter was supplying, especially the sources, Sylvia Yarrow would drive her husband to OSS headquarters at Grosvenor Street, and the two would stand by at the Message Center where their information was sent directly to Donovan and through him to Roosevelt, bad spelling and all.

On 14 October 1944, in one of his many memoranda to Donovan, Bernard Yarrow wrote, "We were invited by the King and Queen to spend the weekend at their country place which they recently bought. I would like to report at this time that our relationship is most friendly. The King often calls me in for consultation and I am trying to use my best judgment under the circumstances. The King complained to me of the intrigues of his mother who was attempting to undermine his authority with the aid of old Serb politicians."[3]

Sylvia Yarrow recalled how King Peter's mother, Queen Maria, demanded that he return to her the crown jewels of Yugoslavia, which he had brought with him to London and which Claridge's refused to store in the hotel safe because of the danger of bombings. "He brought out the most beautiful diamond and emerald tiara I have ever seen," she said. "He let me wear it for a little while, and I marched around the apartment feeling like a queen, and wondering to myself how much such a treasure would bring on the open market!"

In one of his notes home to General Donovan in Washington, Bernard Yarrow expressed his appreciation: "Mrs. Yarrow and I are both kept busy. It is a privilege to participate to some degree in the present developments. We hope some of them are of value to our country."[4] Among the papers that Sylvia Yarrow showed me from her own files was one dated 19 January 1945 from the American ambassador, Richard Patterson Jr., who wrote to her husband, "You have done a grand job. The OSS reports, and your help in London have been of more value to me and to my embassy than all the other agencies combined and I am grateful indeed."

The young king's influence with Churchill began to wane at this point in time. In desperation he looked toward the United States for support, and he used Bernard Yarrow as his conduit to Roosevelt. In the end, Tito took control of Yugoslavia, the monarchy was dissolved, and Roosevelt sided with Churchill. In remembering those later days, Sylvia Yarrow described the king as an immature, skinny boy, harassed by his political advisers and by his Greek mother-in-law, who also dominated her sickly daughter.

Bernard and Sylvia Yarrow's tour was ending in the spring of 1945. In submitting an expense account for their year in London, the following items were noted:

Living: $7,638
Entertaining: $1,980 (including membership in the exclusive Bucks Club at Clifford Street)
Travel: $430
London office expenses: $150
Gifts to contacts: $290

They left London in March 1945. Bernard Yarrow was to be a delegate to the historic San Francisco conference that established the United Nations as an international body "to save successive governments from the scourge of war."

Sylvia Yarrow returned happily to her children and her art. She wrote a letter of resignation, dated 26 March 1945, a copy of which she showed me during our visit:

Dear General Donovan:

Now that the mission entrusted to me has been completed, I feel I should formally tender my resignation. May I take this occasion to express my deep appreciation of the opportunity for serving with the Office of Strategic Services and to thank you personally for affording me the opportunity to contribute my small share in the war effort.

Sylvia T. Yarrow

There were other OSS women in London who worked long hours, even during heavy bomb raids, in such mundane yet basic support functions as the motor pool at Reeves Mews. Here some one hundred vehicles were housed, tended by twenty-three maintenance personnel and twenty-two drivers. Anne Mary Cairns was one of those drivers.

A British woman educated abroad in Germany and France, Cairns fled the Continent just ahead of the German armies and ended up in Cheltenham working at an aircraft factory where Typhoons, Hurricanes, and the first British jet aircraft, the Meteors, were manufactured. She was just twenty years old when she started this work.

"It was pretty dull," she recalled. "When the Yanks began to pour into England, I learned that they needed drivers for the London motor pools. Anything to get where the action was! I talked a family doctor into giving me a certificate stating that I needed 'open-air work,' and I was able to leave the factory. The day I reported to London for work, a bomb hit the Marble Arch! It was the start of a great adventure."

She was sent back to Cheltenham in the hills, where she underwent strenuous training in and out of bomb craters in a country where once, before the war, she had ridden on fox hunts. During the course of her training she overturned a jeep in one of the craters and broke two ribs. In September 1944 she returned to London to report to what was described as a "rather secret" organization. She was then briefed in keeping her mouth shut, driving with eyes straight ahead, and ignoring whoever was riding in the back seats of the staff cars, private cars, lorries, and ambulances that she learned to maneuver through the blacked-out London streets with hooded headlights, a helmet on the seat beside her.

Once, early in her job, she was told to pick up two civilians at Paddington Station. When they were settled in the back seat, they started to speak in French. Not wanting to eavesdrop, she told them she understood the language. They switched to German, and she told them she spoke German, too. They then lapsed into Russian, and she drove them to their destination in silence.

"I began to learn something of OSS as I worked in the pool," Cairns said. "I had to sign an Official Secrets Act form and wore a U.S. drivers' patch but no rank insignia on my tailor-made uniform." Among other things, she learned that she had to sign each trip ticket, which included the name of the person riding in the vehicle and the trip mileage. "One night I was given a ticket with the name of General William Donovan on it. He would be outside the United States embassy, and I would take him to Claridge's," Cairns recalled with a smile. "I was terrified. I said to the dispatcher, 'Jesus Christ, not me!' But it was me! I remember polishing the big black Buick, unfurling the flag with two stars, praying we wouldn't get stuck in an air raid, that I wouldn't run off the road. But I shouldn't have worried! He saluted me as I opened the door, all spit and polish and a friendly smile." On the way to the hotel he chatted with her, asking where she was from, why she had chosen the motor pool for a wartime career, and what her postwar plans were. "It was difficult, talking and driving, but we made it safely, and he wished me luck!"

Cairns made another trip she would never forget, driving an ambulance with six silent passengers. The trip ticket was made out to a place well known to her from student days: Aldermaster, nestled near an old millpond where she had spent many weekends swimming and eating strawberries and cream. "It was lovely in those days, and I looked forward to revisiting it. I assured the motor pool dispatch officer I could find it, although it was a long way from London, west through Reading."

"When we were almost there," Cairns recalled, "I was ordered to pull off the road in a nearby woods. The six men changed into German prisoner-of-war uniforms with a big *P* on the back, and long-billed caps. They began to speak German." The drive resumed. Cairns's memories of the idyllic millpond picnics were shattered when she drove up to the compound surrounded by chain-link fences, cluttered with Quonset huts, guns mounted on the walls. Beyond these walls were masses of pushing, ranting German prisoners, screaming obscenities at her and the guard who accompanied the six OSS "prisoners." At the gate the agents were handcuffed and driven to the Administration Building, where they were shoved into the noisy compound. "I was terrified! The prisoners were so belligerent, cursing the 'miserable English' and 'Jew-loving Roosevelt' in German. At the same time, they were screaming for chewing gum and chocolates, in bad English."

Several weeks later Cairns returned to pick up the OSS men. She learned that they had posed as Germans to ferret out those prisoners who might be "turned" and used eventually in the invasion of the Continent. They were looking for anti-Nazis who wanted to rebuild a new homeland when the war was over. Many were identified and successfully utilized.

One of Cairns's treasured memories was another adventure more inspiring than her POW trip. In March, three months before D-Day, the dispatcher called her in and told her she would drive a lorry at night to a site two hours out of London, toward Sussex. Five persons laden with equipment boarded her truck and huddled quietly with their gear on their laps. After a long, dark drive they arrived at an open field. By moonlight Cairns saw the silhouette of a high-wing monoplane, the only one on a barely distinguishable runway. The plane was dull green, and a few dim lights indicated its takeoff path. "We hung around until nearly midnight," she recalled, "waiting to see if they would have to abort. Finally the men hoisted their heavy gear and moved to the aircraft. In a few moments they were bouncing down the field, and the plane took off into the moonlight. Somewhere in France they would land and be met by men and women of the resistance. I left the field slowly, to find my way home with the help of a jolt of Benzedrine to keep awake."

Today Anne Mary Cairns, vivacious, still full of the pizazz that made her a feisty member of the London OSS motor pool, lives in Alexandria, Virginia, with her American husband, William Ingraham, whom she met through Canadian cousins. In recent years she has boarded foreign exchange students attending schools in the Washington area.

Cairns has never forgotten those years when she put up a brave front to cope with the daily trauma of the streets of London. Others, such as Evangeline Bell, faced an even more exacting routine. Bell supplied cover stories and documentation for agents like the ones Cairns drove to airstrips and to resistance nets in Europe. A minor mistake could cost them their lives if an alert Nazi sentry spotted one error in their papers.

CHAPTER 10

Cover and Documentation

Evangeline Bell, who helped set up the London station and watched it grow from a handful of people to thousands, was the slim, attractive daughter of a Foreign Service officer. She was born in London in 1914, attended schools in Paris, Stockholm, and Rome, and was fluent in French. She was graduated from Radcliffe College and in 1941 joined COI, the Coordinator of Information, where she worked on the French desk, processed agents for the field, assisted in operations, and acted on incoming cables. Her salary was $1,200 per annum throughout her service in OSS.

Bell was working in the Censorship and Documents Branch of Counterintelligence (X-2) when David Bruce reported to the station. Fisher Howe, who helped establish the OSS station in London before her arrival, claims that he was the "stupid Cupid" who introduced them.[1] According to Bell, however, Bruce remembered her from an earlier time, before she left for London, when she had just started working with Ambassador Phillips, although she herself didn't remember knowing him at that time. Bell did recall that Bruce and Donovan came through her office in July 1943, and Donovan asked her if she would like to serve in the OSS office in New Delhi, which was just opening up. She replied that she would serve her country wherever she was needed; she had no ties. After the general left, Bell once told me with a smile, "David Bruce came back to my office and told me it was absolutely ridiculous for me to even consider going to New Delhi. I was urgently needed in London!"

In the months ahead the romance between Bruce and Bell developed. As one London OSS colleague, Gertrude Legendre, remembers, Bell was not clothes-conscious during her first year in London: "She wore low shoes, sensible suits. She even dropped off to sleep at parties — one of mine, to be exact. As the romance between them developed, she began to wear chic clothes, especially when she was assigned to Paris. She frequented the best couturière shops there. She couldn't file worth a darn, but she could type as fast as her boss dictated."

Years later Bell still recalled the hectic life of wartime London: "Sometimes I would burst into tears because of the combined tension of the bombings and work. I remember the German planes flying up the Thames like angry hornets. When I heard a V-1 coming, I would put my hands over my eyes, thumbs in my ears because of the intense noise. I had the feeling that I had to make the most of the days I was living. You mostly saw people you cared about. This feeling was heightened as bombs continued to fall. I seemed to live on the surface."

The trauma of daily living was exacerbated by food shortages and blackout conditions. "It was sometimes frightening, walking home from work to my Mayfair apartment during a raid," Bell recalled. "We carried flashlights with blue bulbs in them. The taxis all had blue headlights capped on top to cut down on reflection. We shopped for food at our commissary, but meat was rationed to four ounces a week. Fruit was nonexistent, although we occasionally got strawberries and sometimes cream from Ireland. There were plenty of potatoes, and we received one 'reconditioned' egg a week. Candy was a prized item."

Bell's office, Cover and Documentation (C&D), was behind the headquarters building at 72 Grosvenor Street, former residence of Charles de Gaulle. It was headed by Willie Reddick, who held a degree in journalism from the University of Illinois and was a printer and advertising man recruited by OSS. His job: to establish a print shop in London to produce forged documents.

This mission took some time, but eventually heavy presses were set up on the concrete floor of the garage. The engraving plant was in the kitchen, for easy access to a water supply. There was a tailor shop in the attic, reached by a rickety staircase. Bell was one of some twenty people working in this once elegant building, three stories high with carved moldings, leaded windows, and tiled fireplaces. There were engravers, retouch artists, and photographers who put together the cover stories for teams going behind the lines in France, and later Holland and Germany. The clandestine agents were provided with counterfeit identification documents and clothing suited to the area of operation.

Bell worried a great deal about her work:

One mistake, and our people could be executed. Their lives depended upon what they wore or carried, either manufactured by Reddick's shop or collected from refugees who had fled occupied Europe.

It was our job to transform ordinary Americans into Dutch longshoremen, French factory workers, even a member of the Nazi SS police. If I was outfitting a French farmer, I looked for patched blue work clothes, heavy hand-knitted socks, sabots, a beret. Even his buttons were sewn with parallel threading, rather than in the American cross-stitch style.

Bell worked with several very competent women in these C&D shops. As D-Day approached, they were supporting an important preinvasion operation, the Sussex Plan. This plan included 120 agents divided into teams of two: one observer, one radio operator. Sussex was a tripartite operation: French, British, and American teams whose job was to report from key points in France on German troop movements prior to D-Day.

Bell explained:

Stamps were important. People couldn't move around occupied areas without proper identification. Stamps had to fit an agent's cover story and his credentials. He needed permits to own a bicycle, for food rations or travel orders. C&D even had a facility for dirtying up French franc notes, always in small denominations, such as a French farmer would stuff in his shoes. Sometimes women in C&D were asked to wear the notes in their brassieres to soften them. Agents were instructed how to smoke French cigarettes, right down to the stub. One agent had been spotted by an alert Gestapo guard because he tossed away a half-smoked cigarette, something no frugal French *paysan* would ever do.

Tension and excitement dominated OSS headquarters in London during the spring of 1944. Everyone sensed that the invasion of Europe was imminent. By the end of May thirteen Sussex teams, including women, were in place in France: seven American, six British. Radio contact had been established.

"You also had to back up a cover story with tangible proof," Bell continued.

A hospital certificate for a recent illness would explain why you were not at work or in the army. A letter from a friend deploring the death of a family member would tell why you had traveled from your home. Civilian apparel bought from refugees to the United States was shipped back to OSS in London and studied for American laundry marks that might betray the wearer. OSS New York was asked to search secondhand shops in the Lower East Side for German fountain pens, battered suitcases of European manufacture, even religious symbols.

We never knew who the agents were, and only our radio reports from behind the lines indicated that they were in place. It was a terrible responsibility, knowing that one small mistake might cost them their life.

Bell wryly recalled that her concern about security was not alleviated one day when she was asked to take some top-secret papers to General Donovan at his Claridge's Hotel suite. She found him perusing other equally secret documents while being shaved by his barber, who could easily have read the reports over his shoulder.

David Bruce himself reported back on one of the Sussex teams that had been captured at Le Mans. Bruce was on his way to Paris after D-Day. He and Donovan had participated in the invasion. In his diary he wrote, "We have overrun here one of the Sussex agents, a woman, who had been parachuted. Her companion was captured by the Gestapo on July 31 and was tortured in the most horrible manner before he died."[2]

Among other OSS women working with Bell in both London and, later, Paris was Beatrice Phillips, whose cover had been blown before she left Washington for her London assignment. In a New York gossip column written by Igor Cassini in November 1942 it was noted that "Beatrice Phillips, beautiful daughter of former Ambassador to Italy, William Phillips, is now doing some work for Bill Donovan's OSS."[3]

Phillips, later Mrs. Ellery Strauss, worked in Biographical Records, where her knowledge of German was important. She recalled her impressions of General Donovan, whom she knew: "He was socially very full of himself, but he was clever, daring, imaginative. He had to fight for everything he could get."

Sue Gordon Hannifin, now a Florida journalist, was also working in the preparation of covers for agents, checking false documents and bona fide wardrobes. She recalls one of the difficulties: in some areas of occupied France the inhabitants didn't wear underclothing — a problem for some of the Americans going in behind the German lines.

Marjorie Levenson was assigned to C&D in London in August 1944, after the bulk of the OSS personnel had moved to Paris. She was ordered to draw a WAC uniform and a small tent colloquially dubbed a "shelter half" and be ready to join Bell and Phillips in France, but a week later the decision was made to leave some OSS personnel behind in London. Agents were still being dispatched from aerodromes outside this city to assignments behind the lines in occupied Europe. As Levenson told me later, "I was left with a huge pile of detritus that Evangeline Bell had collected. It was almost like a secondhand shop: clothes to match any cover story we dreamed up, including German uniforms, clerical habits, and students' outfits."

Levenson had lived abroad and attended school on the Continent. She spoke French and German and knew Western European lifestyles. She too was concerned about carelessness in outfitting agents, but she never met any of them and was never told what happened to them. "I used to worry about *kennkartes*," she said. "That was the basic German ID card. We had over one hundred authentic *kennkartes* filed geographically. For example, if a person was from Berlin, his ID had to match the area and had to include proper signatures of authorities. Also, the bearer carried other identification cards. Some Germans belonged to sports clubs; everyone had to have travel permits and ration cards from the area in which he lived."

Levenson pointed out that all documents had to appear authentic. There were German typewriters in one office where typists were supplied with paper that had been replicated in the United States with proper watermarks. OSS forgers reproduced stamps for permits; if a stamp had a scratch in one corner, this was duplicated. Authentic ink was used. Nazi Party membership cards were forged. Blank travel orders, to cover contingencies, were prepared. "Our main concern was to get them past German security once they reached Europe," Levenson said.

Levenson's supplies of documents and clothing were augmented when a separate collection unit was set up in Paris in September 1944, headed by Griselda Martineau, who had joined OSS a month earlier. Martineau, the wife of a British army major attached to the Supreme Headquarters Allied Expeditionary Force, was fluent in French and had lived in France before the war. OSS scouts working for her in C&D bought a large collection of wrist watches, razors, underwear, pens, even suitcases and briefcases. Martineau also forwarded up-to-date examples of passports, consular rubber stamps, and French identity and ration cards. She acquired German documents through army intelligence and examined, edited, and sent these on to London base. She was decorated for her work after the war.

Most of the women in the C&D unit in London transferred to assignments in France and Germany before returning to their homes after the German surrender. Evangeline Bell returned to the United States in 1945 and married David Bruce, who had obtained a wartime divorce from Ailsa Mellon Bruce. They had drifted apart long before Bruce was assigned to London. The war was to take its toll on many marriages in OSS. As Dr. William J. Morgan, a clinical psychologist and one of OSS's highly decorated paratroopers, explained in his book *The OSS and I*, "There is a tense atmosphere during wartime that develops a sense of freedom from personal responsibilities. It not only applies to OSS personnel, but to all men and women serving overseas. There was pressure engendered by danger, not knowing if there would be a tomorrow. In this atmosphere, affairs between OSS men and women happened around the world, starting with a fleeting moment of intimacy and shared love, ending in divorce and remarriage."

Evangeline and David Bruce served their country in the postwar years in important diplomatic missions ranging from Paris and London to China. After her husband died in 1977, Evangeline lived on as one of the grandes dames of Washington society until her death in 1995.

One of the beneficiaries of Bell's support service in London was perhaps the most famous of all OSS women spies: Virginia Hall. She twice entered France to organize, train, and supply French resistance efforts while simultaneously operating an "underground railroad" to assist the escape of downed Allied flyers to neutral or friendly countries. Decorated for her heroism by both the British and American governments, she was known to her French Maquis comrades as "la Dame Qui Boite," the Limping Lady. She had only one leg.

CHAPTER 11

The Limping Lady

The OSS agent code-named Diane was scheduled to leave England for the Brittany coast on 21 March 1944 on a fast British torpedo boat, putting ashore by dinghy somewhere on the Cotentin Peninsula. She could not parachute in, because of her wooden leg.

Virginia Hall had transferred to OSS from the British Special Operations Executive (SOE) on 1 April 1944, entering the American service with high marks from the British. In the name of King George VI she had been awarded the Member of the British Empire (MBE). But the OSS London Cover and Documentation group (C&D) faced a challenge with this American agent about to enter occupied France: her cover had been blown while she was working for SOE establishing agent nets in occupied France between 1941 and 1943, and she was known to the Gestapo. The Gestapo had circulated a fairly accurate sketch of her from descriptions supplied by French double agents. The drawing depicted a handsome woman with shoulder-length hair, a determined chin, and eyes set wide apart. The orders issued by the Gestapo in France were terse: "The woman who limps is one of the most dangerous Allied agents in France. We must find and destroy her."[1]

Tall at five feet seven, Hall was slender, with high cheekbones and a warm smile that belied her toughness and leadership ability. C&D could not convince her that a radical alteration of her features was indicated for her own safety. But she was a good actress as well as an expert undercover operator, and she opted instead for a more subtle manipulation of her persona. At thirty-eight, she would become an older woman, a sharp-faced French peasant whose horizons had never reached beyond the farms where she tended cows and goats. Her soft brown hair was dyed a dirty gray-black, pulled tightly up from her neck and anchored with a wooden hairpin. This new coiffure gave her young face a severe, almost anile look. To hide her slim figure she was outfitted with full skirts, designed with peplums to add to the illusion of weight. Ample woolen blouses and a drab over-sized sweater further disguised her trim figure and provided protection against the cold weather of the mountainous regions where she was to work. Hall couldn't conceal her limp, but she learned to walk with a swinging motion that modified her gait.

Hall reentered occupied France from the sea, carrying a radio transmitter and her wardrobe in a battered suitcase. She was to serve as radio operator to the agent net Heckler. With her was another OSS agent, Peter Harratt, code name Aramis, in charge of setting up Heckler in the Haute-Loire region of central France. The two appeared to be a typical French couple, trudging into the railroad station at Brest, but the money they used for purchasing tickets to Paris had been flown out of France to London for OSS, and their *cartes d'identité* were forged.

Thus began the six-month mission in which Hall succeeded in organizing, arming, and training three units of some three hundred agents that took part in sabotage operations against the Germans. She also maintained radio communication between London OSS headquarters and resistance forces in the Haute-Loire district. A year later, by direction of President Harry Truman, Hall would be the first woman and civilian awarded the Distinguished Service Cross for "extraordinary heroism in connection with military operations against the enemy."[2]

Virginia Hall was born in Baltimore on 6 April 1906. She was the youngest child of Edwin Lee Hall, who had married his secretary, Barbara Virginia Hammel. Her grandfather, John W. Hall, ran off to sea at the age of nine, stowing away on one of his father's clipper ships. Later he made his fortune in Baltimore, and his family enjoyed the privileges of wealth and education. Virginia, or Dindy, as she was nicknamed by family and friends, was graduated from the exclusive Roland Park Country Day School in Baltimore. She attended Radcliffe and later Barnard College from 1924 to 1926.

Virginia Hall's niece, Baltimorean Lorna Lee Catling, remembers her as very poised, very sure of herself, and always surrounded by admirers; to young Lorna Lee, Dindy was "awesome." In addition to his banking interests, Hall's father owned several movie houses in Baltimore. "Dindy used to get me and my brother in free to see the shows," Catling recalls. "She loved sports — baseball, hockey, and tennis." At school she participated in dramatics at the early age of eight. In college she was editor of the school paper as well as being elected president of her class. She was described in her college yearbook as "different and capricious."

Hall's college interests ran to languages — French, Italian, and German — in addition to courses in philosophy, English literature, and economics. Catling recalls Hall's mother telling her daughter that nothing she ever learned to do would be wasted. The family spent summers at their Box Horn Farm in Parkton, Maryland, where Hall learned to milk cows, a talent she later put to good use in France where she lived her cover as a milkmaid.

Like her grandfather, Hall had a yearning for adventure and travel. After college she persuaded her father to allow her to continue her studies in Europe. She spent a year at the Ecole des Sciences Politiques in Paris and two years at the Konsularakademie in Vienna. She also studied for a short time at the Universities of Strasbourg, Grenoble, and Toulouse. With her flair for languages, she became fluent in French, Italian, and German. Returning home in 1929, she took additional courses in French at George Washington University in Washington, D.C.

The Baltimore social whirl was of little interest to Virginia Hall, who found living abroad more exciting. In July 1931 she took a position as clerk at the American embassy in Warsaw, at a salary of $2,500 per year. Later she served in Talinen, Estonia; Vienna, Austria; and Izmir, Turkey.

While stationed in Turkey, Hall suffered a grim accident. She was snipe hunting with friends outside Izmir when the gun she was carrying slipped from her grasp. Grabbing for it, she hit the trigger, discharging shot into her left foot. When gangrene set in, a surgeon was rushed from Istanbul to save her life, but he had to amputate the leg just below the knee. Fitted with an artificial limb, Hall had a pronounced limp that led to the nickname "la Dame Qui Boite" (the Limping Lady), bestowed by her companions in the French underground. She dubbed her wooden leg Cuthbert.

Hall was denied an appointment as a Foreign Service officer; at that time the State Department had a closed mind about women in the career service and a regulation that stated, "Any amputation of a portion of a limb or resection of a joint is cause for rejection in the career field." Dissatisfied, Hall resigned her clerk's position in May 1939 in Venice to travel in Europe. When World War II broke out that year, she was in Paris and joined the French Ambulance Service Unit as a private second class. After France fell in June 1940, Hall left the Ambulance Service in Valenchy and made her way to England via Spain.

She was working as a code clerk for the military attaché in the U.S. embassy in late 1940 when she was recruited by the British SOE. In this elite service she was trained in basic trade craft: weaponry, communications, and security. Under Maurice Buckmaster, head of the French (F) Section, Hall became the first woman in SOE to establish resistance networks out of Vichy France, beginning in August 1941. Her cover in SOE was that of a stringer for the *New York Post*. Since the United States was still neutral, Hall was able to work openly in Vichy France, then headed by Gen. Henri Pétain, under Nazi control. She reported freely, and her articles were not censored.

In a special wire story to the *Post* from Vichy,

dated 4 September 1941, Hall wrote, "The years have rolled back here in Vichy. There are no taxis at the station, only half a dozen buses and a few one-horse shays. I took a bus using gazogene, charcoal instead of gas, to my hotel. Vichy is a tiny town used once by summer visitors to take the cure. It is an infinitesimally small place to accommodate the government of France and the French Empire which has commandeered most of the hotels." Of living conditions she wrote, "I haven't seen any butter and there is very little milk. I also see little clothing in the shops and that is extremely dear. Shoes, however, are abundant and gay with their cloth or crocheted uppers and painted wooden soles. Women are no longer entitled to buy cigarettes and men are rationed to two packages a week."[3]

In a story from Lyons, dated 24 November 1941, Hall reported that a law had been passed forbidding Jews to become stockholders, barbers, publicity agents, merchants, or real estate agents or owners. And finally on 22 January 1942, from "somewhere in France," Hall sent one of her last reports by airmail, in which she noted that petty larceny, theft of food and transport, had assumed undreamed-of proportions. "Owners don't blame the culprits," she noted. "They know the poor people are hungry. The average weight loss today is 12 pounds per person not only from lack of food, but increased physical activity and mental strain . . .

people separated from their loved ones . . . prisoners of the Germans."[4]

Seventy-five miles away in Lyons, Hall set up her SOE operations, working out of her apartment at 3 place Olliers. Always a cautious agent, she maintained a second escape retreat in a local convent and helped to organize an SOE network under Buckmaster's F Section. She established contact with the French underground in Paris and assisted the return to England of escaped prisoners of war and downed airmen. She located drop zones for money and weapons for the resistance and recruited French citizens who in turn established safe houses for agents and supplies.

Hall continued to write for the *Post* as a cover, but when the United States entered the war, she became an enemy alien. Despite this danger, she continued her clandestine work with SOE for fourteen additional months, meeting contacts only at designated bistros and restaurants, discreetly studying the Vichy surveillance system, and making valuable contacts that lasted throughout the war.

The invasion of North Africa brought German troops pouring into unoccupied Vichy France in November 1941, and Hall was ordered to leave France. She hired a Spanish guide and, in the company of two Frenchmen and a Belgian army captain, began the arduous crossing to Spain by foot, in winter weather over the Pyrenees. During this flight her partially amputated leg became very painful from the cold and the rigorous climbing. In a message transmitted to SOE headquarters, London, she commented, "Cuthbert is giving me trouble, but I can cope." The reply, from an unknowing London colleague: "If Cuthbert is giving you trouble, have him eliminated."[5]

Lacking entry papers, Hall and her exhausted comrades were immediately arrested at the border town of San Juan de las Abadesas and incarcerated in the notorious Figueras prison. Here Hall shared a cell with a friendly Spanish prostitute. When this woman was freed, she smuggled out a letter from Hall to the American consul in Barcelona. Within six weeks Hall was released, and she reported to her SOE contacts in Madrid.

Hall was assigned to the D/F Section of SOE, known as the escape organizers. With new cover in Madrid as a correspondent for the *Chicago Times*, she was to seek out potential safe houses and agents and to act as a courier for the local SOE network after establishing her cover. (It was during her brief stay in Spain that she was awarded the prestigious MBE for her service in France.) Although Madrid was the center of clandestine intrigue and strategic maneuvers between Allied and Axis powers, life in this colorful city did not stimulate Hall. After four months she requested a transfer back to F Section, to return to France. In a letter to headquarters she wrote, "I thought I could help in Spain, but I'm not doing a job. I am living pleasantly and wasting time. It isn't worthwhile and after all, my neck is my own. If I am willing to get a crick in it, I think that's my prerogative."[6]

In November 1943 Hall returned to England. Wanting to improve her usefulness for a prospective assignment in France, she requested training as a wireless operator. It was during this period that she also decided to move from SOE to OSS. With the help of an OSS friend, Capt. William Grell, one-time manager of New York's St. Regis Hotel, she was transferred to OSS with the assimilated rank of a second lieutenant. Her salary would be forwarded to her mother in Baltimore, a process not feasible under SOE.

By the time she left for France, Hall had become proficient in new OSS radio transmission equipment and techniques. She had also spent some time studying American parachute-packing operations at the Peterborough packing station north of London. An OSS colleague, William T. Hornaday II, remembers meeting her there. "She was just back from Spain for SOE debriefings," he recalls. "She sometimes carried her detachable brass foot in a pack or leg bag. I have always had the greatest respect for that lady. Her courage knew no bounds."

Along with Hall's OSS Heckler mission, she also serviced SOE in France, reporting to the British mission called Saint. She would join the resistance in the Haute-Loire region of central France and organize sabotage and guerrilla groups, supplying them with funds and materiel.

Hall began her second tour of duty in occupied France by contacting underground associates in Paris with whom she had worked under SOE. Arriving from Brest with Peter Harratt, she immediately went to the home of an old and trusted friend, Mme. Long, at 59 rue de Babylone, who placed her flat at Hall's disposal. Long also located a room for Harratt in a nearby pension where the landlady was a Gaullist and he could avoid having to fill out the required registration forms.

Hall and Harratt were now ready to begin operations, with D-Day only three months away. The Gestapo was in control of the main French cities, and during her tour Hall managed to evade their nets three times. While in France, Hall's *carte d'identité* listed her as Mlle. Marcelle Montagne, a Parisian serving as a social worker with the Vichy Secours National. Her birth date was given as 3 March 1910; her father was Clément Montagne, a commercial agent, and her mother a housewife. Their address was 5 rue des Sources, Vichy, France.

The Heckler team of Hall and Harratt set up their initial operations about 160 miles south of Paris in the districts of Cher, Nièvre, and Creuse. In her report Hall wrote:

Aramis accompanied me to Creuse, in spite of a very painful knee which he sprained during our landing on the coast. At Maidou in Creuse, I contacted farmer Eugene Lopinat who found a little house for me with one room, no water or electricity, located by the side of the road at the other end of the village from his farmhouse. He arranged for me to eat and work at his own house. Here I cooked for the farmer, his old mother and the hired hand over an open fire as there was no stove in the house. I took his cows to pasture, and in the process found several good fields for parachute drops. Aramis returned to Paris to start his own work and to arrange a courier service to come to me at Maidou.[7]

The OSS had trained Hall early in basic security tactics, which meant moving as often as necessary before Nazi direction finders zeroed in on her hiding place. Hall was constantly in motion during the weeks before D-Day. Early in May she moved to the Nièvre region, where she lived and worked in the attic at the home of Col. and Mme. Fernand Vessereaux. The colonel was, conveniently, head of the local gendarmerie and had once been chief of protocol in Edouard Deladier's cabinet.

Forced to relocate once again because of increased Gestapo activity, Hall changed her radio location to her new hiding place in a garret at the home of eighty-four-year-old Jules Juttry and his daughter-in-law, Estelle Bertrand. Here she exchanged her cows for a trip of goats, which she dutifully tended along the road where she could observe German troop movements. A stooped peasant, faded kerchief around her gray head, leaning on a shepherd's staff, she successfully avoided Nazi surveillance. She also delivered goat's milk as a cover to contact resistance colleagues. After she took her goats back to the stable, Hall radioed messages to London from the farmhouse attic. When contact was made and a rendezvous for a plane drop established, she drove a donkey cart to reception areas where she and her resistance teams recovered parachutes and supplies.

Her next hideout was a farmhouse at nearby Surry-en-Bois, where she arranged for two drops of arms and other supplies for the resistance group in Cher Nord. These supplies included a radio set, battery chargers, soap, money, tea, and a badly needed pair of medical stockings to cushion her leg. In all, during her stay in this region she arranged fifteen air drops for the Maquis.

Shortly after D-Day, in early July, Hall was ordered to report back to the Haute-Loire district, a mountainous area covering roughly two thousand square miles in south central France. Her mission: to establish a new French resistance group and maintain radio contact with London. After a risky beginning when her first agent disappeared and her backup failed to provide a safe house, she moved to Chambon-sur-Lignon and launched her operations.

Chambon-sur-Lignon is a village surrounded by rolling hills, pine forests, and small farms and hamlets. It was settled four centuries ago by the Huguenots — French Calvinist Protestants who perpetuated an austere, melancholic, pious community. Chambon was the center of resistance in the Haute-Loire during German occupation, with headquarters in the capital of Le Puy. A small old-fashioned railroad linked it to the Rhone Valley, but there was no efficient way to reach larger cities in that section of France. It was also difficult for Allied pilots to make accurate, pinpoint drops to the rugged terrain.

Hall's first stop was a brief one at the farm of Mme. Leah Lebret, whose husband was a prisoner of war and who was trying to raise two small children by working the family farm. She sheltered Hall until she found an unused house and barn owned by the Salvation Army. There were three bedrooms; Hall's radio equipment was conveniently lodged in the barn. Working alone, she organized reception committees for incoming agents, arranged for distribution of funds and supplies, and began to organize resistance groups. She reported, "My life in the Haute-Loire was different and difficult. I spent my time looking for fields for receptions, bicycling up and down mountains, checking drop zones, visiting various contacts, doing my wireless transmissions and then spending the nights out waiting, for the most part in vain, for deliveries."[8]

In spite of intensive Gestapo efforts to locate the Limping Lady and her transmitter, Hall maintained regular radio contact with London. Between 14 July and 14 August 1944, she transmitted thirty-seven messages to London with intelligence on German troop movements. It was Hall who first reported that the German General Staff was moving headquarters from Lyons to Le Puy.

Hall's efforts were eventually supported by a Maquis group of thirty men under the leadership of Lt. Raoul Le Boulicaud, known in her dispatches as Bob. He was one of her most trusted colleagues. This group provided Hall with security, helped her mark drop areas, and retrieved materiel that, as often happened, fell several valleys away from the designated zone. They also maintained her radio and batteries.

At this point Hall was halfway through her adventurous life: thirty-eight years were behind her, with thirty-eight more ahead.

By mid-July 1944 the Allied beachheads along the northern fronts in France were being joined. Gen. Charles de Gaulle was recognized as the head of the French provisional government. Cherbourg fell to the Allies, and the liberation of France went forward despite desperate German resistance.

On 15 August, ten weeks after D-Day, another Allied force hit the Mediterranean coast, and several hundred thousand American and French troops landed at Saint-Raphaël, Saint-Tropez, and Marseilles in Operation Anvil. The invasion supported the Allied forces fighting eastward from the Normandy beaches toward Paris and the Rhine. The Germans offered only token resistance as they spilled north to join the final battle for their homeland.

At this time Hall's position was strengthened by the arrival of a three-man team from North Africa composed of one American and one French officer and an American enlisted-man radio operator. This group was part of the secret British SOE/OSS infiltration operation code-named Jedburgh. Supplies were also coming from Algiers, including radio equipment that had to be modified because of the mountainous locale. Jerome Wisniewski, who worked for OSS logistics in Algiers, remembers supplying Hall with the longer antennas that were needed to send clearer and stronger signals, and also sending her financial support in the form of gold pieces and local currency.

With the added help of this Jedburgh team, Hall began organizing, arming, and training three battalions of Forces Françaises d'Intérieur (FFI) that later took part in successful guerrilla-warfare and sabotage operations against the retreating Germans. The work of the resistance took on added importance as the battle lines shifted. Hall and her colleagues provided daily intelligence on local conditions, harassed the retreating Germans, and destroyed their lines of communication. Hall had never been trained in guerrilla warfare, partly because of her physical problems, but her common sense and managerial talent were more than adequate for her to plan and organize these operations.

Her final reports to headquarters were impressive: four bridges destroyed, freight trains derailed, a key rail line severed in several places, and telephone lines downed. Nineteen members of the detested militia had been taken prisoner, men who had betrayed their own countrymen to the Nazis. As the Germans withdrew from Le Puy, their retreating convoys were hindered by the blown bridges. In ensuing skirmishes the FFIs killed some 150 Germans and took 500 prisoners.

Hall's next orders sent her to Bourg near the Swiss border, where she and a small FFI group from the Haute-Loire were overtaken by Gen. Jean de Lattre de Tassigny's French First Army. Among the OSS agents accompanying Hall was her future husband, Paul Goillot, an amiable second lieutenant from New York of French extraction who had parachuted into the Haute-Loire area to join her circuit.

At Bourg, Hall turned over her unit weapons and ordnance to the French Ninth Colonial Division. She and Goillot moved on for a spree in liberated Paris, returning to London on 25 September 1944. During her brief sojourn at OSS headquarters there, she met Lt. Rene Julian Defourneaux, who had taken over her watch at Cosne-sur-Loire with two other agents when she had moved on to the Haute-Loire.

"A friend arranged for me to have lunch with her, since I only knew her by reputation," Defourneaux told me.

I was completely surprised at her appearance. She looked like an old lady with dark gray hair, dressed completely in black, with a black pearl choker which relieved to a degree the severity of her appearance. However, she still looked like a queen. She exuded authority, an eighteenth-century dowager, though she was only thirty-eight at the time. She had just returned from France, and there was alertness about her, as if she were still watching for an ambush. I had the feeling that she was so iron-willed that the Germans didn't really want to tangle with her!

Defourneaux also noted that she carried an umbrella that doubled for a cane. "I met her again several years later," he said. "At this second meeting she had completely changed. She was wearing a gay floral dress, her face was bright and cheerful, her hair was soft brown. She seemed like a *jeune fille*."

Hall's last assignment for OSS was scheduled for the Innsbruck area of Austria where she would head a small team that included Goillot. Expecting last-ditch Nazi resistance, OSS officials proposed to infiltrate OSS teams into Austria. Hall's code name was changed to Camille; for her cover she became Anna Muller, a German subject born in Turkey. The collapse of the German forces caused Allied officials to cancel the operation, however, and Hall returned again to Paris with Goillot from Caserta, Italy, from where the operation was being mounted.

In Paris they set out to locate their former French colleagues and to collect radio transmitting material still in the field. Most of the people they had worked with were safe and unharmed, but some had spent time in Buchenwald; others had been executed by the Nazis. One traitor had been a Gestapo agent, the Abbé Alesh, who posed as a member of SOE and was responsible for the deaths of at least four members of Hall's circuit. Hall had never trusted the abbé, and it was through her efforts that he was picked up by American forces and turned over to the French.

Hall never wrote home about these days in France; she once told her niece, Lorna Lee Catling, that she had seen too many corpses of colleagues who had talked. Catling recalls just one letter that Hall's mother received from her daughter that upset her. The letter described the bodies of resistance leaders spiked by their necks to iron fence posts.

For Hall's heroic work in France, Col. James R. Forgan, OSS commanding officer in the European theater of operations, nominated her for the Distinguished Service Cross, the army's highest military medal after the Medal of Honor.

An American WAC detailed to the London office of Maj. John Rafferty, where official recommendations for citations were written, remembers Virginia Hall vividly. She was Mary Donovan Corvo, who recalls that Hall reported to her office to pick up her citation. "I personally gave her the citation," Corvo remembers. "I had read her reports and was anxious to meet her, being so impressed by her great courage. But Virginia Hall's outstanding characteristic was that she had no outstanding characteristic. Also, she was unnecessarily terse, as if she was not particularly impressed with being awarded the DSC."

Hall's citation made its way up to General Donovan's office in Washington. On 12 May 1945 he sent a memo to President Truman: "Inasmuch as an award of this kind has not been previously made during the present war, you may wish to make the presentation personally." But Hall herself demurred, refusing any publicity on the grounds that she was "still operational and most anxious to get busy."[9] Donovan and Truman acceded to her wishes, and on 27 September 1945 Hall and her mother went to OSS headquarters in Washington where the medal was presented to her in the privacy of Donovan's office.

In the postwar years Hall continued her work in intelligence. She served again in Europe as a contract "field representative" for the newly formed Central Intelligence Group, to become the Central Intelligence Agency in 1947. Her passport for these operations was stamped Switzerland, Italy, Palestine, and Cyprus. In the latter part of 1948 she returned home and settled in New York City, where her fiancé lived. Here she joined the National Committee for Free Europe, a CIA front organization and an adjunct to Radio Free Europe. As part of this work she interviewed refugees from Albania, Yugoslavia, and the Baltics and prepared radio propaganda in support of resistance groups operating in those countries.

In 1950 Virginia Hall and Paul Gaston Goillot were married, despite protestations from her mother, who considered Goillot "too uneducated, eight years younger, and not good enough for her daughter," according to Hall's niece, Lorna Lee Catling. (Earlier, before the war, Hall's father had broken up a budding romance between his daughter and a dashing Polish officer she had met in Vienna during her tour at the embassy there.)

Paul Goillot was born in Paris on 10 July 1914. His parents emigrated to New York when he was fourteen, and he grew up in Manhattan. In 1936 his parents decided to return to France with their daughter, but Paul, then twenty-two, elected to remain in the United States. He returned to his native land as a second lieutenant in the army during the war and parachuted in as an OSS agent on 4 September 1944, to join Hall. After the liberation he was reunited in Paris with his mother and sister, whom he had not seen in nine years. His father had died.

Catling remembers Goillot as a funny roughneck with a delightful sense of humor who always spoke with a French accent: "He was shorter than Dindy, but their early married life was fun. They found a great deal of happiness in shared memories. He was good for her. He lightened her life. If she asked him to take a few days off with her and go fishing, he was always ready and obliged."

In December 1951 a forty-five-year-old Hall started work for the CIA in Washington. She was assigned to the Office of Policy Coordination as an intelligence officer on the French paramilitary desk. She entered as a GS-13 at a salary of $8,360 per year. In December 1952 she became one of the first women operations officers in the newly created Office of the Deputy Director of Plans. In this job she was responsible for countries in Western Europe.

She prepared political action projects, interviewed exiles, and planned stay-behind resistance and sabotage nets to be used in the event the Soviet Union attacked Europe. In 1954 she was assigned to the paramilitary staff because of her wide experience during the war in covert action. In 1956 the agency made her a member of the select Career Staff; she was one of the first women to achieve this distinction, but only after working six years as a contract employee.

Hall had several temporary duty assignments abroad but was based at headquarters for her entire CIA career. She traveled to England, Germany, and Switzerland in 1956 to prepare project plans for Southeast Asia. The records show that during this assignment Hall had a nondisclosed dispute with her supervisor. She returned to Washington, and for the nine years left of her CIA career she held down a desk job, with eventual promotion to GS-14 and a salary of $14,120.

In her earlier years at the agency a former CIA official, Angus Thuermer, recalls Hall as a "gung-ho lady left over from OSS days overseas. Young women in sweater sets and pearls listened raptly to Virginia Hall gas with muscular paramilitary officers who would stop by her desk to tell war stories. She was elegant, her dark brown hair coiled on top of her head with a yellow pencil tucked into the bun. She was always jolly when she was around the old boys. She was a presence!"

E. Howard Hunt, another CIA colleague in the Western Hemisphere division, recalled a different Virginia Hall during her later years: "I was distressed at the insensitive treatment accorded Virginia Hall toward the end of her career. No one knew what to do with her, and she was usually at a lonely desk in war plans or the paramilitary offices." He continued: "She was a sort of embarrassment to the noncombat CIA types, by which I mean bureaucrats. Her experience and abilities were never properly utilized. At the very least she should have been lecturing to trainees at the CIA indoctrination 'farm' near Williamsburg. She was out of the loop, the proverbial round peg, and through no fault of her own. I really ached over her and her low-level status."

Virginia Hall turned in her agency badge in 1966 upon reaching the then mandatory retirement age of sixty. Because of a series of medical problems she took disability retirement and for the next sixteen years lived on a farm in Barnestown, Maryland.

Catling recalls those early retirement years: "Dindy was a great gardener. She planted thousands of bulbs at her Barnestown home, which reminded me of a turreted French château. She also like to bird-watch." Neighbors remember Paul Goillot in a leather apron searching for mushrooms on hands and knees. He had become a restaurateur, briefly utilizing his excellent skill as a French chef. However, he was a bad businessman, and the enterprise failed after a few years. Paul Goillot became a "house husband."

"Dindy and Paul had five beautiful French poodles," Catling remembers. "Dindy would sit them all down in front of her and feed them each from a silver ladle. She also kept several cats in the basement, but they were 'mice' cats, not family pets. But she loved all animals. I remember her foisting a huge goose upon my family at Box Horn Farm. It chased me all over the yard."

Hall made excellent goat's milk cheese and also mastered a handloom, weaving her own cloth. She was a crossword-puzzle addict, and as the years went by she read a great deal. Her library was filled with history and travel books, especially spy stories.

Toward the end of her life Virginia Hall succumbed to bad health. Her husband suffered a severe stroke that changed his personality. Hall died in 1982 at the Shady Grove Adventist Hospital in Rockville, Maryland. The cause of her death was not reported. As the *Baltimore Sun* reported, "With simple services that contrasted to the drama of her World War II career, a Baltimore school girl who became the French underground's 'limping lady' was buried at Druid Ridge Cemetery in Pikesville, Maryland."[10] Her husband died five years later.

Virginia Hall was a legend to many of the

OSS women operating in and out of London, and to this day she is revered as one of the true heroines of the war. Gertrude Legendre, head of the OSS London Central Cable Desk, still remembers seeing Hall's code name, Diane, in dispatches that crossed her desk from occupied France.

The two women never met in those exciting days in the autumn of 1944. They were both posted to a liberated Paris and were in the crowds that cheered Gen. Charles de Gaulle when he marched in the victory parade down the Champs-Elysées. Hall's adventures were winding down, but Legendre was destined to end her OSS career in a bizarre and potentially dangerous situation. She was captured along the fluid front lines en route to Luxembourg by a German army patrol retreating before advancing Allied forces.

CHAPTER 12

The Agent Who Lived Her Cover

In early October 1944 Radio Hamburg broadcast an announcement that the first American woman prisoner had been captured on the Western Front near Wallendorf, forty kilometers from Luxembourg. She was Gertrude Sanford Legendre, an interpreter for an American naval officer.

The International News Service picked up the story, but it was quickly killed in Paris by military censorship. The Germans never knew that they had captured the former head of the OSS London Central Cable Desk, recently transferred to the same job in Paris. Gertrude Legendre had no authorization to make the trip to the front lines; she had five days' leave coming, and, a lover of adventure, she wanted to "smell the fighting."[1] Of more importance was the capture, with Legendre, of Maj. Maxwell J. Papurt of X-2, the OSS Counterintelligence Branch, who had controlled important enemy agent operations in Italy for OSS.

News of their capture went straight to the top echelon. In London, Col. Stewart Menzies, chief of England's Secret Intelligence Service, coordinated with Eisenhower's chief of staff, Brig. Gen. Walter Bedell Smith, and his British deputy, Sir Kenneth W. D. Strong. General Donovan, upon receiving the information, strode up and down in his Washington office in a rage. As reported by his aide, Edwin Putzell, "He was first of all concerned with the capture of Papurt, but he was equally concerned that Legendre might talk. He called her a loose cannon."[2]

OSS leaders in the field expressed confidence that Papurt would not break under interrogation. He had a wealth of counterintelligence experience in Italy and what Putzell called an "instinct for bluffing." In the end, Papurt was killed by an Allied air attack on a German hospital where his captors had taken him after wounding him at Wallendorf. Legendre maintained silence about her OSS connection during six months of intensive questioning in captivity. Her only security briefing had been on-the-job training.

A vital center at OSS London headquarters was the Cable Desk, established there in 1943 to organize cable and code-room traffic. Here incoming and outgoing messages were handled and distributed, information from all over the world regarding agent names, sources, and the location of agent networks.

Legendre, a graduate of Foxcroft in Virginia, spent a year in Washington at OSS headquarters at the Message Center and Cable Desk before her London assignment. Her husband, Lt. Comdr. Sydney Legendre, was serving in the Pacific; the two small Legendre children were living with an aunt and nanny in New Orleans. Their historic plantation, Medway, in Goose Creek, South Carolina, was closed for the duration. Legendre worked up from file clerk to head of the Washington Cable Desk. Years later she told me, "At first, the business of learning office routine seemed strange and frightening because of the responsibility and small margin for error. On my desk was a battery of stamps: Restricted, Confidential, Secret, Top Secret. There was the necessity for supplying the field instant information upon request. It was exacting, fascinating."

Legendre arrived in London in September 1943 "full of high anticipation and earnestness of purpose." Because of her Washington experience she was assigned as chief of the Central Cable Desk. She immediately began to set up files and organize the necessary machinery to handle message traffic for thirteen London OSS branches. There was endless routing, delivering, and verification of intelligence. "The door between my office and the cable room itself seemed to carry as much traffic as the busiest London street," she recalled.

Within a few months of her arrival she reported that the Cable Desk was running smoothly. As traffic increased, her staff also increased to six people, including three WAC secretaries. The steel safes in her office were filled with secret and confidential files from North Africa, Italy, Sweden, India, China, Ceylon, and the top-secret agent outposts in occupied France. When she arrived in London, Legendre shared a large flat with OSS station chief David Bruce and Col. Thomas Hitchcock, air attaché at the U.S. embassy in London; Hitchcock was a polo-playing friend of Legendre's brother, Laddie Sanford. Later Legendre moved to her own house with a Swiss cook, where she was able to give small but elegant dinner parties for influential friends serving in the European theater of operations.

At one such party her guest list included American ambassador John G. Winant, Gen. William Donovan, Gen. Carl Spaatz, Gen. Lewis M. Brereton, and other well-known figures. "I remember that night well," she told me later. "One of the generals, new to the theater, said he had not yet seen a buzz bomb. Hardly had he said this than we heard the familiar putt-putt of an approaching deadly 'doodlebug.' As the chugging grew fainter, I knew it had overshot my house. So many irreplaceable men would have been killed if it had hit us."

In September 1944 Legendre was transferred

to the Paris communications center. She was issued a WAC uniform on express orders of SHAEF (Supreme Headquarters Allied Expeditionary Force) headquarters. It was mandatory that all civilian OSS personnel be integrated into the military establishment in France. It also enabled them to have access to canteen privileges. "I donned the uniform of a WAC second lieutenant, my assimilated rank. I didn't even know how to salute," Legendre said. Because OSS Paris headquarters at 80 Champs-Elysées were being renovated, Legendre found herself wandering aimlessly around Paris, "feeling useless" despite the lure of a city just reasserting its identity. During this period she checked in frequently, looking for work. She was finally issued a five-day pass, her first freedom in twelve months. She had five days before her to do anything exciting she wished.

An opportunity turned up unexpectedly at the Ritz Hotel bar, where a group of war correspondents were talking about new assignments with Third Army headquarters in Luxembourg. Legendre looked up from the group to see an OSS colleague, navy commander Robert Jennings, just in from London and looking for excitement. Their moods meshed, and Jennings came up with a plan to get to the front and back in five days. He knew where he could get a vintage Peugeot, recently liberated from the Nazis, that just might make the trip. The next morning, 23 September 1944, they set out from a rain-drenched Paris on their way to Luxembourg, and to the wavering front beyond, not yet stabilized.

In the official report she made from Bern, 28 March 1945, Legendre stated that the pair had to spend the night in a Luxembourg hotel when the ancient Peugeot broke down after a day's rugged travel over bombed-out roads.[3] Eating breakfast in the hotel on the morning of 25 September, they met a friendly stranger, Maj. Maxwell Papurt of OSS, who had a jeep and driver. He was on his way to Wallendorf, which was in American hands, according to a situation map he had just checked.

The following day Jennings, Papurt, Legendre, and the driver started out for the small German village. Legendre was at last beginning to "smell the excitement" as they passed bombed-out fields, cows on their backs, dead, feet straight up, and houses burned to the ground. Before the war Legendre and her husband had been big-game hunters, tracking down specimens all over the world for museums, zoos, and their own collection. In a sense she had been disciplined to danger, to situations that required extreme confidence and courage.

This discipline became important in the next few minutes. As they approached a signpost marked Wallendorf, they were suddenly sprayed with machine-gun fire. The jeep was an open target. There was no cover. Papurt leapt out and crept toward a hedgerow, pistol drawn. There was more enemy fire. Papurt yelled that he was hit in both legs and crawled back to the jeep. He told the driver to turn the car around. At that same moment, the driver was shot through both legs and arms. Jennings and Legendre, now hiding behind the jeep, shouted to them to take cover. The men wormed their way on their stomachs to the rear of the jeep and crouched together in a mud puddle.

The gunfire was becoming heavier and more accurate. They had no choice but to hoist a white handkerchief on the end of a rifle barrel and at the same time coordinate their cover stories. Papurt was an ordnance officer, Jennings a naval officer, and Legendre a file clerk at the American embassy, serving as an interpreter for Jennings. Legendre calmly collected their passes, her own blue SHAEF pass, and some incriminating OSS papers. As the snipers inched toward the Americans, Legendre dug a hole and burned these articles, then covered the ashes with dirt. Unfortunately Papurt had failed to give her one sensitive document that revealed his intelligence connection. It was this paper that later almost cost Jennings and Legendre their lives. Legendre was busy sprinkling sulfa powder on the wounds of her companions when the enemy soldiers appeared with guns lowered.

The Germans and Americans together carried the two wounded men across a small stream and through a farm to what was left of Wallendorf. Allied guns were booming over the hill from town, occasionally hitting open land and throwing dust and dirt into the air. American planes were circling overhead, with the battle still in progress. The German soldiers commandeered a horse-drawn wagon and transported the wounded men up a steep ridge to a stable where more Germans were huddled. The two Americans were bedded down in straw and eventually were evacuated to a field medical unit.

Legendre and Jennings were then escorted to a bunker where a German lieutenant and radio operator were seated at a table. The interrogation began. Who were they? Why were they at the front? Legendre, in French, repeated her cover story. She was from the American embassy, acting as translator for Jennings. They had been misinformed that Wallendorf was in American hands.

After this initial briefing, Legendre and Jennings were ordered to leave for an unspecified destination. They would never see Papurt again, but the driver, listed only as Richard in the reports, survived the ordeal of captivity. A troop carrier picked Legendre and her companion up, and they were off on a wild ride away from the front lines in what Legendre's report described as "driving through thunder and lightning, with guns booming and flashing as we bumped along muddy and gutted roads on springless seats." After this perilous flight through the Siegfried Line, they reached their destination about midnight. They were in Trier, in the foothills of the Hunsrück Mountains near the Moselle River.

Legendre's second interrogation began when she was ushered into a dreary brick building on the outskirts of town. In her memoir she wrote that a "wizened little man with weasel-like eyes" started questioning her in German, with a young soldier translating awkwardly into French.[4] She stuck to her story. As a clerk with the American embassy, she filed requests for typewriters and stationery, all sorts of office supplies. Why a civilian in uniform with no insignia? Headquarters regulations! There was no variation in the questions; they followed the same pattern as the earlier ones. "Weasel Eyes threw one surprise query towards the end," Legendre wrote. "He asked me whether I was frightened? 'Why should I be frightened?' I replied. 'I understand the Germans treat their prisoners as properly as we do.' "

As she recounted in her official report, Trier was the start for Legendre of a haphazard and often dangerous journey through war-ravaged Germany, just beginning to crumble before the Allied invasion. First they were sardine-packed into a tiny Opel and driven seventy-five kilometers due north to Witlich, where they were told brusquely that there were no facilities there to house them. Then, without sleep or food, they were hustled on to the small village of Flammersheim.

Here Legendre was searched, and a soldier confiscated her Leica camera (which he accused her of stealing), light meter, film, driver's license, and first-aid certificate. She was placed in a filthy cell with a flea-infested straw pallet for a bed. She had no soap, toothbrush, or toilet paper. In the morning she was given five slices of bread with a pat of ersatz butter. She would occasionally get a bloody sausage or some watery potato soup for lunch. Dinner was ersatz coffee. It was during this twelve-day internment that Legendre was informed that an incriminating document found on Papurt made her own future uncertain. She said she began to sense a different feeling in the way the Wehrmacht treated her. They were more suspicious, as if she had suddenly become a dangerous spy instead of a crazy American girl who had ventured too close to the front lines just for a lark.

Her next internment confirmed her apprehensions. Shortly after her interview, Legendre and Jennings were placed in a chauffeur-driven Buick limousine, with two officers as guards, and driven to the village of Diez near the Lahn River. The Buick climbed a steep hill and stopped before the gates of a picturesque thirteenth-century castle. They were ushered into the foyer by a suave Wehrmacht lieutenant, speaking fluent English with just a trace of a New York accent.

Legendre and Jennings were again separated, and she spent the next six weeks in Cell 38 in the castle. Each evening Legendre met with the Wehrmacht officer, a man of about forty with a polite but firm method of interrogation. In her later report Legendre wrote that the first encounter was blunt: "He came right to the point and said I was considered a very dangerous spy. If I didn't tell him everything, he would get it out of me. The Germans had ways of making people talk."

The interrogation continued into the night. The lieutenant said that Legendre had been implicated with Major Papurt, who was carrying an incriminating paper listing the names of thirty agents in the employ of SCI. He handed her the paper to read, a plain letter-size sheet of bond paper. "What does SCI mean?" he asked her. She shook her head and said she wasn't up on all the funny letters the government used. As she spoke she felt her pulse quicken, and she bent her head to the lamp to hide her face. How often had she seen it in cable traffic: SCI, Special Counter Intelligence Units, a joint U.S.-U.K. organization composed of OSS and British MI5.

As she studied the list she recognized the name Haas, which she had seen in cables coming across her desk. Stubbornly she shook her head and vehemently told the lieutenant that she had no idea what she was reading. The interrogation continued for six consecutive meetings. It finally centered on a detailed questionnaire about her family background. Whom did she know? She admitted that she knew General Patton, General Spaatz, and Ambassador Winant socially. At this point she felt a change in the lieutenant's attitude. She wondered if these contacts might be considered useful by the Germans and if she might be used later as a possible intermediary for negotiations.

The lieutenant did not question her too deeply concerning her connection with Jennings, and she continued to repeat that he was a friend of her husband but that she had never seen him prior to being assigned to him as an interpreter. The questioning became more relaxed. The lieutenant said his name was William Gosewisch. He had lived for eighteen years in the United States running a lunch counter, was married to an American, and had two children. In 1939 he came home to show his wife Germany. Because he was not yet an American citizen, he was caught up in compulsory military service and had never been allowed to leave.

He also told her that he had taken his bachelor of arts degree at Columbia University in New York City in psychology. Because of this training, he boasted, he knew that Legendre was telling him the truth. He also said that it was unfortunate that she had been captured, and that he would make every effort through his influential friends to have her released. He said that the SD, or Security Service, of the Gestapo was trying to get hold of her for questioning, but because she had been taken on the Western Front, she was a prisoner of the Wehrmacht and therefore his responsibility.

At the end of six weeks Legendre and her captor were on a first-name basis. She reported, "Bill would come down to my cell and get me after he had finished work and take me upstairs to his office. Here, over cognac or wine we would chat from about nine o'clock to two or three in the morning. He told me that he was an SS officer, the German abbreviation for Schutzstaffel or Defense Echelon, Himmler's elite quasi-military security organization. He was second in command at the castle. He said he loved his native Germany but was opposed to the war and hoped that democracy would eventually prevail."

Several weeks after their arrival Jennings was escorted to Legendre's cell to say good-bye. In a low voice he told her that Gosewisch had also interrogated him, and that he had been convinced that Jennings was actually in naval ordnance. Jennings was being sent to an officers' prison camp. He had lost considerable weight, but he was in good spirits. (The next time they saw each other, quite by accident, was on a

New York City street during the V-E Day celebration in May 1945.)

One day Gosewisch called Legendre to tell her that he had been ordered to the front for three weeks. He would try and clear up her case as soon as possible and keep her out of the hands of the Gestapo. After his departure, events began to move swiftly. The next day the commander of the castle prison walked into Legendre's cell and ordered her to get ready for immediate departure. Within an hour she was on her way to Frankfurt in a wood-burning car driven by two men in civilian clothes. From there she was escorted by train to Berlin. From the station she walked with her guards through deserted city streets, flanked by bombed-out buildings, to an address she knew too well from OSS cables: 8 Prinz Albert Strasse, Gestapo headquarters!

Legendre was subjected to further interrogation during the next two months at a prison in Wansee located between two lakes in the Berlin suburbs. The prison had once been a large estate and was now the guest establishment for officials of the International (German) Criminal Police Department and a detention center for political prisoners. Two women guards were assigned to Legendre during her stay. The interrogation was identical to the questioning she had undergone at Diez. She noted in her report that she began to think what she was saying was actually true: "My imaginary life as an embassy clerk was real. I could see the room, the steel filing cases, a table littered with requests for typewriters, drawers and drawers of manila folders, lettered alphabetically. Even my women colleagues I invented began to assume a personality of their own."

As in the past, Legendre one day was ordered to prepare for immediate evacuation from her prison room. This time the route was by car through devastated country where Allied planes were daily bombing Cologne and Bonn. Their destination was the Rheinhotel Dreesen in Godesberg, once the summer resort on the Rhine of well-to-do Prussian and Hessian families. The building — five stories high, with a sweeping mansard roof and gardens stretching down to the river — still retained some of the elegance of a former era. Legendre was assigned a small room with a washstand, cold running water, a wooden armoire, and a small radiator that did not work. To her surprise, the bed was quite comfortable, and she slept right through to late breakfast call.

That morning she went down to a large salon. Following the sounds of conversation and the rattle of coffee cups, she found more than a hundred men and one woman. To her amazement, they were all speaking French. A kindly man stepped forward and introduced himself as Gen. Maxime Germain. He was the ranking officer among some 130 interned French nationals, mostly officers either retired or on the inactive list of the French army at the time of their arrest. They had been taken into protective custody four months previously to prevent their recall or to render them ineffective in the resistance. The only woman present was Mme. Alfred Caillau of Saint-Etienne, the sister of Gen. Charles de Gaulle. In her memoir Legendre described her as "generally despondent and intensely religious." She worried constantly about her sons in the French army and her family in Paris. At times, though, she could be distracted with questions about her famous brother; then she brightened up and extolled *"mon frère Charles"* as the savior of France.

Legendre enjoyed her almost comfortable prison days with the French, but that ended when units of the U.S. First Army attacked and finally captured Godesberg and Bonn. The French were hustled out of the hotel to an unknown destination, which Legendre later learned was Essenberg in Bohemia. Her own last prison stop was to be Kronberg, where she was given a room at the home of Dr. and Mrs. Hans Grieme. Dr. Grieme was head of a large machine-tool factory, and he had influential friends in the Foreign Office. Through his connections Legendre was able to establish contact with Gosewisch at his office in Diez Castle, and he came immediately to see her at Kronberg. It was at this meeting that Gosewisch planned Legendre's final panicky escape into Switzerland, with the help of Dr. Grieme.

Legendre was picked up in a small Opel and driven through war-ravaged Frankfurt to the German-Swiss border at Konstanz. There she boarded a train for Switzerland, shadowed by a tall stranger in a light overcoat. Once aboard, she obeyed orders to keep out of sight, hiding behind empty seats. At one point she ducked into a toilet to avoid a trainman swinging a lantern. Finally the train started to move, inching its way slowly over battered tracks. When it stopped and she moved slowly toward the door, she could see the white gates of the frontier in the bright moonlight. The train had stopped short of the gate on the German side of the border.

Legendre slipped out the train door and moved slowly along an adjacent line of freight cars. As she pondered her next move, she turned to see the mysterious man in the light topcoat. "Run," he half whispered and gestured with his arm toward the Swiss guard post. As she started to run she looked back, but the unknown friend had disappeared.

Legendre was in full sprint when she heard a shout behind her: "Halt!" It was an armed German border guard. She kept on running toward the Swiss gate as the guard's footsteps grew closer. The Swiss sentry shouted, *"Identité! Identité!"* all the while raising his gate. "American passport," she screamed, and passed under the lifted barrier. The German border guard was shouting with rage. To this day Legendre doesn't know why he didn't shoot her.

Once safely inside Switzerland, Legendre was detained by the chief of the Swiss police in Kreuzlingen, Otto Ragganbass. He checked her story and identity and finally notified the American legation in Bern. Legendre had more trouble at the legation than she had had with the Gestapo and the Kreuzlingen police. After being warmly greeted by the staff she was questioned on where she had been employed when captured. She could not mention OSS, and her Paris-embassy-file-clerk story would not stand up. It was at this juncture that a man from Allen Dulles's office appeared. Tracy Barnes, Dulles's executive officer, knew all about Gertrude Legendre. In short order they had driven to Herrengasse 23, a gray sandstone mansion with gardens on the River Aare, where Dulles lived. She was shown to a charming bedroom, were she tidied up for tea.

As she recounted in her memoir, Legendre was voraciously eating thin cress sandwiches and chocolate-covered sponge cake in the spacious living room when the door opened and Dulles walked in, smoking his pipe, with a wide smile on his face. He greeted her warmly and said how surprised he was to see her standing before him, safe and in good health. When Legendre began to thank him for getting her safely out of Germany, he shook his head.

"OSS did not dare to touch you, nor did the Embassy. You were too hot," he told her. He also explained that there were still OSS agents in Germany, and if OSS had attempted to rescue her or contact her through these channels, there could have been the chance of a slip. The agents would have been tortured and murdered.

That evening, after what Legendre described as a splendid French meal, she sat down with Dulles's secretary, who took shorthand notes as she described her six-month experience as a German prisoner. Both Dulles and Barnes listened carefully, prompting her and asking leading questions. When she reached the part about prison life on the Rhine with the French prisoners, she whipped out her pocket knife and ripped open the sleeve lining of her overcoat. She produced a crumpled paper with a list of 130 names meticulously printed by one of the French prisoners.

Dulles took the paper, read it carefully, and then asked her if she had read the list. She said of course she had, and Dulles smiled. "I mean, have you read what is written in German?" The message said, "To the attention of Mrs. Legendre: In order that you will not have a bad opinion of Kreuzlingen and the Swiss Border Control, we inform you herewith that we have examined the enclosed list of names while you were in our custody. Since we realized that it is only an act of charity in behalf of imprisoned acquaintances we are replacing the manuscript in its original hiding place. Travel well and our greetings to America." It was signed by O. Ragganbass.

Meanwhile, Dulles and Barnes made arrangements for Legendre's transportation to Paris and then home. Barnes would drive her to Geneva, where army orders would be cut for her. She would be driven to the French border and down to Lyons to catch the Paris Express — arriving in Paris, coincidentally, on her birthday, 29 March. Both men warned her not to speak to the press and not to report to OSS headquarters in Paris.

Meanwhile, cables were being sent to Donovan in Washington, to the OSS office in Paris, and out to Honolulu, where Legendre's husband was contacted at sea.[5] Dulles cabled Donovan:

All formalities for G.L.'s leaving Switzerland were handled on basis she was military escapee and turned over to me 27 March. Stayed at my home until departure. Able to minimize any publicity about her escape. I impressed upon her the instructions to give no interviews. Gertrude is rather contrite, I think. She made no effort to make excuses for her escapade. She has obeyed instructions implicitly while she was with us and impressed me as being a person with a great deal of resourcefulness.

Cables from Paris OSS headquarters again stressed that Legendre must be sent home immediately and not venture near the headquarters in Paris. General Donovan himself cabled Honolulu: "For Cmdr. Legendre, husband of Gertrude Legendre. She being returned to Washington immediately via Paris. In view lives of other prisoners in danger greatest security must be maintained including her association with this agency and the entire situation of her escape. Your assistance is earnestly requested."

Gertrude Legendre and her husband were reunited in New York City with their two children. Shortly thereafter he was mustered out of the navy, and they returned to Medway Plantation in South Carolina when war ended.

It wasn't until 1950 that Legendre was able to help her German friend, Lieutenant Gosewisch. She said she found him and his family destitute, as were so many in postwar Germany. She was able to get them to South Carolina, where he was given a job working for her husband. They often met and exchanged reminiscences, and he always sent her red roses on holidays. William Gosewisch died the day before the Berlin Wall came down, a historic incident Legendre knew he would have loved to witness.

The war in Europe was fought for seven long, bloody months after Legendre was captured. For two months before she left London she had seen terse reports coming over the Cable Desk detailing the names and operations of French underground teams working with OSS units out of Algiers after the August invasion of southern France. Her knowledge of these activities could have been vital to Nazi planning at the time German forces in France were being ambushed and scattered by the French resistance with OSS support.

Some of these cables also gave the code names of women agents working out of Algiers and southern France for OSS. Legendre knew who they were and where they operated. They rescued downed Allied flyers, reported on troop movements, determined the locations of parachute drops, and located safe houses for OSS agents. One remarkable woman even helped turn a German agent operating a clandestine radio set near the French-Spanish border.

CHAPTER 13

Turning a Nazi Agent

On 15 August 1944, ten weeks after the invasion of Normandy, Allied forces hit the beaches of southern France. On that day some one thousand vessels stood off the Mediterranean coast, and several hundred thousand American and French troops went ashore at Saint-Raphaël, Saint-Tropez, and Marseilles. Their mission: to push north through the Rhone Valley and join Allied units fighting east from the Normandy beaches. This operation was code-named Anvil/Dragoon.

Unlike Normandy, these landings were virtually unopposed, and many of the Germans offered only token resistance. They were already retreating on some fronts, pushing north to join the final battles for their homeland. They were also meeting the organized French resistance, backed by British, French, and American units under the Sussex Plan, which had successfully infiltrated a large part of enemy-held France.

Much of this early invasion planning originated from OSS headquarters in Algiers. Here, in this French possession about four times the size of Texas, men and women were trained and infiltrated into southern France to make contact with the resistance — at beach resorts, in châteaus in the wine country, in the mountainous terrain bordering Italy and Spain.

OSS operations were established as the provisional 2677th Regiment in Algiers under Col. William A. Eddy, an American who had grown up in France and thought like a Frenchman. The first women destined for this assignment landed in North Africa in 1943.

One woman, Ann Willets, writes that Algiers "was a beautiful city, particularly at night with the white villas nestled against the dark hills and the sun shining below on naval craft, blinking signals."[1] Willets, assigned to the French desk, was the first woman to become an office administrator trusted with the important task of packing parachutes and supplies for agents bound for southern France. She worked out of the parachute training camp at Pine Club.

OSS WAC sergeant Rachel Giese was another outstanding woman who began her career in Algiers, ended up in Bern winning the Legion of Merit. At OSS headquarters she was assigned to X-2, the Counterintelligence Branch, where she analyzed reports coming in from southern France. These she painstakingly pieced together to produce an accurate, integrated study. Edwin Putzell, Donovan's aide, had nothing but praise for Giese's thoroughness. Her reports, he told me years later, included even the addresses of thirty-two brothels in Marseilles and the names of the proprietors. (Prostitutes were often part of the French resistance.)

Sergeant Giese was multilingual, a one-time Columbia University professor described by one of her colleagues as "businesslike, but a lovely high-class lady who kept to herself." Giese was named in a theater commendation as part of the intelligence team "whose work provided probably the fullest and most detailed material, which was extraordinarily accurate."

Another OSS operative, Helen Osmun, was a special assistant to the X-2 chief in Algiers. She was assigned liaison duties with the French and was able to extract important intelligence, with their collaboration, for Anvil/Dragoon operations.

Dolly Corbin also worked with agents in Algiers, where she was headquartered in a villa that had once been the home of Napoleon III. The daughter of an American general, she had been educated abroad and spoke fluent French. Corbin was assigned the job of outfitting French agents who had volunteered to return to their homeland prior to the invasion of southern France. She also briefed them on the names and locations of the resistance groups they would contact in the field and the intelligence requirements levied on them by OSS.

In occupied France, citizens at all levels of society took part in various resistance movements, giving those groups a broad power base and wide-ranging objectives. Many Frenchwomen worked for OSS and reported to Algiers. Hélène Deschamps was one of these top agents. The daughter of an officer in the French colonial army, she had no special training, but once she took the responsibility of reporting on Nazi activities along the Mediterranean, she soon learned the skills needed for survival.

"I covered the territory from Avignon to Montpelier to Marseilles," remembered Deschamps, who reported under the code name Anick. "I spied on German defense works and fortifications, on the strength and movement of enemy troops, and on the transport of equipment and ammunition. I spotted the airfield locations and bicycled along the shores of the Mediterranean to detect coastal defenses and to locate German mines, antiaircraft guns, and camouflaged redoubts."

Another Frenchwoman, Lt. Jeanette Guyot, won the Distinguished Service Cross for operations against the Germans from 8 February until 26 August 1944. Guyot parachuted, wearing civilian clothes, into enemy-occupied France as a member of the Pathfinder mission. She was charged with locating parachute fields, organizing reception committees, and arranging safe houses and local informants. Her citation read, "Because of her great courage and initiative she undertook the most dangerous assignments, such as reporting Gestapo activities and verifying reports of the arrest or execution of any agents. Lieutenant Guyot's work and conduct were beyond all praise."[2]

One of the most effective operations before and during the invasion phase of southern France was conducted by an OSS officer, Maj. Geoffrey M. T. Jones, who parachuted into the Basses-Alpes and joined the Maquis in that area in late July. His mission was to organize and coordinate French resistance to receive the Allied airborne spearhead of the Anvil/Dragoon landings along the French Riviera. Jones not only accomplished his mission but was able to organize a most effective self-contained OSS special-intelligence and covert mission that eventually became OSS Nice. "We were able to build a multinational group of over 120 volunteer men and women from local residents and refugees," Jones recalled. "These people served as translators, cooks, couriers, and counter-intelligence and *coup-de-main* agents complete with a network of clandestine radios, ski patrols, and a small fleet of sail and motor boats." An American expatriate, Isabel Pell, was responsible for organizing the effective female cadre working at headquarters.[3]

One of Jones's key staffers was the Marquise Claire de Forbin, born Claire Charles-Roux, whose father had been the French ambassador to Russia before the war. She had worked with the resistance since 1943 and became Jones's chief of intelligence, processing reports from more than one hundred of the volunteer field agents, which were translated, as required, into French, Italian, English, or German. Five women assisted her in this work.

Of all the women who took part in the Anvil/Dragoon operation, the name Betty Lussier surfaces most often. Years afterward, when World War II was becoming just a memory with the next generation who followed us, I stumbled upon her trail by accident.

"Of course I remember Betty Lussier. She helped set up an extensive double-agent net in Perpignan, France. I was her boss." That boss was Roger Goiran, head of X-2 operations in France and Spain. Now in his mid-eighties, his voice came over the phone from Dunedin, Florida, rich and throaty: "Betty was very intelligent. She had a powerful memory. She was capable of extraordinary discipline. She never let her emotions get the better of her. She was a perfect X-2 agent, well trained, well educated."

Then, recalling the excitement of that world war of fifty-odd years ago, Goiran conjured up something of the spirit of those days: "The people assembled by Donovan were dedicated, excited; their work transcended any previous experience. This was true of men and women who worked to the maximum of their capabilities. We were well integrated. Betty was an outstanding example of the almost mystic *joie de vivre* we all had."

With Goiran's help, I met and interviewed Betty in New York City. She still matched Goiran's description of the unflappable agent. She was tall and thin, with steady hazel green eyes and a face-brightening smile. She had come in for our interview from Staten Island, where she lives alone, though she still keeps in touch with her four sons around the world, and did so too with her estranged husband in Spain until his death.

Lussier's was a story of high adventure and excitement, of delivering coded messages and tracking down collaborators and stay-behind Nazi agents as the war moved from France into Germany.

"I was always adventurous," she told me. "I was born in Canada but got over to England in 1942 to win the war all by myself." She smiled. "I loved to fly and joined the Air Transport Auxiliary, which was seconded to the Royal Air Force to collect new planes at factories and deliver them to aerodromes in Scotland, Wales, or England. We also delivered groups of men pilots to their combat stations in the United Kingdom and flew planes in need of maintenance back to inland bases from combat zones in Britain. Sometimes we piloted VIPs around the country for meetings or inspection tours."

Much as she loved flying, Lussier resigned from the Air Transport Auxiliary in 1943 when she was told that women pilots would not be permitted to fly into combat zones on the Continent once the ground invasion of Europe took place. She joined OSS that year.

"It was an easy move for me," she explained. "My father, Emile John Lussier, and Sir William Stephenson were Canadian pilots during World War I in Squadron 73, the Royal Flying Corps. They were great friends, and Sir William was also my godfather. He was head of the British Security Coordination headquartered in New York City during World War II. Known by his code name, Intrepid, Sir William had been instrumental in arranging the training of Americans by British intelligence. He was also a personal friend of General Donovan."

Lussier was accepted by OSS and sent to Saint Albans, north of London, one of the first group in OSS to be trained by the British in counterespionage and code work. There were five men and five women in this first class.

Most of this training was based upon a new system of cryptography. Before Britain was brought into the war, SIS, the British Secret Intelligence Service, had managed to obtain the basic German cipher machine, Enigma, through Polish contacts. Later, code manuals and additional apparatus were captured. Possession of the Enigma machine saved countless lives during the war and enabled the British to read vital German military radio communications traffic in and out of Axis-held territory during hostilities.

"Possession of Enigma was one of the most closely guarded secrets of the war," Lussier said. "The British called this system Ultra, which was the ability to decipher messages using the intricate machine. The Americans called it Ice. The British kept the actual code reading in their own hands but trained a few Americans authorized to deliver Ultra messages to combat headquarters. This was the training for which I was accepted, and which enabled me to work at various military headquarters in Europe for the rest of the war."

British intelligence created the security system by which Ultra material could be transmitted to military commanders in the field. These agents were called special liaison units, or SLUs, and were posted to major military headquarters. There were only twenty-eight American SLUs in the European theater of operations.

The training at Saint Albans was rigorous. Teams reviewed all radio traffic that had come in and been decoded during the previous twenty-four-hour period. The messages were divided into areas of mutual interest, and trainees then were taught to analyze the traffic, each desk concentrating on a different geographical area. Lussier's specialty became North Africa.

This was an elite unit. The job they were learning at Saint Albans was to collect the "Ice" destined for American consumption from daily British transmissions. Ultra messages, having been decoded, translated, evaluated, and given appropriate priority, were once more encoded and sent to the designated liaison units in the field. There they were decoded and passed to authorized recipients.

The SLUs performing this task needed to be close to American headquarters but also secure from outside attention. A suitable cover story had to be devised, as the presence of a small secretive group of British near an American headquarters might provoke curiosity. In some cases the problem was best dealt with by having an American attached to the team. Thus, Lussier's affiliation with OSS's hush-hush X-2 was double insurance against security breaches.

After three months of training, Lussier was sent to Algiers in North Africa, where she spent another three months on the job before the invasion of Sicily in July 1943. She continued her work in Algiers until Naples was taken in October by the Fifth Army. As the Allies advanced up the Italian boot, North Africa became less strategic, with shipping moving to Naples and other Italian ports.

Lussier went in with the first X-2 unit to Naples as fighting continued toward Rome. The Allies made their triumphal entry into Rome in June 1944, and Lussier was posted there shortly after it was taken but was called back to Naples to await the coming invasion of southern France.

That invasion came in August, when Allied forces landed between Toulon and Cannes in Operation Anvil/Dragoon to establish a second front in France. Lussier's X-2 unit was ordered to go in shortly after the invasion. Her boss, Roger Goiran, assured her that she would hit the beach with the group and promised her that her position as an SLU working with Enigma/Ice messages would guarantee her acceptance by the Seventh Army when it secured Toulon.

The unit took off for Toulon, but Lussier was left at the port of embarkation, bags packed, credentials in order; Goiran had not been able to swing the deal. It was her first brush with military regulations forbidding women to serve on the front lines.

Lussier was furious, she recalls, especially when she later learned from an X-2 buddy, John Marquand (son of the author J. P. Marquand), that the landings had been "a piece of cake." Marquand, who went in on the second lift, told her there was hardly any resistance. It was like invading Palm Beach; girls were on the shore with champagne, waving flags.

Lussier returned dejectedly to OSS headquarters in Naples that night and, as she put it, "did the only thing I could do":

There is always a way of solving a problem if you work at it. And in wartime there was always an agreeable Air Corps pilot who was susceptible to mild flirtation. I met such a pilot who flew one of our generals around in his private plane. He believed me when I said I was a radio technician needed at the front. He flew me to Grenoble in southern France; then I made it to Strasbourg, the French city in northeast France on the Rhine River. Here I attached myself to the Seventh Army's intelligence unit, passing Ice/Ultra data from British to American army units. It was much more exciting than Toulon, and I even got a pass to visit Paris, liberated earlier in August.

It was during this visit that Lussier was reassigned to X-2 and sent to Nice to help set up a French-Spanish border counterintelligence unit. En route, her unit passed through Monaco. "Our arrival was not without its humor," she remembers:

Allied troops were swarming into this hilly little municipality wedged into the French coastline. Americans burst into the famous Casino through the front doors as German troops were exiting hurriedly through the rear. The old-time players and croupiers at work at the casino tables merely looked up curiously, a trifle disturbed by the undue activity, and then continued their gambling.

The French permitted Monaco's ruler, Prince Rainier, then a twenty-one-year-old lieutenant in the French army, to enter the country with them and take possession of his homeland.

Lussier's workload increased when she was assigned to Perpignan, a hotbed of political activity and smuggling between the French and Spanish borders, located in the Pyrénées-Orientales province of France. X-2 headquarters was a château in Thuir near Perpignan, owned by a collaborator who was happy to change sides as the fortunes of war improved for the Allies. Thuir was a typical French provincial village, picturesque but seething with intrigue.

The chief of the X-2 unit at Thuir was Ricardo Sicre, whose nom de guerre was Rick Sickler. He was characterized by his X-2 comrades as a "wild Catalan" whom Lussier had first met briefly in Algiers. Sickler had fought in the Spanish Civil War with the Republicans against Franco, and had managed to escape to London, where he got a job on a freighter bound for the United States. Eventually he was hired by OSS and assigned to an X-2 unit in Algiers, where he met Lussier. His group was headed by Donald Downes, a Yale graduate, history buff, fluent linguist, and daring leader. Lussier and Sickler became an operational team, organizing an extensive net of double agents and also exposing collaborators who had worked with the Nazis. At war's end their wartime camaraderie developed into romance and marriage.

Lussier and Sickler complemented each other: she applied basic common sense to problems, while he followed his instincts. Between them they spoke French, Spanish, English, Catalan, and Italian. Their method of operation was to integrate into the community where they were searching for Nazi stay-behinds and collaborators.

"You enter a town as closely as possible behind advancing liberating troops," Lussier explained. "You immediately set up an enquiry office, talk to anyone who wants to report something. Sometimes you unearth a genuine agent. Often the tips you get are based on grudges or vengeance." In the south of France where they were working the usual enemy agent with a radio set would be someone of Algerian-French blood, for example, someone who felt mistreated by the French. Usually this type of agent would be working for money, not out of patriotism. His job would be primarily to report Allied military activity.

The agent would have been supplied with a clandestine radio set, special codes, and a scheduled transmission time. He would also have an alarm code to use if captured, to warn his contacts that his net was "blown." For this reason, surprise was an important element in capturing an agent; you had to catch him before he could sound the alarm code. This code was the first thing the captured agent would be induced to reveal; then he would be intimidated or lured into becoming a double agent if he was deemed useful by X-2. A case officer would then be assigned to live with the double agent, to take care of his needs and monitor his transmissions. (Morse code transmission, like handwriting, is highly individual and cannot be replicated; recipients can immediately detect any change in the characteristics of the sending "fist.")

"Ours was a very fluid method of operating," Lussier pointed out. "We invented it as we went along; it changed from day to day. It never became routine."

She recalled one example of how she and Sickler handled the problem of mysterious radio signals emanating from the Perpignan area, transmitting damaging intelligence direct to Berlin. "We just couldn't get a handle on this problem," she remembered:

We started asking questions. Who had moved into town in the past two, four, or five years? I had access to police and town hall files. I spent hours scanning the lists and finally came up with a tentative lead. A highly decorated young French air force officer had moved into a remote farmhouse in

271

the past year with his wife and child. Ricardo agreed that we had a prospect. Why had he retired so young? Why is he living in the country in a farmhouse? Could he just be a disillusioned Vichyite, or could he be working for the Nazis? And why?

Sickler and Lussier decided to visit the officer, over the protests of others in the unit who saw the young Frenchman as a patriot sitting out the war. Wearing civilian clothes, they took a jeep early in the morning, driving through deeply rutted farm-cart tracks. The Frenchman's home was L-shaped. One wing housed the animals and farm equipment; the other was well-kept living quarters. The house was plastered pale yellow, with green blinds, and a spring bubbled up into a pool in the courtyard.

They parked their vehicle; Sickler bounded out of the jeep to the front door. When he knocked, the French aviator himself answered. Sickler calmly asked him in perfect French, "Where is the radio set?" The suddenness of the question caught the man off guard. He blanched, then pointed toward the wing of the house where the animals were stabled. They followed him past a flock of irritated chickens and a hutch of rabbits. He revealed the clandestine radio in a suitcase hidden by a bale of hay. In the days that followed, Sickler and Lussier learned from the agent that he had grown up a rich, decadent youth in Paris who preferred the Nazi pattern of life and eventually cast his lot with the Germans.

The X-2 office assigned a case officer to the French lieutenant. He was Gordon Merrick, who was able to maintain complete control over his suddenly cooperative double agent. X-2 had seized the agent's wife and child, threatening to kill them if he betrayed them. Turning this agent probably saved hundreds of Allied lives because OSS was able to send false information to German headquarters about the location of Allied troop advances.

Lussier recalled another operation. A captured German civilian was suspected of collaborating with the Nazis but refused to talk. French intelligence handed him over to the British, who in turn gave him to the X-2 unit. Lussier and Sickler finally broke him down, discovering that his great ambition was to go to Hollywood; he fancied himself another Charlie Chaplin.

"Sickler told the man that he thought this could be arranged," said Lussier, smiling as she recalled the incident:

> After a few days we told him we would send him to Hollywood as soon as the war was over. All he had to do was tell us about his connections with the Nazi agent network.

The collaborator complied and admitted that he was paymaster for a network of thirty-five agents left behind to cover the French-Spanish border. He had their names and addresses, and we were able to turn about eight of his agents. The others were jailed. Unfortunately, our informer never made it to Hollywood. We gave him back to the French, and I believe they shot him.

Lussier and Sickler worked together for nearly three years, becoming the best of friends. Nine months before the war ended, Sickler located his family in Toulouse. They had escaped from Spain.

"The two of us went to see them," Lussier recalled, "and on that trip Rick asked me to marry him. When we got back to X-2 headquarters, our unit was sitting around one night at dinner, and I blurted out that I was going to be married. Someone asked who was the lucky man? They didn't have a clue. Rick and I were married first in a civil ceremony with his parents present. We didn't announce it until after the war, because a husband and wife could not serve in the same theater, according to military rules. Then in 1945 we had a real army wedding." Later they returned to Spain, where Ricardo Sicre became the founder of a profitable import-export business.

In looking back over her adventures, Lussier said she never thought the Germans were as intelligent and clever as some believed. "I got this impression over the years reading their cable traffic. Their messages were banal, trivial; much of it was about social plans. It never seemed to occur to them that their agents could be captured and turned. They had a certain arrogance about them that you couldn't miss."

That arrogance was most evident in Eastern Europe, especially in the Balkans, where Nazis controlled subject people and their destinies. Pockets of resistance in these areas smoldered, briefly flared up, and were quelled by swift and cruel retribution by German soldiers.

In the mountains of Czechoslovakia, British SIS reported increasing partisan activity during the summer of 1944. Before mounting any operations, it was necessary for the United States to ask Russia for permission to deploy an American military mission to Czechoslovakia under the pretext of rescuing downed Allied aircrews. Russia had already begun to stake out areas of future political influence. In mid-September the OSS Dawes Mission was dispatched to the Tatra Mountains in what is today Slovakia. Its assignment: to aid the resistance there and collect intelligence on Nazi movements. Years later the young Czechoslovak partisan, Maria Gulovich, would remember her part in the rescue of two American OSS agents from a German ambush.

CHAPTER 14

Through Enemy Lines

Blonde, blue-eyed Maria Gulovich stood at attention as the West Point corps of cadets came to a measured halt before the reviewing stand. It was a sunny mid-May afternoon in 1946, and a crisp breeze swept up from the Hudson River. She was just twenty-four years old, the first woman ever to be honored by a review of the academy cadet corps. Her wartime chief, Maj. Gen. William J. Donovan, stepped up to her, his bright Irish eyes twinkling, and presented her with the Bronze Star. It had been authorized by President Harry Truman for her work behind German lines with OSS agents between October 1944 and May 1945. The citation read:

Maria Gulovich, Czechoslovak partisan guide and interpreter, Dawes Team, Company B, 2677th Regiment, OSS, for meritorious achievement in connection with military operations in Czechoslovakia.

Maria Gulovich, who served with the

Czech brigade in the heart of enemy territory, was recruited 30 October, 1944, to assist an American intelligence mission in that territory as guide and interpreter. She served with the mission until the capture and subsequent execution of most of its members, and then, in company with two American OSS enlisted men, made her way through enemy lines to Russian forces.

Enduring great suffering from exposure to the elements and extreme hazards from enemy action, the mission contributed intelligence of value to the war effort and effected rescue of Allied flyers downed in enemy territory. Maria Gulovich, through her complete disregard for danger, her faithful and effective performance of duties, was instrumental in making these contributions.[1]

Maria Gulovich remembered these events as she watched the parade pageantry and these young cadets marching smartly off the field at the close of the ceremony. Only nineteen months earlier another group of young Americans had been huddled in an icy encampment in the Lower Tatra Mountains. Because of the subzero weather, the treachery of Gulovich's own people, and the Nazi net thrown across the mountains, those other young Americans never came home. Of her group just two survived, stumbling toward Russian lines with her, starving, frostbitten, ragged, and confused.

Her two companions remembered her well. In a report they submitted to OSS headquarters in Italy in 1945, Sgt. Steve Catlos and Pvt. Kenneth Dunlevy wrote, "Her courage and abilities are admired and appreciated by all the men, especially us, whom she accompanied through the lines. She is responsible for our being alive today."[2]

Maria Gulovich had not planned on being a partisan in the Czechoslovak underground.[3] She was born in the Slovak village of Jakubany where her father was a Greek Orthodox priest. She was the eldest of five sisters. After finishing secondary school she left home for Prešov, a cultural center in eastern Slovakia, where she attended a teachers' training college. Fluent in Russian, Hungarian, German, and Slovak, she was given her first teaching job in Jarabina, a village near her home. When war broke out in 1939 and male teachers left for war or concentration camps, Gulovich was transferred from one teaching assignment to another, each farther away from family and home.

Her first brush with clandestine operations was a simple family dilemma. While teaching in the village of Hriňová, her sister brought a young Jewish woman and her five-year-old son to her. They were fleeing the Nazis and needed asylum until they could safely move on. Overcome by their tears and fright, Gulovich hid them from authorities in her flat.

That act of kindness was the first step in her involvement in the internecine upheavals that lasted in Czechoslovakia until long after war's end. As Gulovich remembers the politics of the time, Czechoslovakia in 1939 was an independent state sold out to Nazi Germany through the Munich Pact, an act of appeasement mainly by Britain. Hitler never sent an army of occupation to the country, but the German presence was very visible. "He told our officials, 'Control the state, or our armies will.' There were Nazis overseeing the government, and from positions of power inside the government they were able to track down dissenters, particularly those with allegiance to the Allied cause." Gulovich points out that the Germans controlled all Czechoslovak railroads. When the Nazis moved against Poland and, later, the Soviet Union, they used the railroads as their own transit system, with Germans having priority over Czechoslovak civilians.

The situation became even more confusing when, in 1943, the Russians began to infiltrate military missions into Slovakia, working with Czechoslovak soldiers trained in the Soviet Union in partisan warfare. The party members also blacklisted those who were working for the Nazis and began to establish the base for a communist state in Czechoslovakia.

Meanwhile, intelligence operations by both British and Americans were hampered by lack of contacts in Nazi-controlled Czechoslovakia.

It was not until 1944 that the first OSS mission penetrated the country after news of a Czech resistance movement reached OSS London headquarters. Encouraged by Soviet advances in Hungary and Ruthenia, two divisions of the Slovak Independent Army revolted. They seized Baňská Bystrica, a small Slovak town of seventeen thousand, in late August and radioed appeals for help. Contact was made with Czechoslovak army headquarters in London by OSS, and hasty arrangements were made to infiltrate a liaison team and aircrew rescue unit to Baňská Bystrica from Italy.

At this point in Gulovich's young life, she gave up her teaching profession and joined the Slovak national uprising in Baňská Bystrica. The Czechoslovak military forces were in the hands of partisans and western-oriented officers; the political leadership was represented by Slovak nationalist and communist elements and the Soviet military.

Gulovich's immediate superior was a colonel in the Soviet army, who kept her busy on a twenty-four-hour schedule translating front-line intelligence from Slovak or German into Russian. Headquarters was a large building where partisans, intelligence teams, and military reported. The Russians worked, ate, and slept in this building. Later when Americans and British teams arrived they were quartered in local hotels and in private homes. It was at this headquarters building that Gulovich first met the members of the OSS Dawes Mission.

The partisan redoubt in Baňská Bystrica did not survive. That part of Slovakia became an unexpected anti-Nazi theater of war, and the uprising kept several German divisions tied down for eight months in the Tatra Mountains. Gulovich, in a later report to OSS headquarters in Bari, Italy, stated that Baňská Bystrica was circled by Germans on 27 October 1944 as resistance was collapsing.[4] She described the atmosphere in that quaint little mountain town with yellow houses and ancient churches as "noisy, exciting, and frightening. Long columns of Czechoslovak Army vehicles carrying food and supplies were moving out of town bound for Donovaly, a ski resort in the Tatra foothills 25 kilometers away."

On her last visit to the abandoned headquarters that afternoon, Gulovich saw a large crowd of people in front of a nearby liquor store. They were soldiers with no one to give them orders and partisans weary from the rigors of mountain patrols. "When I passed by this liquor store," she reported, "the unbearable stench of alcohol hit me. I shall never forget the picture I saw there: people with glassy eyes and red faces, bottles in their hands. They were singing, stumbling, using obscene language. Stoppers had been ripped out of whisky kegs and men were lying on their stomachs drinking the whisky as it trickled on the ground. At that moment I lost my idealism. They were my countrymen but they didn't care for whom they were fighting. They were destroying everything around them."

Two Czechoslovak officers, four enlisted men, and Gulovich were the last of the rebel staff to leave a town abandoned by everyone except the hopeless, drunken townspeople. The next day Germans and "patriot" units occupied Baňská Bystrica after incessant bombing attacks on the valleys through which the partisans and the military staff were fleeing.

Gulovich recalls that the days and nights that followed were like a nightmare — a frigid nightmare. The mountain headquarters in the small resort village of Donovaly was evacuated almost as soon as it was established, when the leaders learned that several German divisions, independent battalions, and Wehrmacht units were invading Slovakia to break up the rebellion. The Czechoslovak army staff, plus Gulovich, the Soviet mission, British and American intelligence teams, downed Allied fliers, partisans, and refugees, all pushed deeper on unmapped trails into the Tatra Mountains, always eastward toward the Hungarian border where Soviet forces were fighting.

As they rested outside the snow-covered village of Slovenská Lupča, scouts reported that Germans were only a few hundred yards away. "Exhausted, we started out again toward the higher mountains," Gulovich remembered. "It was a starless night, and we had to slip by the

Nazis. After a superhuman effort we succeeded in slowly sliding down a precipitous hill, knee-deep in mud, often unable to maintain our balance." About ten o'clock that night, they stumbled into a valley where other refugees from Donovaly were bivouacking. More than 400 were crowded into bunkers built for 150 men. "It took about an hour to pass from one end of a twenty-foot room to the other," Gulovich said. "With all the windows closed, the air was beyond description."

The next morning, 30 October, groups began to form and take off toward the Russian front. Lt. James Holt Green, head of the OSS team, recruited Gulovich that day to help lead his group, to act as interpreter and forage for food in the villages en route. This OSS mission, code-named Dawes, consisting of twenty persons, had arrived in Czechoslovakia in September and October to support the insurgents, establish liaison, and evacuate Allied aircrews. In addition, Associated Press correspondent Joseph Morton and a British Special Operations Executive representative, Guilliam Davis, were aboard. Fifteen members of the OSS team would die on the mission, tortured and executed without trial at the Mauthausen (Austria) concentration camp in this last winter of the war. Morton, the AP reporter, was also killed.

After the team fled into the mountains, they abandoned their radio equipment. The men split up for greater safety but regrouped from time to time during the retreat from the Nazi net. Gulovich described the ordeal in her report:

We marched the entire day through rain and gale force winds. No one knew where we were. We looked at maps which didn't mean anything. We reached bare mountain cliffs where the wind was bitter. Our wet clothes were frozen, our shoes were hard as stones. All that day I marched beside OSS Lt. Tibor Keszthelyi who spoke Hungarian. His mother was Italian, his father Hungarian. We marched in silence and we helped each other to get up when we slipped on the frozen ground.

About eleven that night we finally reached the floor of a valley. We made a fire near a small stream and shared soup from canned rations. Lt. Keszthelyi had a few crackers and a small can of Spam that he shared with me. The following morning, with nothing to eat, Lt. Keszthelyi and I set out to look for food, and after considerable difficulty, found some beans, a beef bone and a little flour in a neighboring campsite. Here, we also found several downed American flyers and the correspondent, Joe Morton.

With these supplies we were able to cook up a scanty soup and were finally forced to eat part of a dead horse we found in a stream. We roasted the black meat on sticks above the fire. That night we slept under a makeshift shelter of pine branches.

A great deal of Gulovich's time was spent foraging for food. The OSS team was supplied with ample funds for this purpose, generally in gold. One lucky day on the outskirts of a village she and two OSS men came across a barn where they found four chickens and a calf, which they quickly purchased from the farmer. "The road back to our cabin was slippery with mud and the calf was very obstinate, unwilling to go with us," she wrote. "When we finally reached camp, you can't imagine the cries of joy that went up when our starving companions saw food on the hoof!"

Whenever possible, the group would camp for a few days in huts in the mountains, but German patrols were everywhere. They would escape from one narrow brush with the enemy only to be warned by loyal townspeople of another sweep by the well-equipped Germans. Sometimes the warning came too late. Gulovich reported a black 7 November: "Our first calamity happened. Six members of the OSS group were captured while looking for food, and partisans warned us to move out of our bivouac immediately, as more Germans had been sighted."

The only escape route was, as always, up the steep cliffs, always in the direction of the Russian front. "I shall never forget that November march for the rest of my life," Gulovich said:

> Germans were closing in on us. The mountain slopes were covered with ice and snow. Our packs weighed us down. There were no trees and we knew the enemy could see us very well outlined against the snow. Often we crawled on all fours. After five hours we reached the mountain top where a heavy snowstorm was raging. Our eyebrows and hair became icicles. Men's beards froze solid and clothes and shoes were stiff with ice. I didn't have any gloves and I could feel my hands freezing. We all suffered frostbite. My right leg became swollen and black, and the pain was terrible.

Gulovich credits AP correspondent Morton with saving her life. The flesh on her right leg was beginning to flake away where gangrene was setting in. Morton had stashed away some sulfa powder in his hatband against just such a crisis. He poured a small amount of it onto Gulovich's blackened flesh, and within a week it had healed.

The group pushed on down the slopes for another seven hours. Partisans with them said they were within five kilometers of a small village. Gulovich, with Lieutenant Keszthelyi and a patrol, cautiously trudged up to the outskirts of the group of small snow-covered dwellings.

The villagers were friendly and said there were no Germans billeted in the area. To Gulovich the name of the town, Hriňová, had a familiar ring. Then she remembered that she had taught here briefly and that a schoolteacher colleague, Zuzka, lived here. They had worked together earlier in Hriňová and had become good friends. She was able to locate her friend's house and led the small group cautiously up to the front door.

Gulovich was wearing a bulky army coat; her legs were bandaged and her face reddened by the weather. At first Zuzka couldn't believe that the apparition in front of her was indeed the slim, stylish teacher with whom she had worked. Recovering from her surprise, she warmly invited the party in, fed them, and alerted her neighbors. The group returned at three in the morning to their base loaded with food and medical supplies. Gulovich and Keszthelyi stayed that night with Zuzka but were warned the next day by townspeople that anyone caught giving refuge to a partisan would suffer severe reprisals from the Nazi patrols. They also told Gulovich about an abandoned manganese mine not far from town where the group might seek shelter.

In mid-November, Gulovich and her team moved to the mining camp, where they discovered about eight hundred people already gathered in makeshift barracks and in the mines. There were partisans and also members of a

Czechoslovak army brigade. Here too, fortunately, were medical facilities and partisan doctors and nurses who treated the frostbite patients. The nurses were especially appalled at the condition of the OSS team and their guide. These same nurses were later shot when the Nazis learned that they had taken care of refugees.

Gulovich and her OSS team remained in the area for a week before pushing on toward the Russian front as the bitter weather grew worse. There were villages scattered throughout these mountains, but they were usually separated by deep valleys and snowdrifts and were often occupied by Germans and their collaborators. Occasionally the OSS team would find an abandoned hunter's lodge, a deserted farmhouse, or more underground mines long out of commission but offering some shelter from the cold. Waves of refugees swept through these mountains, heading eastward toward the Hungarian border. The people set up makeshift camps and bought or stole food from villagers. Some died of starvation, and many more were betrayed and turned over by Nazi sympathizers. For the latter, it meant torture, detention camp, or death before a firing squad.

At one time the OSS team was hiding in an underground mine where a partisan doctor diagnosed two of their members as having symptoms of pneumonia. He directed them to a healthier area three miles into the mountains, where a cabin could provide shelter. "It was a hard trip," Gulovich reported, "and when we finally made it to the cabin, we found four Jewish refugees huddled there. Soon so many other people began drifting in that there wasn't any place to sit down. Word of these havens got around quickly. Partisans made a fire in the middle of the room and started to cook their meal. I foraged around in the cellar and came up with some potatoes, cabbage and onions. I made a rather bad soup but since we hadn't eaten all day it tasted pretty good."

That night Gulovich forcibly made room by the fire for Keszthelyi, who was shivering, pale, and having trouble breathing:

He'd been in the cold and rain all day and I was afraid he wouldn't survive. The people around the fire wouldn't budge. They kicked at us, swore, stepped on our frostbitten feet. I was finally able to get the lieutenant near the heat. He slept in the mud with his head on my knees, all through the night. I somehow managed to stay awake and prayed. Early in the morning when he woke up he said he was feeling better and there was some color in his pale cheeks. I realized that I had become very fond of him.

At this point the OSS team had split up. Lieutenant Green was billeted with part of a British A-Force mission several kilometers

289

north from Gulovich and her smaller group. It was early December when another tragedy struck. Lieutenant Green sent a letter ordering Lieutenant Keszthelyi and Sgt. Jerry Mican to go to the nearby town of Mýto. They were to deliver a note to a local orthodox priest, known to a woman attached to A-Force, Margaret Kockova, who had assured Green that the priest was trustworthy. The note requested assistance in obtaining horses to evacuate British and Americans in need of hospitalization. Kockova was an American with nursing experience who had been caught up in the war while in Czechoslovakia caring for her ailing grandmother. Her knowledge of English and Slovak was useful to the British A-Force members who had been in contact with the OSS team since the evacuation of Baňská Bystrica.

Gulovich recalled the incident sadly and bitterly. The young Americans had become her dear friends. "I had a foreboding and begged them not to go that night, as I had a dream that they would be captured by the Germans. But they only laughed. I was very disturbed the whole day long, certain that something had happened to them." When they failed to return, Gulovich and Lt. James Gaul, an OSS Secret Intelligence officer second in command, determined to go down to Mýto and reconnoiter. "The first people we met were frightened, but they confirmed our fears. The Germans had been in Mýto and captured two Americans."

Gulovich was furious. She was determined to accost the priest at the risk of betrayal. Changing from her heavy Czech uniform and topcoat into a woolen skirt and blouse that she borrowed from a friendly family, she went directly to the priest's house. At first he denied that any Americans had been there, but when his wife came in Gulovich bullied her into telling what had happened. She said the OSS men had delivered a letter to her husband. After they had been fed, her husband invited them to spend the night. Early the next morning the priest's maidservant led the men to a road at the edge of town, where they were captured by waiting German soldiers. The American prisoners and captors went back to the priest's home with the traitorous maid. They searched the entire house, threatened to send the priest and his wife to a concentration camp, and presumably recovered the incriminating letter from Kockova.

The Americans knew that the Germans would be searching for them, and so there was nothing to do but move on. Their next destination was the mountain resort of Velký Bok, where the British had established headquarters that they shared with the rest of the OSS contingent. "It was a killing march," Gulovich remembered:

No one believed we could make it with our frostbitten feet and swollen legs. Again

we sloughed through mire and snow, climbing slippery slopes, crawling on all fours
down the mountain. Once we almost
walked into a German patrol. In our fatigue
we had become careless and had taken a little road that led toward a village. We were
concentrating on survival and didn't spot
the German patrol until they were within a
few yards of us. Then we hit the bushes on
the side of the road, not daring to breathe
until they had marched on in the opposite
direction.

After six hours Gulovich's group finally
reached the rendezvous cottage in Velký Bok,
halfway up a mountain slope with a large resort
hotel at its peak.

"Oh God," Gulovich said. "What a happy
moment it was when we hesitantly opened the
door and found them all waiting for us, after
weeks of separation, the British and Americans.
It was then, too, that I met Kockova, the
woman who wrote that damned letter that betrayed our boys to the Germans." Gulovich was
not impressed with Kockova. "Ever since that
letter she had been anathema to me. She was
very tall, skinny as a stick, pale-faced, with col-
orless eyes and an ironic smile. She was about
thirty-five years old, vicious, domineering, and
to top it off she had absolutely no sense of
humor, which was so vital in those trying days."

Despite the friction between the two women,

the British and Americans settled down to a fairly stable routine. Some were quartered in the hotel on the mountaintop, where they tended signal fires at night awaiting a long-promised air drop of food, medicine, and ammunition. The British A-Force had been able to make contact with the OSS detachment in Bari, Italy. The drop was finally made, but unhappily it fell into German hands in the nearby Hron Valley.

Meanwhile the men went on daily patrols looking for food and staking out enemy positions. Gulovich and Kockova did the cooking and cleaning. The weather had turned warmer, the moonless skies were starry, but the town in a nearby valley that had supplied them with food was now sealed off by a German garrison.

Gulovich admits that thanks to Kockova, the British and American teams celebrated Christmas with food and drink. Kockova had friends in the nearby town of Malužina; Lieutenant Green and two OSS men followed her directions, knocked on the right doors, and were able to return with supplies for the holiday, including dress material for the two women, whose clothes were in rags. Sgt. Joseph Horvath, the Slovak interpreter, cut down a small pine tree and dragged it back to the cottage. "We had some candles," Gulovich reported, "which we used in place of our flashlights with their dead batteries. We decorated the tree and celebrated Christmas Eve. After supper Lt. Green prepared a drink he called 'Sumadinsky caj' which he learned to make when he worked with Yugoslav partisans. We drank, sang carols in Hungarian, Slovak, English, and German. We danced, trying to forget the war around us."

On that same Christmas Eve, the Soviet armies were fighting on the outskirts of Budapest in a battle that would end on 13 February with the surrender of that Hungarian city, a surrender that eventually facilitated Gulovich's escape.

On Christmas Day the entire British and American teams arrived for the dinner that the two women had prepared. "We even baked a cake to make the boys feel more like Christmas," Gulovich recalled. "And after dinner we prayed with Lieutenant Gaul. We prayed for all those who were not with us anymore, for those who might be dead or suffering in prisons. We prayed for the families of those whose loved ones were so far away, and we prayed to God to help us all, to help us stay alive. But our prayers were not to be answered."

Late on Christmas Day Gulovich had a final flareup with Kockova and knew she could no longer stay in the same cottage with her. She asked Lieutenant Green to transfer her to the hotel on the top of the mountain, where she offered to cook and clean for the men who were on guard there. Green agreed, and Gulovich packed her small knapsack, together with her

Christmas present of precious dress material, and climbed to the hotel on the mountaintop, a move that saved her life.

Early the next morning, 26 December, Gulovich and two OSS companions had started out from the hotel on reconnaissance when, to their horror, they spotted a squad of Germans, led by sympathizers, surrounding the rustic cottage below that she had abandoned the night before. Through binoculars they watched the soldiers bring out their companions, hands tied behind their backs, and load them into lorries. Kockova was with them. The Germans set fire to the cottage and regrouped for the climb up the mountain to the hotel.

"We fled as quietly as we could. It was the same old way of the Cross: mountains, snow, cold," she remembered. "After half an hour of evasion, we joined some Czechoslovak army officers and partisans. We passed through a valley to Ráztoka, and from there we could see the slopes of Velký Bok and the blackened area where our cottage had stood and where the hotel was still smoldering."

In the twenty-three days that lay ahead before they crossed into Soviet lines, Gulovich and her small band suffered continuing hardships, hunger, and near capture across a fluid battle front. With her were the last of the OSS party, Sgt. Steve Catlos and Pvt. Kenneth Dunlevy. From the British A-Force were Lt. Guilliam Davis and Lt. Steve Zenobian.

On this last desperate push toward Hungary, they had become infested with lice, their clothes were rotting away, and frostbite again hampered their progress. At the end Gulovich was carried on the back of Lieutenant Davis to their final hideout, another deserted mine. As her health improved, Gulovich was able to forage for food across the border of Hungary. Once she encountered Germans in a partisan's house: "They questioned me rudely. Why was I carrying so much food? Where was I going? I was wearing a peasant dress and pretended to be a frightened young girl, which I really was. I told them I was trying to get back home across the lines, and they finally let me go."

On 23 January the refugees were huddled together in a damp mine shaft when a courier from the village of Bystré shouted down to them that the Germans had abandoned the village, but no military units had come to occupy it. He told them he would return when there were new developments. At about eleven in the morning, after waiting for what seemed an eternity, Gulovich heard him yelling to them in Slovak. "He said we were free, that the Rumanians and Soviet forces had occupied the village of Bystré."

"We grabbed our belongings, crept out of the hole, and started to kiss each other with joy." Gulovich remembered looking up at the bright blue sky. "At this point in my happiness there was only one regret: the memory of our comrades who had not lived to see this day with us."

Gulovich's story should have ended here with her triumphal return across Allied lines with the two OSS men and the British agents who had escaped with her. But it would be five months before she could help arrange another escape, this time from the Russians and their KGB interrogators in Hungary.

The front between Hungary and Czechoslovakia was fluid: Germans were retreating; Rumanians, Hungarians, and Russians were integrating their commands. On 25 January, after several confrontations, Rumanian soldiers loaded Gulovich's small group into a truck and took them to Russian headquarters at Rimavská Sobota. Here they were interrogated for two days.

Gulovich, the only captive who spoke Russian, maintained the OSS cover throughout the twelve hours of grueling questioning. They were an American military mission sent to rescue downed Allied fliers and help the Slovak rebellion. This was her story, and she never deviated from it. Her OSS companions were the first Americans to pass through Russian lines at this point. Gulovich felt that the KGB authorities might have had reasons to interrogate her in depth. There had been too many betrayals along the way from Baňská Bystrica to Budapest, their eventual destination. Too many intelligence missions, both British and American,

297

had been penetrated by KGB operatives.

At no time did the Russians tell the Americans or Gulovich where they were being sent. Once they were admitted to a hospital in Lučenec, suffering from dysentery and exhaustion. After ten days they were loaded into a lorry and taken to Jászkisér, on the way to Budapest. Here Gulovich was billeted in a single room. "But when the KGB interrogators began to call me at all hours of the night, I was afraid to live alone and moved in with Dunlevy and Catlos."

The Russians continued to evacuate them eastward. At one point Gulovich was ordered to remain behind to act as an interpreter at their headquarters. "They told me I could not proceed with the group because I was a Slovak citizen. I rushed back to my comrades who luckily found the answer to this dilemma. If I were married to a British subject, Lieutenant Davis, for example, my status would be changed and they would have no control over me." Davis gallantly volunteered to satisfy the formal requirements of marriage in order to arrange Gulovich's release. "At the Russian headquarters we signed the necessary documents, and two Dutch officials who were interned there signed as witnesses, and I was free again."

The group were told that they were bound for Budapest en route to the Russian port of Odessa on the Black Sea. Despite their continued requests to notify American and British authorities or the International Red Cross, no action was taken. Gulovich realized that once they reached Odessa, on Russian soil, escape would be impossible.

After two and a half days aboard a slow train to Budapest, they finally reached the outskirts of that once beautiful city. The royal palace, Romanesque churches, theaters, and river promenades had been blasted by German bombers during a fourteen-week battle that was eventually won by Russian and Rumanian troops. Once in the station, teeming with refugees from all over Europe, the British and Americans with Gulovich decided to make a desperate effort to reach the Allied Control Commission, which had the authority to order their release.

Gulovich was elected spokesperson. Wearing a nondescript Russian uniform, she eluded the guard who had been assigned to the party and made her way to the Russian commandant's quarters. Here, after an impassioned plea, she was given permission to remain in Budapest overnight. They were billeted in a camp into which hundreds of refugees had been herded, including some women who had worked for Phillips Petroleum, a Dutch conglomerate. Three women told Gulovich of having been abused and raped by Russian soldiers. One of them was seven months pregnant.

That night the three planned a desperate escape. Catlos slipped out to try to contact the

Allied Control Commission, with help from some of the internees. "The word," Gulovich said, "was stall! Do anything, but don't get on that morning train to Odessa."

The next morning Gulovich figured out an evasive action. She and the pregnant Dutch woman disappeared into the ladies' room while their Russian guard stood outside. Gulovich called out that the woman was having labor pains and that they would remain there with a nurse "who happened to be present." Meanwhile, Catlos had been able to contact American authorities. He sidled up to the ladies' room and whispered through the door to Gulovich in English, "Stall some more. Come out when I whistle 'Yankee Doodle.'"

Gulovich had never heard "Yankee Doodle" but was able to stall in the rest room for another hour, until she heard the tune she would never forget. She emerged, dramatically, putting on a good act and half-carrying the woman. Within an hour British and American authorities had stormed the building, rescued their countrymen, and, with Gulovich, sped away before the Russians realized what was happening.

Gulovich was flown to OSS headquarters in Bari and was later assigned to OSS detachments in Caserta and Salzburg. Meanwhile, when news of this escape reached headquarters in Washington, General Donovan himself arranged to bring Maria Gulovich to the United

States as an exchange student, where she enrolled at Vassar, graduating in 1948.

Before leaving for her new life in America, Gulovich arranged with OSS to return to Czechoslovakia, now under Russian control, in hopes of seeing her family. She wore an American uniform when she reached her home and knocked on the door. "It was a wonderful but traumatic experience," she recalled, smiling sadly. "My family thought I was dead, and you can imagine their surprise and joy when I walked into the living room, after five years."

Gulovich now lives in Oxnard, California, where the climate is kind to her still-numbed limbs, which never recovered from frostbite. Married to Hans Liu, a manufacturer's representative, she has two grown children and works in a real estate office. Documentation of her part in that long-ago war is now on exhibit at the Slovak Museum of the National Uprising at Baňská Bystrica, together with her Bronze Star citation.

Yugoslavia and other countries in the Balkan peninsula were under Nazi repression from almost the outset of World War II. Their citizens were impressed into German armies and became conscript laborers. By early 1942 Axis armies in North Africa and southeastern Europe threatened to encompass the eastern Mediterranean in a giant pincer move. Preparations had to be made against this possible Axis incursion. The importance of neutral countries — Spain, Egypt, Switzerland, Turkey — became obvious. A great deal of successful OSS planning was focused on those spy-ridden havens in a war-torn world.

CHAPTER 15

Espionage in the Twilight Zones

Some of the most difficult and successful OSS missions were carried out in the neutral countries of Europe and the Middle East, in those twilight zones where loyalties were suspect, stakes high.

The possibility of German occupation of Spain represented a major strategic danger to the Allies, especially in the months after the North African campaign in 1942, when supply lines were stretched taut from French North Africa to the Tunisian front. OSS agents began their operations in Lisbon and Madrid in April 1942 under State Department cover as oil attachés. In the months that followed, expanded nets of OSS operatives successfully carried out three major assignments levied by the Joint Chiefs of Staff. They secured irrefutable evidence of military cooperation between Spain and Germany, including use of Spanish military airfields by Axis aircraft. OSS also proved that Spain was supplying German submarines with harbor facilities and fuel. Extensive economic support was uncovered between Madrid and Berlin, as well as flagrant joint espionage efforts between Spanish and German officials. By V-E Day the files of X-2 (the OSS Counterintelligence Branch) alone identified nearly three thousand enemy agents.

Basic yet complicated, multilingual clerical support for OSS missions was managed in large part by a handful of women. X-2, responsible for most of the counterespionage work, was set up under cover of the American Oil Mission, and the office system was organized by the efficient Grace Tully, a fugitive from James Angleton's office in London.

Some of these OSS ladies of Spain did considerably more than clerical tasks, translating messages in many languages from agents in the field. Lucie Clark Killin spoke French, Spanish, and Portuguese; Jane Cabanas was fluent in Spanish. Others worked as reports officers and analysts: Elizabeth Sanford, Patricia Fowler, Mary Louise Green. And there were those indispensable "good-in-math" girls who spent long hours in the code room: Rebecca Conally, Marian Blair, Eileen Sullivan.

There was one lady spy in this group, a Hattie Carnegie model from Pearl River, New York, who later became better known as Aline, Countess of Romanones. In her undercover days she was Aline Griffith, pseudonym Butch. She started out in Madrid in the X-2 code room in 1943, on call night and day to encipher messages. She also handled a small agent net that spied on the private secretary of a minister in the Spanish government.

Most of her exciting work was done after hours, when she developed an extensive social life, reporting on the gossip she had overheard after a night of partying, often with Spanish aristocracy. She was beautiful, she was smart, and the National Archives files reveal some of her operations: "Prince Max Ernst zu Hohenlohe-Langenburg received mail last week through the Swiss diplomatic pouch. I learned from one of his sons that they had recently heard from their friend, the president of Mexico, who said he'd send the Prince a private plane if he could get as far as Cuba, and he would then get him to Mexico."[1] (Hohenlohe was a Sudeten German who had married into a wealthy Spanish royal family; he was an apologist for the Nazi government.)

Three years after the war Aline Griffith married the handsome count of Quintilla (later Romanones) in a ceremony that was one of the social events of postwar Madrid. William Casey, a wartime colleague and later director of the Central Intelligence Agency, wrote, "She accurately reflected the sensitivity of the clandestine intrigue and strategic maneuvers that marked the struggle between the secret services

. . . and the atmosphere of the high social life in wartime Spain."[2]

Early in the war OSS was organized in the Middle East to prepare for a possible Axis invasion of the entire African continent. A base was established in Cairo in 1942 to direct Secret Intelligence, Counterintelligence, and Research and Analysis activities in Egypt, Turkey, and other Middle Eastern countries as well as Greece, Czechoslovakia, and the Balkans. Cairo continued to be a primary OSS base in this territory until Italy opened up and OSS moved to Caserta, Bari, and Rome, with the posh villa of millionaire Mrs. Harrison Williams on the Isle of Capri set aside by Donovan for R&R (rest and rehabilitation).

Thirty women staffed the offices in Cairo. Some worked in the code room. Others handled secret intelligence intercepts or were office administrators. Still others were assigned to the Secret Intelligence Branch for specific countries: Louie Leas and Lolly Fending, for example, were specialists on the Balkans, and Louise Hepburn, an admiral's daughter, eventually headed the SI branch when it was transferred to Caserta. Jane Smiley and Nancy Chamberlain worked long hours, often well after midnight, when cable traffic in the code room backed up, and they were expected to paraphrase messages at breakneck speed.

On her first OSS tour in 1943 to Cairo,

before she went to China, Virginia Rathbun was assigned the job of establishing an OSS library, which later became a vital part of all research work for the area. "When I first saw it, the 'library' was a room full of junk, boxed files, and unsorted reference material, and no one was in charge," Rathbun explained to me years later. "We managed to bring order out of chaos, to establish categories for information by country and classified material from confidential to top secret."

In order to coordinate properly a basic library structure, Rathbun and her staff also had to understand what was happening in the Middle East. "We faced the challenge," she recalled, "of learning the delicate state of Egyptian politics and personalities, intrigues in Istanbul, internecine warfare in Greece. Also not to be ignored was the intransigence of the British in Egypt, who resented the American presence in what they considered to have been their territory since the early 1900s."

Rathbun, who was among other OSS officers later assigned the task of writing the official history of the Cairo station, noted in her diary that as of December 1944, twenty-nine undercover agents had been developed in the Middle East, a chain of five hundred subagents had been trained, and more than five thousand reports had been filed, especially from the Istanbul office.[3] Here Ellin Balliet and Blanche O'Connell, dispatched earlier from Cairo, had kept detailed records of German and other enemy agents working within the Turkish capital.

Cairo, seat of one of the world's oldest civilizations, meant many things to these women of OSS. To Rathbun it was a panorama of "sights and sounds, cultures and languages."

"The pyramids and Sphinx I expected," she told me later. "But I was bewildered by the confusion: roads filled with lorries, jeeps, mule-drawn carts; the colorful but noisy bazaars; veiled women, sophisticated Egyptians, deposed royalty from the war in Europe."

To Laura Tuckerman, a Washington socialite trained for SI work on the Cairo cable desk, Cairo was a dusty city with high winds. She remembers the contrast in living conditions: on the one side of Cairo life, elaborate dinner parties in gardens on the Nile, where guests wore white gloves and ate beluga caviar flown in from the Caspian Sea; on the other side, a native family sleeping in the gutter, with their spitting camel on the sidewalk, or a donkey that, from the tragic hee-haws on the street below her apartment, sounded as if it were starving. "I had a sense of hopelessness at times," she remembered.[4]

North Dakota–born Florence Larson, who worked in the OSS Finance Office taking care of payrolls, first learned about Egyptians from her recruiter in Washington: "They are the same as we are, under their sheets."[5]

Perhaps the most entertaining aspect of life in Cairo was King Farouk and his pursuit of attractive OSS girls. "Fleeing Farouk" was a buzzword that never made cable traffic out of that Egyptian city. Farouk had succeeded his father, King Faud, in 1937 and was destined to be the last of the Egyptian pharaohs, the monarchy being abolished in 1953. Cairo gossip had it that Farouk had been injured in an automobile accident while still a handsome, slim young man, and from that time on his entire character was changed. Formerly a "personage," British-educated and serious-minded, he became a fat, self-indulgent playboy who also showed a great deal of dash and capriciousness.

Farouk was Egypt's single largest landowner, and his income was around £2 million annually. His wife, Fatima, whom he married in 1937, had her own quarters in nearby Alexandria. He himself had two palaces, four yachts, a squadron of airplanes, and carloads of erotica. And he liked young, preferably blond, American women.

One pert British cipher clerk, Irene Gurney Orr, who later joined OSS, remembers Farouk as a neighbor. Irene the Cypherine, as she was called, and her women colleagues all lived aboard a yacht moored next to Farouk's on the Nile. "Farouk also owned the Auberge de Pyramides, a posh nightclub where we all liked to dine and dance," she recalled.[6] "It was open to the skies, wall-to-wall flowers, and Farouk was usually there. He was heavy-lidded and seemed to mentally undress you. If he saw something he liked, he sent his equerry to request that she dance with him."

Laura Tuckerman, who often attended functions at the American legation and who was a friend of the minister, S. Pinckney Tuck, remembers some of the swank embassy dinners that started around 11 P.M.: "Farouk often attended, and on the evening I first met him, he began to follow me around the room. He was well padded, most unattractive, and when he approached, I would move away. Eventually it almost became a game, until he realized how absolutely puritanical I could become. Then he became formal and merely bowed to me."

Jane Smiley, who later married diplomat Parker T. Hart, was in charge of all intelligence coming out of Greece for the Cairo station. She also remembered Farouk:

> He was a dull, lonely man who had a wonderful red sports car. He would show up at our billet as late as 10 P.M., looking for Josephine Britton, whose father-in-law was a judge of the supreme court in Egypt. Farouk really had a crush on her. Josie was terrified of him, but he was always asking her to go out nightclubbing. She would ask us all to go with her so she wouldn't be alone with him. We would accompany her, and Farouk

would pay the bill. Britton became so desperate she finally told her boss about the problem, and he shipped her out by special plane for a two-week R&R on Capri. By the time she returned, Farouk's antennae were focused on another blonde American.[7]

The young lady from North Dakota, Florence Larson, finally became acclimated to Cairo life and remembers seeing Farouk at the Auberge: "He was in his twenties, but big and heavy. Liked to dance and drive flashy red sports cars. When he tipped a waiter, he slithered the coins across the floor. I heard that his lifelong ambition was to go to Hollywood and meet Ginger Rogers."

Much of the activity in the Middle East was downgraded as OSS stations moved north to Italy, France, and finally Germany. However, a great deal of high-level espionage, counter-intelligence maneuvers, and penetration of Axis territory was to be carried out from one of the most important neutral countries in Europe: Switzerland, with OSS headquarters in Bern.

Cordelia Dodson's orders were explicit. She was relieved of her duties with X-2 in London, where she had been stationed since September 1944. She would proceed immediately to Bern for new assignment. En route she would escort two Swiss socialists who had been attending a convention in London and were returning

311

home. The cabled order was signed 110, code designation for Allen W. Dulles, chief of the OSS station in Bern. Dodson's departure date was set for 18 December 1944. The Battle of the Bulge had been raging for two days, a last effort by twenty-five Nazi divisions to sweep through to the coast and split the Allied armies in the Ardennes.

Dodson and her two Swiss charges were trucked from blacked-out London to a secret airport where a motley crew boarded an OSS twin-engine C-47, a converted DC-3. One of the passengers was a young American fighter pilot, Charles (Chuck) Yeager, who three years later was to become the first person to break the sound barrier. Yeager was on his way to a mission so secret that he didn't know what was involved.[8] Also aboard were two "turned" German prisoners of war, escorted by an OSS officer whose job it was to infiltrate them into Germany for ongoing intelligence operations. The plane was flown by a military pilot who had been taken off combat missions because of a shrapnel wound. Their destination was Lyons in central France, where the Seventh Army had established advanced fighter bases near the Swiss border. Blizzard weather conditions were forecast for that area.

The plane was tossed about in turbulence along the coast and over central France until the pilot finally slipped down between the clouds to a fighter strip outside Lyons. Here

OSS representatives met Dodson's group and arranged for temporary quarters for the OSS contingent at a "Joe house," a safe area set aside for agents. Yeager was picked up by an American air attaché from Bern, Peter De Paolo, a former racing-car driver, and sequestered at Lake Annecy on the French border, where they discussed the possibility of rescuing downed American airmen from Switzerland, a project soon abandoned.

Dodson and her charges spent two nervous nights in Lyons. Although Dodson spoke French and German, her concern was to maintain her anonymity and to keep her Swiss companions from speaking in their German-accented French. Another problem: she had no papers permitting her to escort them to Switzerland. After two days in Lyons, Dodson was able to hitch a ride for herself and her friends in an army command and reconnaissance car that her OSS colleague had commandeered to escort his agents to the German border. Her cover was simple: she was his French girlfriend and was to act accordingly if halted en route to the border. Their main fear was the edgy French Maquis units on the lookout for escaping Germans as the Battle of the Bulge raged to the west.

The trip took half a day of steady driving on bomb-scarred roads through bitter winter weather. Finally they reached the Swiss border at Saint-Louis. Across the darkness was Geneva and the safety of neutral Switzerland. Here Dodson and her two charges disembarked at the border station and waved good-bye as the command car headed toward Germany. "I couldn't believe we had finally made it," Dodson recalled some fifty years later. Her memories of the operation were still vivid. "How did we get to Geneva from the border town? The Swiss called a taxi, of course!"

Switzerland was a time warp in the war-torn continent of Europe. It was almost stodgy in a self-contented way, well stocked with food and drink, a bright contrast to Dodson's London post, where winter winds had whistled through her bomb-cracked office walls and she had to wear mittens with fingertips cut out to facilitate typing. "Switzerland's towns were intact," she recalled. "We drove at night with lights on. In Geneva that evening we dined at an elegant restaurant where the martinis were served in proper glasses, not paper cups, and the napkins were real linen, not Kleenex. The dinner was superb, the wine excellent. Later we took the train to Bern. It was a comfortable, smooth ride, and we actually arrived on time!"

Dodson's boss, Paul Blum, met her at the station in Bern on 22 December. He handed her a key to her own private apartment in a hotel overlooking the Aare River and told her he was looking forward to working with her. There was lots to be done.

Dodson remembered Blum as a charming

314

gentleman. He was forty-six years old at the time, chief of Bern's newly established X-2 branch. Earlier he had set up counterintelligence branches in Lisbon, then had worked in London's X-2 shop, where Dodson had met him briefly.

Blum was born in Japan to an American mother and a French father. After graduating from Yale, he went into the import-export business, becoming a world traveler and in later years a collector of Orientalia. His French was perfect. As a teenager during World War I he had been awarded the Croix de Guerre for driving an ambulance in France. Blum later made contact with German officers in northern Italy on the secret surrender operation engineered by Dulles, code name Operation Sunrise.

The Bern that Dodson knew was a quaint medieval city with shopping arcades, cobbled streets, busy hotels and restaurants, bright geraniums in window boxes outside sandstone apartment buildings, an ornate clock tower in the center of town, and a hectic work schedule.

Allen Dulles's espionage organization stretched from Nazi Germany to Austria, Yugoslavia, Hungary, Rumania, and Italy. Agents reported secretly to him at his residence at Herrengasse 23, an elegant Swiss burgher's mansion dating back to the late 1600s. There were four apartments in his house, and the rear ground-floor door opened into a garden and

315

grape arbors planted on embankments stretching to the river. Many a visitor had left by this back door to maintain security after secret sessions with the OSS chief.

During both world wars, Switzerland was the main Allied listening post tuned to activities in European enemy and enemy-occupied countries. Swiss neutrality afforded easy access to the intelligence services of all belligerents operating there, opportunities seized by OSS. An exceedingly small staff of agents located in major Swiss cities produced some of the best OSS intelligence of the war. Approximately one hundred agents were in contact with hundreds of subagents throughout Europe. Through them OSS provided early intelligence on atomic and bacteriological research, location of the V-1 and V-2 development and testing sites, the planning of the 20 July attempt on Hitler's life, and negotiations with various satellite governments for the surrender of Axis forces in northern Italy on 2 May 1945.

Dodson was one of the early arrivals in Bern. The work to which she was assigned was painstaking and vital to postwar planning. As hostilities waned, the Allies were already organizing data for the trials of the Axis war criminals that were eventually held in Nuremberg. OSS Bern contributed importantly to the depositions at these trials. Dodson had reason to look forward to this day of reckoning. After graduating from Reed College in Oregon, she went to Europe;

she studied in Grenoble and was in school in Vienna when Hitler's troops occupied that city in 1938. "I learned to hate the Nazis from that time on," she recalled bitterly. "They were so arrogant, so merciless, rounding up anti-Nazis all over town, even during opera performances. Their persecution of the Jews was inhuman. It was too much. I returned to the States."

Dodson took her master's degree in German from Reed College, where she was recruited by military intelligence to translate and analyze air order of battle at the Pentagon in Washington. The material she produced was often sent on to appropriate OSS offices. When she requested a transfer overseas, she was informed that she was relieving a man for just such duty. She resigned and joined OSS, where she took a crash course in typing, and two months later found herself in London.

Working with Paul Blum, Dodson appreciated how his earlier career enabled him to handle sensitive intelligence operations dealing with international money movements. With the help of "informers" — business contacts he had worked with before the war — Blum and his staff were able to trace deposits of Nazi gold in Germany and watch them covertly appear in banks in Liechtenstein, France, Spain, and finally South America. Dodson and her X-2 colleagues patiently charted these huge amounts of bullion clandestinely on the move from a collapsing Reich.

One of Dodson's most nostalgic memories was a rendezvous that Dulles arranged for her at Zermatt, an Alpine ski resort in the shadow of the Matterhorn. Dulles wanted to obtain the complete set of diaries written by Count Galeazzo Ciano, Mussolini's son-in-law and Italy's foreign minister until Mussolini fired him in February 1943. Some of Ciano's diaries had been smuggled into Switzerland earlier by his wife Edda, who escaped from Italy several days before her husband was finally executed. The diaries were photocopied by an OSS agent, Capt. Tracy Barnes, in Switzerland, translated in Washington by Alice Moore, a multilingual OSS reports officer, and used at the Nuremberg trials. Edda Ciano had been accompanied to Switzerland by her lover, dashing Emilio Pucci, away without leave from the Italian fascist air force. The remaining diaries were reportedly still hidden somewhere in Italy. Dulles thought Pucci might be able to help locate them.

While working in her office one day, Dodson saw Pucci's name in the cable traffic. She mentioned to Blum that she had been a classmate of his at Reed College and had later met his parents, the Marchesa and Marchese Pucci de Barsento, in Italy. When Blum reported this lucky coincidence to Dulles, Dodson was immediately called in to Dulles's office, where he then arranged for her to contact Pucci, whose present amour, Edda Ciano, had been confined to a sanatorium under the watchful eyes of Swiss security. Her lover was free and more than willing to renew the acquaintance of an attractive college colleague.

Dodson recalled Pucci fondly: "He was a slender young man, very graceful, and a good athlete. He skied, fenced, danced beautifully. He and I won a dance contest at Zermatt, above and beyond the call to duty! We skied, relived college memories, discussed the Italy that Pucci saw collapsing under fascist rule as we relaxed in front of a roaring fire at one of the resort chalets. But I struck out on the diaries. Emilio did not know where the missing books were hidden. However, he did offer to go back to Italy and look for them." At Dodson's suggestion, Dulles intervened with the Italian air attaché in Switzerland, and Pucci was able to return to his unit in Italy. No disciplinary action was taken against him there, but he was unsuccessful in locating the remaining diaries, which later turned up in German hands.

Remembering her assignment at Zermatt with this enchanting Italian — who later became the aristocrat of the fashion world in Florence and created gowns for such celebrities as Jacqueline Kennedy and Princess Grace of Monaco — Dodson reflected, "At about that time I had met an American assigned to OSS in Bern named William Hood, and that was that!"

Cordelia Dodson Hood remained in Bern until 1948, when she and her husband transferred to the newly established Central Intelligence Agency in Washington. They were later posted overseas to the CIA station in Austria and were on duty at the time the Soviet defector Lt. Col. Pyotr Popov walked into their office and became one of the agency's most valuable sources of intelligence. Hood supervised the case, and Cordelia worked on the reports Popov submitted until he was captured and assassinated by the Soviets in 1963. Cordelia Hood, now retired and separated from her husband, divides her time between her home in New Harbor, Maine, and Silver Spring, Maryland. William Hood, a thirty-year retired veteran of OSS and CIA, is the author of an award-winning book, *The Mole*, which retells the Popov story.

Cordelia Dodson and most of the OSS women employed in Bern worked in nearby offices and seldom saw their busy, peripatetic boss. But one attractive, self-assured agent was in daily contact with Dulles by phone from her Zurich home, or at Herrengasse 23 in the evening, enjoying dinner and perhaps later a pleasant "dalliance" with the OSS chief.

She was Mary Bancroft, who had been recruited in Bern before Dulles arrived, and she remained with his operation until war's end. Bancroft was hired by Gerald Meyer, a scout for Dulles who had arrived two months earlier to establish the OSS office in Switzerland. Proficient in German and French, she was assigned the job of analyzing the German press output and the speeches of such Nazi leaders as Hitler, Goering, and Goebbels.

Meyer arranged for Bancroft to meet their boss in December 1942, telling her that Dulles was "special assistant to the American minister." She was quick to make her own analysis of Dulles: "I met Gerald at the Baur au Lac Hotel in Zurich sitting with a man of ruddy complexion, a small greying moustache, keen blue eyes behind rimless spectacles, and wearing a tweed jacket and grey flannels. My instantaneous impression of Allen Welsh Dulles was that he would never be anyone's assistant!"[9]

Mary Bancroft was handsome, outspoken, and profoundly intelligent. She was a former Boston debutante, a Smith College dropout raised by a loving step-grandfather, C. W. Barron, publisher of the *Wall Street Journal*. She was living in Zurich with her second husband, Jean Rufenacht, a French-Swiss businessman. Her daughter by her first marriage, Mary Jane, lived with them and attended Swiss schools.

Bancroft was also an enthusiastic student of the Swiss psychiatrist Carl Gustav Jung, founder of the school of analytical psychology. She often relied upon his judgment over the years as she became more involved in intelligence work. She wrote in her autobiography, "Intelligence is a mosaic. General material about background and people's interrelationships can be both illuminating and important. Quite often missing pieces of the mosaic emerge that make a previously incomprehensible picture unexpectedly clear. I very quickly learned the value of personal relationships, how important it was to win people's trust and confidence."

When she first met Dulles, Bancroft's marriage to Rufenacht was adrift. He traveled constantly, and she relieved her boredom by writing for Swiss newspapers. Her articles were in-depth analyses of power shifts in Germany based upon source material readily available in Switzerland in still-reputable German newspapers such as the *Frankfurter Zeitung* or in Goebbels's weekly *Das Reich* with its obviously slanted news. Later, when she began to write weekly studies for OSS, her timely and perceptive analyses were of great value to the Morale Operations teams in England and Italy, as well as to analysts in Washington.

Bancroft was thirty-eight years old, Dulles forty-nine, when they met and shortly thereafter combined business and pleasure. As Bancroft wrote in her autobiography, "I can no longer remember exactly when I realized that not only was he in love with me, but I was very much in love with him. How perfectly Allen and I would work together. The speed with which he could think, the ingenuity with which he could find solutions to even the most com plicated problems were thrilling to me. This was tremendously exhilarating." Mary Bancroft's worldly and blasé husband accepted the relationship, and Dr. Jung found it intriguing. He explained to Bancroft that "ambitious, powerful men like Dulles needed to listen to what women said in order to exercise their best judgment. A woman's intuitive capacity is superior to a man's."

By late January 1943 Bancroft was working full-time for Dulles. Her cover was conveniently believable: her ménage in Zurich was an agreeable setting for "visitors" to make friendly social calls, and her occupation as a journalist enabled her to meet contacts publicly. Every weekend Bancroft would travel sixty miles by rail to Bern, register at the Hotel Schweizerhof across the street from the railroad station, and walk through shopping arcades under the arches of the medieval clock tower toward Dulles's ground-floor apartment on the Herrengasse. Here, after cocktails, an elegant dinner, and coffee, they would settle down to discuss her reports, garnered from the press or contacts Dulles had sent to her, and prepare a regular phone-call report to Washington. These calls, monitored by the Swiss, were carefully tailored to leak information that might be of interest to Swiss authorities or other eavesdroppers, with some of the real intelligence camouflaged with American slang.

"When all the business was out of the way,

we'd engage in a bit of dalliance before I made my way back to my hotel," Bancroft wrote in her autobiography. "On these occasions I was impressed by how we were never disturbed. No phone calls and no visitors. Allen had the reputation for being a poor administrator but he obviously knew how to protect his privacy!"

Bancroft's real contribution to the Bern station's intelligence production began in May 1943. Dulles arranged for her to meet Hans Gisevius, who was assigned to Switzerland as a member of the German army intelligence service, the Abwehr. Despite his position, Gisevius was an old-fashioned German nationalist, a snobbish Prussian civil servant who regarded Hitler and the Nazi hierarchy as inferior and despicable. He and Dulles had established a working rapport, although British intelligence warned that the man might be a dangerous double agent.

Determined to check Gisevius out, Dulles arranged the initial meeting with the German and Mary Bancroft. The ruse was a good one: Gisevius was writing a ponderous book denouncing Nazism, which he wanted to publish after the war. Bancroft would translate the manuscript, meanwhile spending all the time she needed to get him to talk, taking note of everything he told her about the decision making in Hitler's high command, then later passing it along to Dulles.

The relationship between Bancroft and her

new agent — a "giant of a man, fair haired, blue eyed, with a healthy tan, so engaging, his smile so beguiling" — developed. During the first few weeks of their work together, Bancroft wrote, "the attraction between us was like that of a high tension power line. He would grab my hand and suggest we go to Lucerne where he had a beautiful apartment for a couple of weeks to work on the book." She always resisted the temptation to accompany him to Lucerne, despite the fact that once Gisevius told her he was meeting Rudolf Diels, an important Gestapo officer and another well-known ladies' man. When she reported this later to Dulles he asked her, "Why the hell didn't you go? It might have been interesting!"

The manuscript that Gisevius brought to Bancroft was in three thick leather-bound volumes, written in very involved and difficult German. She finally persuaded Dulles to enlist the help of two women translators and friends: American-born Mary Briner, wife of a Swiss army officer, Carl Briner; and Elizabeth Scott Montague, sister of Lord Montague of Beaulieu, former ambassador to the United States. Gisevius was particularly enchanted with having a titled English lady, a descendant of Mary, Queen of Scots, working with Bancroft on his book.

Before getting down to the actual translation of Gisevius's tome, the ladies would start a lively after-lunch conversation over coffee to query the now relaxed Abwehr official about current events in Berlin, especially as they pertained to the German high command. The material they were able to elicit proved invaluable in Dulles's reporting back to Washington. Their operation with Gisevius halted abruptly in July 1944, when he called Bancroft to tell her he was going away for a few days; but he did not return to Bern for six months.

Meanwhile, she decided to take a much needed summer vacation in Ascona on the shores of Lake Maggiore with her daughter. As she later wrote, "The work I had been doing, with its necessity of regarding everyone with suspicion or mistrust, had put a terrible strain on my nerves. Also, having to sit down and write up each meeting as factually as possible, while organizing facts in such a way as to give the correct impression, was no small task." On this vacation Bancroft was determined to get the maximum benefit from "no translating, no entertaining authors, no meetings with foreign nationals with complicated stories to tell."

When she returned to Zurich she found waiting for her translation a twenty-page memorandum from Gisevius, which he had entrusted to Dulles. It had been written before Gisevius left for Berlin to take part in the failed assassination plot against Hitler, on 20 July 1944. The memo was based upon the assumption that the assassination would succeed, and Gisevius strongly urged that the German people be allowed to punish the war criminals themselves. Gisevius himself did not appear in Zurich until early January 1945, using OSS-forged identification papers to narrowly escape the countrywide Gestapo net that caught most of the conspirators. The gaunt, gray-haired man whom she barely recognized had returned to finish the last chapter of his book, and to report to her and OSS on the futile attempt of his group of generals and other anti-Nazi leaders to kill the *Führer*. The book, later published in the United States, was titled *To the Bitter End*.

Bancroft stayed on with Dulles in Switzerland until the Allies moved to Germany and he became head of the OSS mission there. He invited her to join him, but she requested only that he arrange for her to attend the trials at Nuremberg where so many of the Nazi war criminals she had written about in reports would appear in person.

She drove to Nuremberg with an OSS colleague, Robert Shea, and an exhausted Gisevius in the back seat. In her autobiography Bancroft described the "strange beauty in the ruins, the reds and the browns, mingled with the blacks and greys of bombed out buildings, [which] contrasted strongly with the lime green buds of the willow trees." During the next few weeks she attended the trials of von Ribbentrop, Goering, Hess, and Keitel, Hitler's chief of staff. The names she had so often transcribed in her interviews with Gisevius had become real people.

Bancroft returned to New York City in 1953, having spent much of her time in Switzerland writing, translating, and editing films. She divorced her husband during this period. In her later years she eschewed espionage for the "byzantine plots and intrigues in local New York democratic politics." She died in January 1997. The *New York Times* obituary described her as a "Boston Brahmin colleen who cut a coquettish swath through 20th century history bewitching men of power even as she did brilliant work in Switzerland in World War II."[10]

During the thirty months that Allen Dulles headed the OSS station in Bern, he masterminded one of the most important high-echelon operations of his career. Code-named Operation Sunrise, it was initiated in February 1945, and it reached a dramatic climax three months later with the unconditional surrender of German troops in Italy.

Operation Sunrise began covertly with the appearance in Bern of an Italian baron, Luigi Parilli, who had come from Rome seeking Swiss and Allied cooperation in opening a channel for peace talks with the German high command in Italy. As a result of this meeting, Dulles was able to arrange a series of secret talks with the man who had requested the audience, Gen. Karl Wolff, commander of the SS

(Schutzstaffel), and German military, political, and police organs in Italy.

As negotiations proceeded, Dulles arranged a series of covert planning sessions with two high Allied officers from the Mediterranean theater: Brig. Gen. Terence S. Airley of British intelligence, and Maj. Gen. Lyman L. Lemnitzer of the U.S. Army. Operation Sunrise progressed slowly through bureaucratic maneuverings in Italy and Switzerland and later at the highest levels in Washington and London. News of these secret meetings reached an irate Stalin, who demanded to be included in all negotiations. In spite of his threats and protests, Russia was not included; the Mediterranean theater was considered an American and British battle zone.

There are many theories as to how Moscow continued to monitor the Operation Sunrise machinations after 11 March 1945, when the Allied governments officially informed the Soviets that Britain and America would handle the deal alone. One plausible explanation (besides the very active intelligence service operated illegally by the Soviets in Switzerland) is that two known communists — Noel Field, an American representative of the Unitarian Service Committee (USC), and his attractive foster daughter, Erica Glaser — were on the OSS payroll.

Field, a former Foreign Service employee, had known Dulles earlier in their State Department careers. When they met in Bern during the war, Field denied that he was a member of the Communist Party, describing himself as "a man of peace." He told Dulles that he had become acquainted with communists and their leaders when he was in Spain during the civil war, heading the USC mission. It was also in Spain that he first met Erica Glaser's parents, who had fled Nazi Germany because of their Jewish heritage. Dr. Glaser had a license to practice medicine in Spain and ended up as a captain in the Communist International Brigade. Penniless at that war's end, Dr. and Mrs. Glaser were granted asylum in England. They left sixteen-year-old Erica with Herta and Noel Field. She was the daughter they never had, and they arranged for her education in Switzerland.

Born in Pomerania, Germany, in 1922, Erica grew up enduring physical and mental harassment about her half-Jewish father by schoolmates and teachers under the ever-growing Nazi domination of the country. Later her experience as a teenaged nurse tending the wounded on the battlefields of Spain with her mother left this feisty, dark-haired girl with a mind of her own and a determination to fight Hitler's regime through whatever channels she could use. She turned definitely to communism as that road when she was a student at the University of Geneva. Her contact in Geneva was a prominent German communist who gave her "political lessons." She later explained to me, "I was already pro-communist, and he taught me background, education and the theoretical side of Marxism. It seemed to me that the communists were the most active opponents to Nazi-ism that I could work with."

Erica completed her studies at the University of Geneva in 1944 and was assigned to work with the Communist Committee to Free Germany. She helped smuggle German communists out of France, across Switzerland, and into Germany, where they were instructed to organize communist cells. Twice she met agents at the French border to receive reports from them for her foster father, Noel Field. He in turn reported to Dulles, whose aim was to establish contact with a variety of undercover agents in Germany: communists, unionists, religious groups. Dulles felt comfortable at that time in history with his communist contacts: they were fighting the same enemy.

Erica was recruited for OSS by one of Dulles's top aides, Gerhard P. (Gary) Van Arkel, former general consul for the National Labor Relations Board in Washington. Dulles himself signed Erica's character references for her job description. She was hired as a secretary and translator, although she had to learn to type before reporting for duty. She spoke Spanish, German, French, and English.

Van Arkel's operations were not limited to labor union activity in Germany. He was case officer for an Austrian socialist working within the German railroad system who regularly reported bombing targets for Allied missions. In another area, his agents carefully monitored daily water levels of the Rhine in case the Germans decided to inundate the lowlands to avert Allied advances. He also read the cable traffic and knew that Dulles was in secret negotiations with General Wolff in Italy; his secretary was also in a good position to scan this intelligence. Later Erica was to admit that she was perfectly willing to fight the Nazis by keeping her communist contacts informed about OSS operations. In his book *Dulles* Leonard Moseley noted, "Noel Field could have told Dulles that Erica worked for the Communist party in Switzerland and that she had taken the post with instructions to report back to the Party on the OSS negotiations."

During the three months Erica Glaser worked in Bern, negotiations were proceeding slowly on Operation Sunrise. After he had been officially notified of the operation, Stalin insisted on smuggling three observers into Bern, but his request was not honored. On 16 March the Soviets demanded that the Americans and British break off negotiations with Wolff. The request was denied angrily by Roosevelt. On 23 March, Stalin wrote an inflammatory letter to Roosevelt accusing the Allies of planning a separate truce with Germany, double-crossing their Russian allies, who had borne the brunt of the fighting in Europe. In his book *Operation Sunrise* Dulles commented, "It is clear from Stalin's letter that he drew upon information which Soviet intelligence had gathered about our discussions in Switzerland, much of it incorrect and probably purposefully distorted." Roosevelt himself wrote Stalin, "Frankly, I cannot avoid a feeling of bitter resentment towards your informers, whoever they are, for such vile misrepresentation of my actions and those of my trusted subordinates."

Operation Sunrise succeeded in spite of Russian intransigence. At two o'clock Italian time on 2 May, German soldiers began to lay down their arms. The war in Italy was over. V-E Day was five days away. Mussolini and Hitler were dead.

Erica Glaser's story became a tangled web of bizarre happenings after Allen Dulles was transferred to Germany as head of the OSS mission and Erica was assigned to Wiesbaden, where she worked with Van Arkel in the Henkel champagne factory.

I met Erica almost fifty years later at her estate, Hopefield, in Warrenton, Virginia. The war years held vivid but devastating memories for her. She laughingly recalled that she had been a terrible secretary in Wiesbaden, working in a glass-enclosed office, spending a great deal of her time interrogating German scientists and other government officials for Van Arkel. Neither she nor her boss could ever find important papers in her files, marked "In," "Out," and "Misc." She also maintained contact with her German communist friends and in 1945 went to Berlin, where she interrogated prisoners of war from the Soviet Union. After the war she officially joined the Communist Party and resigned her job with OSS. As secretary to the communist faction of the Hesse Parliament, she represented this group in dealing with American occupation authorities. And here she met and fell in love with her liaison officer, Capt. Robert Wallach, scion of a prominent Washington family.

As she explained it, during the war years she was engaged in a life-and-death struggle against fascism. Later, when she married Captain Wallach, she became entangled in the politics of the Cold War. In spite of the War Brides Act, she was denied entry into the United States because of her Communist Party membership. She and her husband remained in Europe for two years. In Paris, Erica worked as editor of a Communist Party magazine. Because she disagreed with the party line at this time, she finally resigned in 1948. Her husband, meanwhile, attended classes at the Sorbonne, and the Wallachs became the parents of two children.

During this period Herta and Noel Field were enticed behind the Iron Curtain, and in 1949 they disappeared from Prague and from the world. Believing that her one-time communist contacts could help her find her foster parents, Erica Wallach flew to West Berlin, was lured to East Berlin by false promises, and was promptly arrested as an American spy. Found guilty of espionage, she was given the death sentence, later commuted to fifteen years in a Siberian slave-labor camp. She had been trapped, like the Noel Fields, in a series of intrigues complicated by the fact that she had worked for Allen Dulles and had also been a member of the Communist Party. The Soviets claimed that she was an American agent; certain U.S. government authorities maintained that she was working for the communists. She was caught between conflicting political forces in postwar Europe.

Erica Wallach spent five long, frustrating years in Siberia and was finally released after the death of Stalin, who, it was later learned, had instigated indiscriminate purges against anyone associated with Noel Field. Soviet authorities then declared that Erica was innocent of all charges. Her foster parents emerged from jail, but they chose to remain behind the Iron Curtain. Throughout Soviet prisons in Europe, hundreds of prisoners suddenly reappeared, victims of their association with Noel Field and his OSS connection.

Erica Wallach was granted entry into the United States in 1957. The Department of State and the Committee on Un-American Activities investigated her case and found that she was a bona fide defector from communism. She came home to two young children who did not know her, and to a husband now out of the army and working in international banking. Her son, Robert Wallach, now an architect in Burke, Virginia, remembers his mother's arrival at Hopefield: "It was with great nervousness that I stood at the window in 1957 watching her walk up the front sidewalk. I had been very lucky in that I had an aunt and a grandmother who had raised me with love and caring. However, it seemed only a matter of days before my mother had somehow made me feel as if she had never been gone. And in the years that followed she became my mother, my teacher, my model."

Her daughter, Madeleine W. de Heller, greatly resembles her mother, and she too remembers when Erica Wallach first walked up the path to their home. "When I saw her then, I immediately thought: 'She's my mummy, come home to take care of us.'"

The Erica Wallach whom I met in 1994 at Hopefield was a smiling, slight woman with a face lined with furrows from the years spent in the Siberian slave-labor camp. Her elegant home reflected charm and hospitality. She had two friendly dogs, refugees from the local Humane Society, and a large black cat in attendance. She said she had always loved animals; it went back to her childhood in Germany, when a dog had saved her brother from drowning.

She also loved children and taught French and Latin for eighteen years at the Highland School in Warrenton. Her husband had died in 1990, but she still radiated the warmth and optimism of her early years fighting the Nazi system that had broken up her family and her own life.

When we said good-bye, she lent me a book she had written about her life in the Russian camp in Siberia, *Light at Midnight.* "You must promise to return it," she admonished me. "It's the only one I have." It was the last time I saw Erica Wallach alive, but I did return her book. She died of cancer a few months later on 22 December 1994. At memorial services at Hopefield on 28 December, a neighbor and old friend from OSS days in Wiesbaden remembered her. Harry Rositzke said: "Dying had no terror for her. She believed that this life is *the* life, that you should live it fully, that you should be honest and forthright in your dealings, that you should be compassionate."

And that is how her close friends remember Erica Glaser Wallach.

Most of the wartime colleagues with whom Erica Wallach served celebrated the German surrender on 7 May 1945 and eventually left their posts in Europe for home or reassignment in the China-Burma theater. Here the war would be waged for another three months from Burma to the Pacific. For the twenty-four months beginning August 1943, OSS operated from detachments in India, Burma, and China. During this period teams were infiltrated into Siam, Indonesia, Indochina, and the Japanese-held areas of the China coast. OSS men with little if any Asian background were fighting in exotic countries where the cultures and languages reflected another world, one of strange people and stranger beliefs. At times there was not even a common enemy. A civil war was smoldering in China, and British, French, and Dutch interests were fighting for the return of their colonial empires.

CHAPTER 16

Through the
Transom into India

It was a sizzling 114 degrees in the shade in New Delhi when Joan Bondurant and Maureen Patterson reported for duty in May 1944, at the dentist's office that was now OSS headquarters at 32 Feroz Shah Road.[1] The young women had been assigned to R&A, the newly established Research and Analysis Branch, where Olive Reddick, an old India hand, briefed them on the intramural warfare being waged — not against the Japanese across the Bay of Bengal in Burma, but with the British Raj in New Delhi. It was the first trip to Asia for these recent recruits.

At that time in history India was the crumbling bastion of British colonial power. In August 1943 the revered Mohandas Gandhi and the leaders of the Indian National Congress had launched the Quit India movement, calling for mass civil disobedience if the British did not leave India immediately. The viceroy, Lord Linlithgow, quickly jailed Gandhi, the other Congress leaders, and thousands of their followers all over India. In response to these arrests, violence erupted throughout the country. The British-led Indian army suppressed the uprising and maintained a smoldering peace. All activities by the Congress, India's major nationalist organization, were banned for the next three years.

The American press had for a long time been needling the Roosevelt administration about the situation. Where, journalists asked, was that concept of freedom for oppressed peoples proclaimed in the Atlantic Charter and endorsed by the president? With India in turmoil, how could the Allies concentrate on war against Japan?

As Olive Reddick explained to Bondurant and Patterson, Roosevelt had taken steps to deal with the problem. In early January 1943 the president's personal representative, William Phillips, arrived in New Delhi to help work out a peaceful solution between the British and Indians while also opening the way for OSS to operate in the Far East. Phillips was accompanied by thirty-three-year-old Richard P. Heppner, former head of OSS Special Operations in Europe, a Princeton and Columbia Law School graduate who had served briefly with Phillips when he headed OSS in London. Heppner's job was to establish an OSS station in India if British authorities concurred. In a memorandum he had written for Phillips to present to the viceroy, Heppner stated, "It is proposed that the OSS staff number four men. One officer would maintain liaison with the British Secret Intelligence Service (SIS); the other with the Special Operations Executive (SOE). The remaining two would operate a microfilm facility."[2]

Reddick told her two new colleagues that it took seven frustrating months before permission was obtained for OSS to organize intelligence and research units in India. In 1942 an OSS Special Operations team originally destined for China had been reassigned to Nazira, Assam, in northeastern India by order of Gen. Joseph Stilwell as part of his long-range plan to retake Burma. Never welcomed by British SOE, forward bases of Detachment 101 eventually moved into Burma to become a legendary part of OSS lore. (Detachment 101, created on 14 April 1942, was the first unit in military history organized to conduct unconventional warfare operations behind enemy lines.) Here their teams rescued downed flyers, organized the native Kachins for sabotage strikes against Japanese outposts, and supplied vital target intelligence leading to the liberation of Burma.

After William Phillips's visit, a permanent American presence was established in New Delhi, with a mission headed by career diplomat George Merrill. Attached to this unit was a U.S. military-observer group. As Reddick explained to Bondurant and Patterson, the viceroy considered this representation adequate for what was still the British Raj, and he relied on bureaucratic maneuvering between London and Washington to stall further OSS buildup in India as long as possible.

General Donovan himself attempted to speed up negotiations and only succeeded in locking horns with an Australian, Brig. W. J. Cawthorne, then head of military intelligence for the Indian army. In a stormy interview Donovan told Cawthorne that "if he didn't let OSS in the door, we would come through the transom!"[3]

Phillips was further thwarted in his attempts to accomplish his mission to India. His request for an audience with the imprisoned Gandhi was denied. As he wrote later in his memoir *Ventures in Diplomacy*, Phillips wondered if the stern Scottish viceroy "does not feel the pathos in the appeal of millions of Indians for freedom in their own country. Perhaps he is a chip off the old block that we Americans knew something about back in 1772."

In August 1943 Donovan was able to arrange an agreement with London that permitted OSS to open an intelligence office in New Delhi with the proviso that the British remain dominant partners in all India-based operations. Anticipating such an agreement, Heppner had actually set up Detachment 303 in New Delhi in July 1943 and placed it under the South East

Asia Command (SEAC), led by Lord Louis Mountbatten, who was to establish his headquarters in Kandy, Ceylon, later that year. Eventually Heppner's original request for four men escalated into a staff of hundreds, which included Detachment 505 in Calcutta — mainly a supply depot for Burma and China operations — and Detachment 404 in Kandy, which ran missions into Siam, Burma, and Malaya. As Bondurant and Patterson quickly learned, their assignment to SEAC was irreverently translated by their colleagues as "Save England's Asiatic Colonies," and also as "Supreme Example of Allied Confusion."

In January 1944 a group of OSS scholars organized the first R&A unit within Detachment 303 in New Delhi, headed by anthropologist David Mandelbaum. He was joined by Olive Reddick, who before the war had been a schoolteacher in India and had extensive contacts with Indian politicians and with those Indian residents of Burma who had been forced out by the Japanese invasion. During her tour with OSS she lived with an Indian family.

At first the R&A office in New Delhi was generally assigned to produce background research for Detachment 101's operations on the Assam-Burma border. Later, when Bondurant and Patterson joined the group, they processed Japanese-language materials captured in Burma, forwarding important documents by air to Washington and gleaning details from these materials on potential bombing targets in Japanese-occupied China. But by the beginning of 1945 R&A had begun to carry out research on the Indian political scene, secretly and in contravention of the agreement with the British not to engage in any activities relating to the internal affairs of India. This was intended to circumvent official channels (both American and British) and to provide OSS in Washington with information on the nationalist movement in India. The research was initiated by Bondurant and Patterson, aided and supervised by the veteran Reddick.

The two women were well qualified for this covert assignment. When the Japanese attacked Pearl Harbor in 1941, Bondurant was a student at the University of Michigan. Wanting to join the war effort, she enrolled after graduation in a crash course in Japanese language just started at the university. Patterson, a sophomore there at the time, talked her way into the next Japanese class, although women were generally discouraged from taking it. The consensus at that time was that men would be using the language, not women. Both women eventually mastered enough of the complex written characters to do short translations. After completing these courses, they contacted their former geography professor at Michigan, Dr. Robert B. Hall (later Colonel Hall), reported by the college grapevine to be working for the Oh So Secret OSS. Hall, then stationed in San

Francisco, recruited his former students, and they started to work under him in the Foreign Nationalities Branch of OSS in California.

Here they learned the basic research and analytical techniques that would be of value to them later in India. The women gained access to published materials confiscated from Japanese temples on the West Coast and from homes of Japanese-Americans forced into relocation camps after Pearl Harbor. From returned missionaries and others who had lived in the Orient they collected photographic materials, postcards, travel brochures, and anything else that might identify possible landing sites in Japan. Rather than admit that they were collecting data for the OSS, they were instructed to state that they worked for a "Government Pictorial Agency." In order not to blow their cover, they parked their car and took "diversionary action," as they say in the spy trade, before approaching their target.

Colonel Hall was eventually reassigned to OSS India, and within a few months he arranged to transfer his Michigan students to New Delhi. Following indoctrination in clandestine operations at an OSS training school in Virginia, the women boarded a troopship for the thirty-two-day journey to India, and to what Patterson considers one of the most exciting periods of her life: penetrating the British Raj to help American officialdom understand the goals of the Indian nationalist movement.

"It helped that I had lived in England until I was about sixteen. My father was in the U.S. Foreign Service," she later recounted to me. "I had a genuine British accent which allowed me to quietly infiltrate Delhi society. I did not advertise that I was an American."

Patterson remembers the almost immediate fascination India's culture held for these two young women from the University of Michigan. They worked with Japanese documents at the R&A office during the day but soon began to spend their spare time studying Hindi, one of India's fifteen major literary languages. They advertised for a tutor by placing a notice on the bulletin board of the Lady Harding Medical College in New Delhi. Both had language aptitude, and soon their residence became not only a schoolroom after work but a teatime rendezvous for Indian students with varied political views, all focused upon independence from the British, who had controlled this vast subcontinent since the mid-1700s.

Joseph R. Coolidge, then head of R&A in New Delhi, remembers receiving sub rosa instructions from Washington by the end of 1944: "I was informed by my superiors that Washington did, in fact, want New Delhi R&A to continue to take the pulse of the body politic in India. But I was cautioned that any surveillance had to be done in complete secrecy." OSS had promised the British not to intrude into India's internal affairs. An infraction of this agreement would jeopardize relations between the two countries.

Shortly after Coolidge received these instructions, his superior, Dr. Charles Burton Fahs, who was the chief of the India Section of R&A in Washington, visited New Delhi and directed that R&A intelligence collection include appraisals of Indian leadership potential. Patterson and Bondurant both began to work on this project, knowing full well that they were entering a political minefield. Patterson recalls Fahs's instructions to her to meet as many important Indians as possible, even though Congress leaders were still in prison, and to write reports on political discussions with them.

At about that same time I had been assigned to the Morale Operations Branch (MO) in New Delhi, and both Patterson and Bondurant helped us occasionally by translating Japanese material. Some fifty years later I met Dr. Patterson again, retired after a career as a teacher and researcher on many aspects of Indian civilization, and author of a major bibliography on South Asia. There were still traces of that dedicated, responsible girl of twenty I remembered from our service together.

Our memories first lingered fondly on the exciting life we led during those last years of the war. I chided Patterson about that comfortable bungalow she and Bondurant had rented on Tughlak Road, with spacious living and dining areas, separate bedrooms, a large garden, and quarters in the back for seven servants. What a difference from the crowded girls' billets at the motel-like Taj where I shared a small bedroom with Joy Homer, the contagiously happy daughter of the famous singer Madame Louise Homer, and granddaughter of Winslow Homer! Joy's pet mongoose, Fifi, lived in the bottom bureau drawer of our room, and my English bull terrier, Angel Puss, shared my cot and mosquito net with me.

It was fifty years later too that I fully understood how important that bungalow on Tughlak Road had been for the sensitive operations Bondurant and Patterson carried out in British India. Along with hosting small social gatherings at their residence of a diverse sampling of Indians, the girls attended formal dances at the Imperial Hotel and dinners at restaurants and elegant homes. They met maharajahs, journalists, government functionaries, and left-wing and other non-Congress political leaders, as well as industrialists who were anticipating the postwar economic development of their country. The girls were invited to the Chelmsford Club, established by New Delhi's Indian elite, who were excluded by the British from the segregated Gymkhana Club. And they saw a lot of Muslim League leaders, who were eager to set up a separate state they called Pakistan.

The girls had been warned early by OSS security to be careful of servants who might be reporting to the British. Aware of this, they secreted a shortwave radio in a bedroom and tuned in to the nightly broadcasts from Japanese-occupied Singapore. It was from there that Subhas Chandra Bose, a Cambridge-educated Indian nationalist, advocated a violent overthrow of the British and formed the Indian National Army, which with Japanese help he hoped to use to invade and liberate his homeland. These broadcasts from Sonan (the Japanese name for Singapore) were considered treasonable under the British Defense of India Rules, but Bondurant and Patterson shared the information they gleaned with Indian friends who were unable to listen to what the Raj called subversive propaganda.

Patterson was attracted to India's diverse politics, with its religious and caste overtones. Bondurant was particularly drawn to Mahatma Gandhi's nonviolent strategy *Satyagraha*, or "insistence on truth," the technique that eventually changed the history of India. Long after the war she wrote a book, *Conquest of Violence*, a classic interpretation of Gandhi's beliefs.

Later Patterson contrived to attend a conference in Simla called by the British to consider the transfer of power to Indians. By then Gandhi, Nehru, and the other Congress leaders had been released from prison and were invited to discuss India's future. One of Patterson's friends in New Delhi had introduced Patterson to Dr. B. C. Roy, Gandhi's personal physician, who suggested that she might enjoy what promised to be a momentous event. She was able to meet and talk with Nehru and many other Indian leaders, and to attend one of Gandhi's famous prayer meetings. She reported to OSS her observations on this important but inconclusive conference.

As part of this much-needed requirement to fill the gaps of knowledge about India in transition, OSS also engaged a young State Department official, Robert Crane, for a book-buying mission. An ardent proponent of Indian independence, Crane, born in India, had a scholarly interest in the country. He was given unlimited funds to purchase, from all over India, books he deemed useful not only to OSS but to the Library of Congress and fourteen other agencies and departments including State, Commerce, and Treasury. These huge purchases contributed greatly to the information base available to analysts during the war and to American academics in the postwar world.

Dr. Marshall Windmiller, professor emeritus of international relations at San Francisco State University and an authority on India, told me that the component of the wartime intelligence apparatus that made the most lasting impact on American perceptions and understanding of India was OSS R&A. He credits Bondurant and Patterson as having been responsible for a great deal of this input. Dr. Cora DuBois, who had headed R&A in Ceylon, later praised the

Bondurant-Patterson extracurricular activities, which she pronounced "well-informed and shrewd appraisals of politics."[4] The fact that they were the only women in OSS who were granted an audience with Mahatma Gandhi — meeting him directly after the war in an ashram outside Calcutta, through the good offices of Dr. Roy — attests to the degree of friendship Patterson and Bondurant were able to develop with their Indian colleagues.

Official records note that no OSS branch in India rendered broader service than R&A. However, during the brief interlude before the end of the war when OSS functioned in India, the MO branch contributed several operations that were run on a shoestring but were well received by the military and Detachment 101. I worked on two of these projects with the help of Bondurant and Patterson, several other OSS colleagues, and enlightened British friends who believed that women could indeed make a solid contribution to the war effort.

CHAPTER 17

Black Mail

New Delhi was my first overseas OSS tour before eventual assignment behind the Japanese lines in western China. I arrived in India in July 1944, with a bright, attractive Morale Operations (MO) colleague, Marjorie Severyns, also slated for China. We were both University of Washington graduates but did not meet until years later at OSS headquarters in Washington, where we established a close working rapport during our training.

At that time in my career I was Elizabeth MacDonald, married to Alexander MacDonald, an adventurous newspaperman from Boston just out of college. He came to what was then romantic Hawaii, looking for adventure, but he ended up covering the waterfront for the *Honolulu Advertiser* and writing an exposé of the moneyed establishment that controlled the islands, *Revolt in Paradise*.

I had grown up in Hawaii. My father, William Peet, was a newspaperman and sports editor for the *Honolulu Advertiser*; my mother, a former Washington, D.C., columnist, became a schoolteacher. Just out of journalism school, I was on my first job as a cub reporter covering sports for my father when I met Alex MacDonald in the city room. Later I left the *Advertiser* and became a stringer for the Scripps-Howard feature service. I also became society editor of the rival paper, the *Star-Bulletin*, in the days when "society" was part of media coverage, especially in small towns such as Honolulu was then.

Alex and I both wanted to go to Japan — like so many of our colleagues, lured by exotic dreams of the Far East. To prepare for this adventure and learn the language we started married life residing with a Japanese family living in Honolulu. The head of the household, Dr. Saburo Watanabe, was the principal of a local Japanese language school. After a year we had picked up a speaking knowledge of Japanese, but we didn't go to Japan to use it; instead, the Japanese came to us. We were asleep on that Sunday morning when Japanese warplanes bombed Pearl Harbor and changed our lives forever.

I covered wartime Hawaii until the Scripps-Howard syndicate offered me a job in Washington covering Eleanor Roosevelt and the White House and writing a daily column, "Homefront Forecast." Alex was in the Naval Reserves and had immediately reported for duty, to be assigned as press officer with naval intelligence in Honolulu. Through my later efforts in Washington, he was recruited by OSS.

By the time I had landed in New Delhi, Lieutenant MacDonald was in training at an OSS facility at Catalina Island, California. He would eventually be assigned to Ceylon, later to Burma and Siam where he started the first English-language newspaper, the *Bangkok Post*. When he was assigned to the South East Area Command, I was sent to China. We were never permitted to serve in the same theater; it was against OSS rules, which could be amended only by General Donovan himself. Like so many other wartime marriages in OSS, ours eventually ended in divorce.

Once established at our billet, the Taj Hotel, Marjorie Severyns and I were anxious to get to work. In a memorandum to Washington, Severyns wrote, "Betty MacDonald and I got in early Monday morning after a rocket flight on the Cannon Ball Express across Africa, the Middle East and Asia. We are still fired up with surplus energy and anxious to establish a real MO service."[1]

I notified the Colombo (Ceylon) base, where Carlton F. Schofield was in charge of operations, "This is just to let you know that MO has raised its ugly head in Delhi and Marj Severyns and I are open for business. We are sort of intelligence service station attendants. Marjorie analyzes material as soon as we acquire it, and I try to develop MO production possibilities."[2]

Our immediate boss, Maj. Harley C. Stevens, reported to headquarters, "The MO team is now in position. They have settled down in a well lighted office right off the dining room, formerly the dentist's bedroom. Grace Mullen, a secretary from Donovan's Wall Street office, is handling the stenographic chores for the team. There are flowers on the mantel and the desks are neat and tidy."[3] No mention was made of our real introduction to office life in India and the perils of encountering resident reptiles. We had liberated a rusty safe from our supply office, and in the process of filing papers in the top drawer, Grace Mullen spotted a small, very agile wormlike snake that leaped out and darted across the floor. A friendly Indian bearer bringing our morning tea tray dropped everything with a crash and fled the room. Later we learned that the snake was a deadly krait. One bite and the victim was lucky to take three steps before dropping dead!

Like Joan Bondurant and Maureen Patterson, we had been briefed about working with the British. Our target was the Japanese in Burma, yet no printing press or Japanese typesetting facilities were available to us. The British in New Delhi and Calcutta had all such assets. MO did, however, have access to two important intelligence sources. One was the joint British-American South East Asia Translation and Interpreter Command (SEATIC). Here American Nisei and British language teams worked on captured material. The other equally important resource was the British prisoner-of-war compound at the historic Red Fort in Old Delhi, where Japanese prisoners were interned.

Severyns and I were busy organizing files into some semblance of order when a smiling young navy lieutenant walked into the office. "I'm Bill Magistretti. Welcome to Per Diem Hill." He dropped a bulging briefcase onto my desk from which he pulled scraps of Japanese newspapers, postcards, and photographs of Japanese soldiers and their families. "There's lots more where these came from."

We had heard of Magistretti before we left Washington. He was one of the most competent Japanese scholars in OSS. He had studied the language in Japanese middle schools and later at Waseda University in Tokyo. He left Japan just before Pearl Harbor and worked as a civilian with the San Francisco Office of Naval Intelligence. After war was declared he joined the navy, was transferred to OSS, and was sent to India with R&A, the Research and Analysis Branch, to analyze and study captured material. In the months ahead we were able to lure him away from R&A. Our MO projects seemed to delight his Italian taste for unbureaucratic approaches to the war effort. He was the first of a number of "bodies" Marj and I induced to develop our MO unit. After him came Indian nationals, American Nisei, and, finally, the head of British overt propaganda production, Maj. Peter Glemser, who remained until his death one of our best friends after the war.

After reviewing Magistretti's treasure trove, nothing would do but for me to go to SEATIC and see for myself. That afternoon after lunch Bill offered to jeep me over. SEATIC had just received a new shipment of captured documents. We drove through a rain shower to the command compound, a series of squat wooden houses surrounded by barbed wire. Barefoot Indian boys were brewing tea over open braziers. Badly ventilated offices were crowded with British and Americans — the British in sensible short-sleeved blouses and shorts, the perspiring Americans in regulation starched uniforms, shirts, and ties. There was a low babel of Japanese and English at the far end of the workroom. "American Nisei," Magistretti explained. "Our GI samurai."

To me the Japanese-Americans in Hawaii occupied a very special niche in World War II. Before the war their records in the Reserve Officers Training Corps had been the highest. They were the backbone of the Hawaii National Guard until that day, shortly after Pearl Harbor, when all men of Japanese ancestry in Hawaii were told to turn in their uniforms and arms. They had reentered the service as volunteer labor battalions and had then petitioned Congress to restore their rights as American citizens to fight in defense of their country. In

Italy the much-decorated Nisei 442d Regimental Combat Team fought valiantly at Anzio. Other Nisei were among the first to break down the gates at Dachau. Still others served with Merrill's Marauders in the Burma jungles, and in the Pacific with MacArthur.

Standing there in that smoke-filled room, I was startled to hear someone call my name. Heads bobbed up from the tables where the Nisei were working, then suddenly several stood up and came toward me. The first one I recognized was Saburo Watanabe, son of my Japanese professor in Honolulu. Others gathered around: Chieko Ikeda, a student of my mother's at McKinley High School; Errol Nagao, who had lived a few blocks from my family; Edward Mitsukada, who had been with Merrill's Marauders and whose brother, Andy, worked for my father in the sports department of the *Honolulu Advertiser*.

A warm exchange of hometown news followed as our little group began to block tea traffic. I was just a trifle homesick when I finally broke away and Magistretti escorted me to the office of British major Willie Clark, in charge of registering and distributing captured field manuals, books, magazines, and newspapers, all grist for the MO mill.

Major Clark was a slim, bronzed colonial who had been doing undercover work for the British in Malaysia when the Japanese overran that area. The major spoke better Japanese than many of the prisoners. Almost immediately he accused Magistretti of bringing in female reinforcements to pilfer his precious collection. Then, relaxing after more badinage, he offered me a cigarette. When I told him I didn't smoke, he leaned forward, smiling: "Perhaps you might consider my application for your cigarette rations?" I readily agreed, and we were on a first-name basis for the rest of my tour of duty in New Delhi. American cigarettes, I learned, were one of the chief barter items in establishing clout in India.

After a cup of sweet dark brown tea served in a heavy mug, the major invited me to rummage through the sacks of rancid, unclean things, mouldy leather bags, and papers still damp from the Burma jungles. I fished out some pitiful mementos: photos of children in bright kimonos and a small silk Japanese flag autographed by well-wishers, carried by a soldier into battle. Near the bottom of the bag I felt something solid and retrieved a leather pouch with a five-cornered Japanese brass star on the flap. Opening the slip lock, I found hundreds of clean, dry postcards.

Willie, as I now called him, identified the cache: "A batch of cards that a Japanese officer ordered his men to write home before their last battle." He read a covering letter, which identified the Japanese field unit, one that Indian and British troops had wiped out a month ago, before the mail had been dispatched. "These postcards we find never have anything of military importance," Willie said, "just the standard greetings from homesick soldiers." He and Magistretti studied several cards with messages scrawled in pencil, in unsteady, basic kanji that even I could read. The addresses were printed on the reverse side and stamped with a censor's chop.

"What a shame the families will never receive these last messages from their loved ones," I was thinking out loud as I thumbed through them.

Suddenly Magistretti grabbed them. "Why can't they be mailed to Japan? They've been censored, haven't they?"

I picked up the idea: "Erase the original messages. Substitute our own. It might be the first black MO into Japan."

He agreed: "It's a cinch. Our 101 boys can slip this mail pouch into the Japanese postal system that's still working in the south. They won't bother to check cards that have already been censored."

Willie was with us: "What will the Japanese at home think when they read about the real conditions in Burma? Their propaganda still tells them the Imperial armies are marching through India."

He selected a card at random. It was written in awkward characters by a soldier with little education. Willie erased words about fighting for the emperor and the country and dexterously replaced them with a different message: "Obasan, where are supplies from home? We are starving in the jungle. How can we fight without bullets?"

There were close to five hundred cards in the lot. As we were leaving, Willie offered to help with Project Black Mail, as we had dubbed it: "If you'll send a car around after working hours, I'll come by and bring some reinforcements."

Shortly after five that evening we heard a commotion beyond the gate, and I looked out to see our Indian *chawkidar* guarding the entrance and attempting to hold Willie Clark and some half-dozen Nisei at bay. Magistretti reached them just in time to assure the confused guard that these were friendly forces, not looking for the long-gone dentist but reporting for work.

The group was ushered into our MO office, with an overflow in the dining room. The duty officer at the front desk tactfully ignored Willie's British uniform. In spite of the long day at SEATIC, my Nisei friends said they didn't mind helping out their *aikane* from Hawaii. Besides, they were rather excited about the job.

I explained briefly that we would hammer the same messages home on each card, like an advertising campaign emphasizing a single slogan. The Japanese were losing in Burma, and the home front was not supporting them. Accuse the people back home of being slackers. Tell of heartbreak and starvation in the jungles. We divided up the cards, and the boys started to work. Later Severyns and I served tea and sandwiches from the pantry, and the team worked until well after ten o'clock to finish the painstaking task of forgery and deception.

Magistretti figured we could deliver the mail sack to Col. Ray Peers, the commander of Detachment 101, who was expected in New Delhi within the week. We had completed about four hundred cards, with translations for Washington and a correct memo in military terminology to satisfy Colonel Peers, reputedly a spit-and-polish West Point graduate. (Many years later, as Lt. Gen. William R. Peers, he chaired the panel that investigated the My Lai massacre in Vietnam.)

Severyns and I expected a grim, craggy colonel of the Blimp variety, but Ray Peers was one of those typical young OSS officers provided by our military services — tanned, slim, with a quick smile dotted by a chin dimple. To our amazement, he listened attentively to our request, accepted the mailbag, and read the covering memo.

"Colonel," I said, "if you could get this pouch reinserted into the Japanese mail, it might be the first 'black' penetration of Japan proper." Severyns told me later that I had just the right quaver to my voice.

Peers read our covering request carefully; this

was followed by an uncomfortable silence as he thumbed through the cards. Then: "As I understand it, you want my Kachins to slip this mail pouch into the Japanese post."

"Yes, sir!"

With a frown he scratched his head. Then he abruptly picked up our mailbag, shoved it into his briefcase, and said seriously, "Check. I'll get it to the boys first thing tomorrow. You know, it's not such a bad idea."

Three days later a courier arrived with a message from Peers himself: "Mission accomplished. Every reason to believe material will reach objective."

The following week Magistretti skipped into our office flourishing a newspaper, the *Delhi Statesman,* and grinning: "Tojo cabinet resigns; Koiso forming a new cabinet. See what you girls have done?"

It was not long afterward that Severyns brought in a sheaf of intercepts that included a military order from the Japanese high command restating the punishments that would be meted out to any soldier who surrendered in battle. She also showed me reports on the morale of the Japanese Eighteenth Division in Burma, where food was scarce, medical supplies exhausted, and news from Japan sometimes five months late in arriving. In addition, there was a terse memo to troops that Koiso was forming a new cabinet after the resignation of Prime Minister Tojo, the same news that had been reported earlier in the New Delhi newspapers.

An idea suddenly hit me. What if the new cabinet approved a more lenient surrender policy? Perhaps MO could produce a forged order involving this concept. While Tojo was in control, Japanese troops were indoctrinated with the fanatical belief that surrender was dishonorable and would bring permanent disgrace to family and emperor. If a soldier surrendered, his birthright, *genseki,* was forfeited. He was declared legally dead, and his soul could not return to Japan's spiritual Arlington, Yasukuni Shrine. If recaptured after surrender, a Japanese soldier was subjected to penalties ranging from death by firing squad to banishment from Japan.

Burma was the furthermost outpost of the Japanese empire. What hungry, homesick soldier in those jungles across the Bay of Bengal from us would not welcome the news that Koiso had decided upon a more lenient policy? Perhaps his mandate would be to conserve Japanese manhood for the postwar years when Japan's propagandists envisioned a Greater East Asia Co-prosperity Sphere under imperial domination.

I typed a draft of a proposed forgery, addressed by the Koiso government to the Japanese high command in Rangoon with instructions to disseminate a new order to all forward units. This order rescinded former caveats regarding surrender and announced a new policy. Under certain conditions, when soldiers were hopelessly outnumbered in battle, unconscious, too ill to fight, or without ammunition, it would now be permissible to surrender and demand fair treatment under the Geneva Convention.

Having restructured certain basic aspects of the Japanese army's field manual, I found that my problems had just begun. We needed a Japanese prisoner, preferably with headquarters experience, to rewrite my order, and we needed a reproduction facility. An offset press — the only one available was under the control of British intelligence — was vital because of the method the Japanese used in printing their orders. We would also need proper ink, paper, and official chops, or seals.

As the days dragged by and we had not found answers to our dilemma, a chance remark by Willie Clark galvanized us to action. Over tea one day, Willie told us that the British had captured a college-educated Japanese who refused to cooperate with them. Perhaps, he suggested, Magistretti could try and reach this recalcitrant prisoner who had already lost his *genseki*. A phone call to Magistretti's R&A office brought him into the plot. In a matter of hours he had made contact with a British associate and received permission to meet the prisoner, who was in solitary confinement at the Red Fort.

Magistretti twisted the jeep expertly through

the narrow streets of Old Delhi. The horn parted phalanxes of hucksters, rug merchants, and bullock carts as we made our way to the Red Fort. The massive red sandstone walls of the fort towered above us, still pockmarked with shell holes from the last great Sepoy uprising against the British in 1857. A guard with fixed bayonet passed us into the stockade, where interrogators strolled along shaded paths with Japanese prisoners in blue denim uniforms with POW in large white letters stamped on the back.

We found the commandant, a British major, having tea in a cool mud-floor office near the prisoners' billets. When we explained our mission, he gulped his tea, wiped a few stray leaves from his bushy moustache, and welcomed us aboard. He described Okamoto, the prisoner we wished to interview, as a stubborn but sad young man. He was disillusioned about what he believed would soon be Japan's defeat in Asia, but he wasn't ready to become an intellectual traitor to his country and write propaganda slanted at his buddies in the Burma jungles.

We followed the major through a pleasant garden to a separate billet with barred windows. A guard unlocked the door, and we entered a bare room furnished with a single cot, chair, and table. The prisoner, Okamoto, was facing the window, a squat, short figure in prison uniform with comfortable Punjabi slippers on his feet. He looked around slowly when

Magistretti greeted him. Suddenly he was staring beyond me, studying Magistretti's face intently. All at once his grim face was transformed by a radiant smile. "Biru-Biru Magistretti!" He pushed me aside and extended his hand. "Otomodachi!" ("Friend!")

Magistretti was equally incredulous: "Okamoto-san?" There followed a rapid dialogue in Japanese. Magistretti finally lapsed into English to explain to us the amazing coincidence: the two had been good friends and students together at Waseda University. From then on, Okamoto became a member of the MO family. I think Magistretti convinced him that his hope for a better Japan lay in teaching the postwar generation to accept the concept of a peaceful world.

Okamoto was an apt pupil and quickly mastered MO techniques. After studying my Koiso surrender forgery, he said he could handle it. Before his capture he had been assigned to headquarters in Rangoon and was familiar with military formats. He told us we would need a chop from the high command in Burma to make the document official. We were able to obtain the chop from Willie Clark's supplies, along with the orange-red vegetable dye used in affixing the seal to the order and the rice paper upon which most official business was cyclostyled. Okamoto spent several days perfecting the forgery. When he turned in his finished copy, Magistretti said it looked like it had come from the headquarters of General Homma himself.

Our next step was to get access to the offset press that was under the control of one Maj. Andre Bicat of British intelligence. The original forged order could not be disseminated until it had been copied, since all orders from the central command were replicated by offset.

Magistretti drove me over to Major Bicat's digs at the Council House, home of the Indian legislature. Here, in a stately rotunda with spiraling staircases and a labyrinth of hallways, we tracked down a portly gentleman with crisp red hair and twinkling eyes. To our relief, he expressed immediate interest in our project. "His Majesty's Government pays me to forge documents and passports and odds and ends for these poor blighters they send behind the lines," he said, gesturing toward a pile of papers on his desk. "In my spare time I make dummy paratroopers for deceptive warfare in the jungles. Have to stuff them myself, it's so frightfully secret."

He examined Okamoto's forgery and confessed that the kanji looked like "hen tracks" to him. But he assured me that it would be a simple job to run off, a matter of a day or so. He seemed rather pleased to get some work that had promise of tangible results. I gave him ten sheets of rice paper, orange ink, the seal, and a glob of wax to affix to the documents. That done, we then had tea.

When Major Bicat's office delivered the product to our office in an envelope heavily weighted down with sealing wax and "Top Secret" stamps, we decided to send up a trial balloon, which Willie Clark arranged. A copy of a "captured document" was routed through channels for translation. Several minutes later a Nisei translator rushed to Willie Clark's office saying that he had a very important document. "It's a new surrender policy," he told his boss. "It should eliminate a lot of last-ditch fighting!"

Willie Clark then reported back to us that he believed that our forgery was technically and psychologically perfect. "But where," he asked me, "do you go from here?"

The answer was the fortuitous presence of an MO team passing through New Delhi en route to Detachment 101 in Burma. Team member Roger Starr, later a writer and *New York Times* columnist, agreed to handle the matter. When he reached Colonel Peers's headquarters, the project was cleared with General Stilwell's intelligence staff, and Starr was assigned to work out a plausible scheme to get the forgery into the Japanese line of command. It was imperative that the Japanese believe that the document attested to a bona fide policy.

Starr found the answer in an OSS Kachin agent, a wiry little man trained to ambush and kill Japanese invaders who had taken over his village. Most of his victims were Japanese couriers who traveled alone along the jungle paths through the fluid fronts of northern Burma. Starr instructed his agent that the forgery must be inserted into an official mail pouch.

Several weeks passed before Starr learned what had happened to the order. He came upon the Kachin by chance, lounging outside a *basha*, a thatched hut that served as an OSS office. Yes, he had placed the forgery in the courier's pouch after he had killed him. He had reported to Japanese headquarters in his village and led them to the body. He watched while the soldiers removed the pouch, then buried the courier. He followed them back to his village, where he saw the company commander open the pouch and sift through the contents. When the commander came to the forged order, he showed it to the other soldiers. There was much discussion, but all in Japanese, and the little Kachin slipped away to report back to 101 headquarters.

In order to assure a larger distribution, a "copy" of the order was "delivered" to the U.S. Office of War Information. It was immediately seized by an alert psychological-warfare team operating in the northern Burmese triangle, and a leaflet was designed showing a photostat of the "captured" order. Our planes papered the jungles and the Japanese with the news.

Reports from Detachment 101 forward headquarters later informed our MO team in New Delhi that they believed that the forgery had a direct effect on Japanese soldiers' will to resist, particularly toward the end of the Burma campaign, when Bhamo fell with hardly a struggle. Many incidents were reported of Japanese soldiers feigning unconsciousness and POW compounds crowded with prisoners who gave up when surrounded. As the Burma operation wound down, there were fewer reports of last-ditch fanatical fighting.

Unfortunately, when the military bureaucrat hammered on the desk and asked for figures to prove what MO had done in Burma, no one could produce any concrete results for Washington's records. The casualties in thought warfare couldn't be estimated as closely as body counts. There are no grave crews to report the doubts planted in the minds of troubled fighting men that make them lose their will to fight.

Very shortly after our MO operations against the Japanese army in Burma, I was assigned to the China theater in K'un-ming, where Colonel Heppner had just taken command. He had left a burgeoning OSS organization in Ceylon that was carrying out operations in Siam, Malaya, and French Indochina. Women played important parts in both the planning and the administrative work required to handle these top-secret operations.

CHAPTER 18

Kandy Was Dandy

The first contingent of OSS women to reach their headquarters in Ceylon sailed on 9 March 1944 from California, aboard the one-time luxury liner *Mariposa*, which in the days before Pearl Harbor delivered tourists to Hawaii. There were nine in the group: Virginia Durand, Julia McWilliams, Rosamond Frame, Eleanor Thiry, Virginia Pryor, Louise Banville, Cora DuBois, Jeanne Taylor, and Mary Nelson Lee.

Thiry kept a diary of the trip.[1] "We girls are the source of curiosity in our army fatigues and steel helmets, sharing a tight ship and meals with hundreds of GIs," she wrote. "We are also occasionally the object of wolf calls and whistles. Julia launched a rumor that we are missionaries, which has helped curb the outbursts. Our cabin holds all nine of us, in three sets of triple-decked bunks. There is one bathtub, one toilet, and one sink, with only salt water for bathing. Somehow nine women live together in this crowded space and get along beautifully."

After taking on supplies in Australia in late March, the *Mariposa* picked up a destroyer escort to cross the Indian Ocean, where a Japanese task force had been sighted. On 8 April, after a zigzag crossing, the girls landed safely in Bombay, where Thiry noted a "mysterious haze hanging over the city." A bureaucratic haze also hung over the destination of the OSS women. Adm. Lord Louis Mountbatten had decided to shift his headquarters from New Delhi to Ceylon, where the supreme commander of the South East Asia Command (SEAC) would re-establish his command at Kandy.

Thiry wrote:

Easter Sunday: Off the ship to encounter a real snafu. Our orders were cut for Calcutta, but overnight our destination was switched to Ceylon. The Bombay U.S. military had not been notified, and to add to the confusion, they did not know we were women!

Until all the paperwork was finished, we spent the next ten wonderful days in Bombay, sightseeing, shopping, and enjoying our introduction to the Mysterious East.

Eighteen days later all the girls (except Frame, who went to New Delhi) reached Colombo, the port town where several OSS installations were located. They were jeeped up to Kandy through lush jungles of palms, acacia, and matted liana to their new billet, the aging but picturesque Queen's Hotel in the center of town. "Our OSS offices are grass shacks or *bashas* in the hills beyond the estate where Mountbatten has his headquarters," Thiry wrote in her diary. "Weapons carriers take us to work from our hotel. The men live in *bashas* within the headquarters compound. Colonel Heppner is our commanding officer, and I am to be his secretary. So tomorrow, to work!"

Ceylon was indeed a beautiful place to work and play, remote from the sordid business of war across the bay in Burma. Mountbatten's headquarters became a byword for elegance and luxury, a place where well-groomed staff, many of them titled, were chauffeured in shiny limousines to offices scattered throughout the lush tropical gardens of a tea plantation. There were some 10,000 men and women under Mountbatten's command in India, and eventually 595 in the OSS detachments in Ceylon.

Most of the girls assigned to OSS in Ceylon were new to the Far East; many had never traveled outside the United States. Newcomer Virginia Webbert, an R&A (Reports and Analysis) reports officer for Burma, came straight from Fort Knox, Kentucky. She wrote to friends, "I can't possibly describe how beautiful it is. I am looking out my office window at coconut palms and papaya trees, up the hills to a terraced rice paddy, past a tea plantation to a native pagoda." She continued: "There's so much to see. Buddhist monks in bright saffron robes and shaved heads; the oxcarts, the rickshaws, the little brown naked babies straddling their mothers' hips; the shops of silversmiths; and in the night sky, the new moon lying upside down in this hemisphere."[2]

Another OSS girl assigned to Morale Operations, Jane Foster, reached the pinnacle of social success when she received an engraved invitation for dinner with Mountbatten at the palatial residence. In her autobiography she wrote, "Not only was he handsome, witty, and intelligent, but he was the most charming man I have ever met. He had the great and wonderful gift, during conversation, of making you feel that all his life he had been waiting for your pearls of wisdom, and that he was sincere, at least for the moment."[3]

Julia McWilliams (later Child) reported in as head of Registry. After her long ocean trip, she wrote to her family of life in this tropical rear echelon:

> I find Kandy has a delightful climate, skin-warm all the time. Life is pastoral. Our office is a series of palm-thatched huts connected by cement walks, surrounded by native workmen and barbed wire. It is somewhat primitive, but airy and far from dressy. There are movies and dances twice a week at the American officers' club, walks in the moonlight. On Sundays there are pic-

nics, golf, tennis, swimming, or a weekend down in Colombo, depending entirely upon the enterprise of yourself in enticing the enterprise of the other gender.

The future French Chef never mentioned Ceylonese culinary customs; that interest would come much later, when the war was long over. However, she did find a way to outwit military censorship, which forbade any mention of location in letters home: she quoted Ogden Nash's now famous mini-poem in a letter to friends in Washington, "Candy is dandy, but liquor is quicker."[4]

In a letter home that she still has, yellowed with age, Millicent Amstutz, a reports officer with the Secret Intelligence staff, described the nightlife of half a century ago in Kandy. After a grueling week writing reports for her boss, Lloyd George, she relaxed on Saturday night at the officers' club: "This club is open on all sides on a hill overlooking the river. The moonlight is so bright it seems like day. On one jolly occasion, an enthusiastic British couple rode a bicycle around the dance floor during intermission! The music always stops at midnight, and everyone hates to leave immediately, so they sing on into the early-morning hours, those wonderful songs: 'Lili Marlene,' 'I'll Be Seeing You.' "

As those lighthearted memories attest, Ceylon was not a hardship post. But important missions were carried out from there against the Japanese. During the twenty-one months that OSS functioned in SEAC, operations were conducted in southern Burma, Siam, Malaysia, the Andaman Islands, Sumatra, the adjacent islands of the Dutch East Indies, and, finally, French Indochina. A total of twenty-four hundred intelligence reports were transmitted to Washington; 215 native agents were trained; and 125 different operations were launched into Japanese-held territory. Despite the tangled administrative structure of the theater in this British-dominated war zone, OSS maintained its status as a purely American agency and supplied American military and State Department representatives with the only regular, independent U.S. source of intelligence on the enemy that was available throughout much of the region.

The most senior OSS woman in Ceylon was Dr. Cora DuBois, acting head of R&A in Ceylon in 1944–45, a lean, handsome woman with a habit of peering quizzically over her glasses as she discussed operations with her staff. DuBois was an anthropologist, a graduate of Columbia University with a master's degree from the University of California. She specialized in Southeast Asian affairs and was an instructor at Sarah Lawrence College when she was recruited by OSS.

There was still something of the schoolteacher in her, trying to cope with military rigidity. Her acerbic cables to her R&A chief in Washington, requesting additional personnel, reveal both her frustration and her perspicacity: "24 August 1944: R&A is poorly staffed in comparison with other operational branches here. It may be an impertinence to tell you that SEAC is the largest unexploited colonial region in the Far East and therefore a potential bone of contention between us and colonial powers in the future." And in an intramural memo to her boss, Colonel Heppner, she had the temerity to suggest an improved modus operandi for the OSS base in Ceylon involving more careful and integrated planning at all levels: "At present I feel that each branch operates in relation to any one project as though it were an isolated abstraction. The tendency for responsible people to gallop madly over the countryside should be controlled administratively."[5]

Colonel Heppner reacted as an officer, a gentleman, and a slightly miffed male. In a progress report to Washington he wrote, "Miss DuBois is an exceedingly brilliant woman. Personally our relations with her are the best. However, she is sharp and tactless and sometimes overbearing. I think you have the usual problems with army officers being placed under a woman's command, which causes trouble."[6] Eventually DuBois's persistence was rewarded, and her concept of integrating R&A into much of headquarters planning was realized. Her branch ultimately participated in almost every phase of OSS operations, from the determination of tactical objectives to training techniques for native agents.

Much of R&A's focus was in support of operations in Siam. DuBois believed that this country was politically the most important postwar consideration in Southeast Asia. Strategically, she maintained, it was of vital importance to Japan in wartime; from a clandestine point of view it was the most accessible. Siam was the crossroads for Japanese troops traveling overland between Burma, Malaysia, Indochina, and China. It was also the spawning ground for the only organized resistance against the Japanese in Asia originated by indigenous peoples.

OSS helped support and organize that resistance by dropping men and equipment into the jungle hideouts and into the very heart of Bangkok itself, where OSS agents were billeted in one of the royal palaces. An R&A report in late 1945 noted that more than two hundred reports a month were filed, including intelligence requirements, location of bomb targets, and descriptions of troop locations and movements.

For her work in support of Siamese operations, DuBois was awarded the Order of the Crown of Thailand after the war, and Colonel Heppner signed off on her Exceptional Civilian Award. DuBois later returned to Washington to work in the Department of State's Office of Intelligence Research before returning to academic life at Harvard and Radcliffe College. She died in 1994.

One of DuBois's colleagues in charge of Burmese R&A was Wellesley graduate Virginia Webbert, the only professional woman staffer working on strategic planning against the Burmese peninsula.

Her reports were also geared toward aiding downed Allied airmen. She developed instructions to these fliers on where to seek help from tribes friendly to the Allies and included amounts and types of currency needed. In addition, she wrote up geographical data for specific operations, both military and industrial. Her town studies were particularly effective, reporting the influence of the Japanese on the political, social, and economic life of a particular town or village. Her work also included estimates of reconstruction requirements after hostilities ended.

One of her colleagues at Washington headquarters, Bernice Hanson, later recalled Webbert's method of operation to me: "She was slow but methodical and refused to perform a task before she fully understood it herself. As a result, her work was painstakingly thorough and accurate and in the end proved she was completely reliable in her reporting."[7]

The men in the organization had mixed reactions to the women who were sharing their assignments in SEAC. Capt. Oliver Caldwell, son of China missionaries, later wrote, "If I were making arrangements for an ideal war, I would insist that no women were permitted in forward areas. Regardless of the gallantry and dedication of individual women, the injection of sex into a wartime situation establishes an intolerable obstacle to discipline, without which not much of anything can be achieved." Lt. Comdr. Edmond Taylor was another critic. This well-known foreign correspondent — author of the classic *The Strategy of Terror*, bon vivant, and aide to Colonel Heppner — was quoted in a 1944 memo to OSS headquarters in Washington, "It is urgently requested that great care be given in the selection of female personnel for SEAC. From now on the women must be healthy, able, and at the same time should have a degree of sophistication and experience that qualifies them for coping with the unusual situations they will find in Ceylon."[8]

But another one-time foreign correspondent for the *Baltimore Sun*, James M. Cannon, disagreed with Taylor, his immediate boss: "Detachment 404 was the first place in my experience where women were given professional responsibility and succeeded very well. They proved they could do the work as well as the men." Cannon, who shared a large office with other Secret Intelligence colleagues, described the work of a young woman lawyer, Charlene Roland, in charge of the Japanese order of battle: "She would sit over in a corner — we had no private offices — surrounded by maps and charts. She was completely engrossed in tracing Japanese troop movements, to the extent that she'd sometimes sing softly to herself. I can still remember one dirge: 'Oh General Nakamura, can't you hear me cry? If I can't locate you, I think that I shall die!' She was of Scotch-Irish descent, with a fine sense of humor."[9]

Roland's job was to make sense out of bits and pieces of information about Japanese rail and troop movements, information received by shortwave radio and filed on index cards. OSS agents infiltrated Japanese-held territory, risking their lives to transmit intelligence data to Ceylon. Many were students from occupied countries who had been studying in the United States when recruited by OSS. One of Cannon's jobs was to brief them before they left Ceylon. He drove the teams in the early-morning hours before takeoff to a remote area of a tea plantation, where they had a last good meal and reviewed instructions. Roland's order-of-battle material was always part of this last briefing.

Roland remembers a report she filed at the end of the war that revealed the discovery of a Japanese labor camp filled with Allied prisoners, starving and sick with dysentery. They had been forced to build a railroad from Burma to Siam. Years later when she saw the Academy

Award–winning movie *The Bridge on the River Kwai*, she realized that she had transmitted to Washington the first report about this unfortunate group of men.

Lord Louis Mountbatten, his staff, and the American military were also briefed by Roland, and at the end of the war she was awarded the Emblem of Meritorious Civilian Service. The commendation noted that "Miss Roland originated and put into effect the Order-of-Battle [O.B.] for SEAC. Her work consisted of keeping records of Japanese and Allied troop movements, writing intelligence summaries, updating the O.B. map in the headquarters war room. She was commended for her superior judgment in fulfilling her duties."[10]

Another field open to very few women overseas was the Communications Branch, involving the encoding and decoding of messages. One of those assigned to SEAC was Barbara Hans, who said she was qualified because she was good at crossword puzzles and acrostics.

Hans had just graduated from Smith College when war broke out and was living with her mother in Mount Kisco, New York. Both women wanted to get overseas, but the daughter was the lucky one. "I wanted to go where the action was," Hans recounted to me later. "And war had drained Mount Kisco of all the eligible bachelors. I took an exam for the

OSS Communications Branch and passed it. The training was boring: double transpositions, garbled messages, one-time pads. But I did go overseas." Hans went to Ceylon aboard a crowded troopship with eight other girls under the strict supervision of an OSS lieutenant commander, Gweneth Zarfoss; her only comment was "Wow." Thirty-two days later they arrived in India.

"Sometimes I wished I had never left Mount Kisco," Hans said. "I spent half my time in Kandy locked up in a cage on night duty, receiving and sending cable traffic to and from the Arakan, OSS drops, and Detachment 101." One of her happy memories of the war: attending a reception at Mountbatten's estate in Kandy. "He wasn't as tall as I had imagined him, but he was very good looking."

Another flashback: "We girls were lined up in Kandy to receive awards after the war was over. Our commanding officer, Col. John Coughlin, very West Pointish, had trouble with a buxom beauty in décolleté blouse nicknamed the Black Tulip. He couldn't find a proper place to pin the ribbon on her bosom, so he finally presented it to her, saluted, and hastily continued the ceremony while ignoring our girlish giggles."

What Mount Kisco failed to do for Barbara Hans was accomplished by OSS. At war's end she met her future husband and OSS colleague, John Waller, who today is a noted author on

World War II operations.

In those faraway days before computers compacted and stored input on wafer-thin metallic film, there was a system known as Index Files, consisting of thousands of five-by-eight cards that often occupied acres of office space.

Voluminous collections of intelligence data were stored under lock and key in OSS registries around the world. In Ceylon, Julia McWilliams was keeper of the secrets and the head of Kandy Registry. As she saw her job, it combined a sense of responsibility, executive know-how, and a trained and imaginative mind. For McWilliams, a sense of humor was also obligatory.

Something of the scope of McWilliams's work can be seen in a report she sent back on 6 October 1944 to the head registrar in Washington, Margaret Griggs:

Our in-and-out material has been snowballing. Of 365 Washington pouches received in September, there are about 600 pieces that had to be accessioned, cross indexed, circulated, filed. This figure does not include our operational and intelligence input from the field.

Our cross index is definitely our soul and savior. We are slowly breaking it up into a uniform, fool-proof locator system, I hope. We have much to do to systematize procedures so documents can be related and our relations with OWI [the Office of War Information], the Theater Commander, Air Force, etc. are clear. We keep master cards on each current subject which means my staff must be completely familiar with what is going on. For example: cards for S.I. include names of all agents, student recruits and their various code names.[11]

McWilliams retained her sense of humor throughout her tour. In a request to Griggs on 9 May 1944 she asked that the Code and Cipher Branch in Washington air-pouch "one of those books you have, giving people numbers and funny names like Fruitcake #385." She added that she kept finding references to these "funny" (i.e., pseudo) names, but no one could identify them. She promised that the book would be kept "very securely in a fireproof Mauser safe and will be available to no one except Colonel Heppner." She often lightened official requests for information with postscripts like this one of 25 May 1944: "If you don't send Registry that report we need, I shall fill the next Washington pouch with itching powder and virulent bacteriological diseases, and change all the numbers, as well as translating the material into Singhalese, and destroying the English version."

One of McWilliams's ablest assistants in Kandy was a young woman from Illinois, Patty

Norbury. As McWilliams described her, Norbury was about five feet five and wonderfully reliable, with a pretty laughing face, nice figure, and glasses: "We had a good time together, especially sending out tongue-in-cheek instructions which every recipient had to read and initial. Once we described in detail our new filing system which we named Bellows-Wellcombe, where all documents were classified under the letter of their last word and the vaults, when full, were sealed. No one ever failed to initial these documents, which were absolutely fraudulent."

The reason Norbury requested an OSS assignment in Ceylon was to locate her fiancé, Lt. Roy Wentz Jr., a bombardier with the Tenth Air Force who had been shot down in Burma and given up for lost by everyone but Norbury. She was certain he was alive. After Burma fell, Wentz was discovered in the Insein jail near Rangoon, starved and ill with dysentery. They were reunited in Calcutta and were married later in Wilmington, Delaware, where Roy Wentz became a lawyer in the Dupont empire.

Another Registry report, carefully filed under "Misc.," gave as its source British reports of Japanese intelligence bulletins, evaluated A-1: "It has been reliably reported that OSS/SEAC is planning some kind of a blow-out commemorating a British-American controversy in the late 18th century. All OSS personnel will participate at Bittersweet Basha, opening the Officers' new day room on July Fourth!" McWilliams recalls that there were plenty of firecrackers and refreshments at the party and toasts to the Stars and Stripes as British colleagues glumly sipped their gin and tonics.

After graduating from Smith College, McWilliams worked in the W&J Sloane advertising department in New York City before joining OSS "because I was too tall to get into the WACs or WAVEs," she claims. She spent one happy year with the OSS Emergency Sea Rescue Equipment Section in Washington, engaged part of the time in developing a shark repellent: "I must say we had lots of fun. I was an executive administrator working with Harold Coolidge, head of Special Projects. We designed rescue kits and other agent paraphernalia. I understand the shark repellent we developed is being used today for downed space equipment — strapped around it so the sharks won't attack it when it lands in the ocean."

McWilliams met her future husband, Paul Cushing Child, when he was posted to Ceylon in charge of Visual Presentation for R&A. Paul was a painter, photographer, mapmaker, art and French teacher, lumberjack, furniture maker, and holder of a black belt in judo. "It was not love at first sight," Julia recalled. "He was very sophisticated. He had lived in France, and I had only been to Tijuana, so I found him very impressive, you see. And he was intellectual while I was a kind of California butterfly, a golf player and tennis person." They were later posted to China together, where "we courted around a bit," as she described their wartime romance. "War was sort of an artificial life, and we wanted to see each other in a home environment. We were married in 1946."

Before leaving China, McWilliams was given the Emblem of Meritorious Civilian Service by Colonel Heppner. The citation read, "Head of the Registry of OSS Secretariat. Important job calculating and channeling a great amount of classified documents. Her drive and inherent cheerfulness served as a spur to greater effort by those working for her."[12]

When Japan surrendered in August 1945, Dr. Cora DuBois summed up the situation in Southeast Asia based upon R&A intelligence reports:

> The Japanese, by breaking up the European colonial system, seem to be advancing the cause of nationalism in Southeast Asia. They have injected a new confidence in the natives and it will be next to impossible for them to go back to their old way of life. The British, French and Dutch have no positive program to offer these people, who witnessed the defeat of the European colonialists at the hands of the Japanese. The United States has a backlog of prestige over here now, but the generalities of our foreign

policy must be made specific or we will soon lose this prestige.[13]

One of the areas DuBois saw as a potential powder keg was Indonesia; and one of the few OSS staffers in Ceylon who spoke Malay and knew the country was Jane Foster, who had gone through training with me in Washington. At war's end she was to be the first OSS woman assigned to Indonesia, days after President Ahmed Sukarno proclaimed the independence of that country.

Foster was an unreconstructed rebel, perhaps in part because of her Irish heritage. The only daughter of a wealthy San Francisco family, she was educated at Mills College and traveled extensively in Europe after graduation. She saw Hitler's Germany and Mussolini's Italy and was sickened by totalitarianism. Upon her return to San Francisco, she met and married a Dutch civil servant from Indonesia who when he took her home to Java introduced her to another of her pet hates: colonialism in the Dutch East Indies. After two years of unsuccessful married life in Java where her own artistic individualism was denied and she was expected to bow to her husband's demands, Foster returned to the United States. Disillusioned and rebelling against events abroad, she joined the Communist Party in 1939. Over the years Foster continued to be a rebel but says that her ties to communism loosened and finally the ideology no longer sustained her.

Her second husband, whom she married in 1941, was George Zlatovski, a Russian Jew whose doctor-father had migrated to Duluth, Minnesota, in 1922. They met prior to World War II in New York City, where they were both active in Communist Party work until Zlatovski joined the Army Corps of Engineers and was sent overseas. Foster was recruited by OSS where, in general, Communist Party affiliations were ignored. At that time in history the Russians were allies, fighting fascism on all fronts, sustaining huge casualties during Hitler's brutal invasion of their homeland.

While in Ceylon, Foster worked mainly in Morale Operations (MO) as both an artist and a writer, assigned to Indonesian targets. Her claim to almost instant fame occurred during an inspection tour when General Donovan and entourage visited Kandy. The general made a stop at the MO *basha* to see firsthand some of the production. His attention was directed to a corner of the room where Foster and two young Ceylonese women were busy at a large table. They were stuffing messages into rubber condoms. Expertly, they blew air into the condoms, tied a quick knot, and threw them, one by one, into a large bouncing pile. Foster hastened to explain to the general, who stood over her with a bemused smile on his Irish face, "These are messages to Indonesians urging them to resist the Japanese. Our agents release

391

hundreds of them by submarine along the coastline." Reportedly General Donovan nodded brusquely, asked no further questions, and beat a hasty retreat.[14]

Jane later confided to friends that she had had something of a problem obtaining the condoms in the first place. She had gone over to the resident OSS doctor's office where navy commander Willis Murphy met her for what he thought was an office visit. His eyebrows arched slightly when she said she needed some condoms. "When I said, 'Yes, Murphy, about five hundred,' he dropped his stethoscope and just stared at me in complete disbelief."[15]

It was on 20 August 1945, shortly after Japan had capitulated to the nuclear attacks on Hiroshima and Nagasaki, that Foster was summoned to the office of the commanding officer of the OSS detachment, Col. John Coughlin. He had succeeded Colonel Heppner, reassigned to the China theater. Coughlin asked Foster if she would consider a risky assignment in Indonesia. He pointed out that she was one of the few OSS operatives who had kept up with the political situation in Indonesia, and who also spoke the language. He could not order her to go; she would have to volunteer her services. The Indonesians were in revolt against the return of the Dutch; there was also reportedly a large contingent of the Japanese army in central Java, ready for a bloody last-ditch stand.

Foster enthusiastically agreed, and Coughlin outlined her duties: she was to supervise repatriation of American military and civilian prisoners; take war-crimes testimony; and observe and report daily Indonesian political developments to OSS headquarters in Washington.

She arrived in the Javanese capital city of Batavia after helping the navigator find the unmarked airport, which fortunately was familiar to her. She recalled that en route, the pilot buzzed the perimeter of the field where American prisoners of war were being held for repatriation. She was billeted at the Batavia Hotel, guarded by Japanese soldiers under the watchful eye of a small force of British Royal Marines. Her OSS boss was Maj. Frederick Crockett, who had arrived shortly before her aboard a British warship. Foster said that he knew nothing of the language and very little of the country, but he was a most engaging officer who allowed her a free hand in carrying out her assignment.

Foster's first job was to interview prisoners and ascertain the extent of war crimes. She determined what crimes had been committed by individual Japanese officers, usually the *kempeitai,* the hated Japanese gestapo, who had by now escaped to central Java with a small contingent of Japanese troops. The Japanese remaining in Batavia were personnel who had elected to accept their emperor's surrender and were willing to work with the Allied conquerors.

Foster processed some five hundred American prisoners — navy, army, and air corps as well as civilian. She worked sometimes twenty hours a day taking testimony. "They were a sorry lot . . . ," she wrote in her report. "Naked, emaciated, infested with lice, yellow from malaria but still dazed by sudden freedom after years behind bars."[16] From intelligence reports Foster had anticipated a shortage of clothing. Before she left Ceylon she took up a collection for women prisoners that she called Janey's Javanese Junkshop. OSS women were generous in their donations, and several crates of clothes and other necessities were shipped to Foster in Batavia.

Acting as an interpreter, Foster also attended meetings of OSS representatives with President Sukarno, leader of the independence movement during the Japanese occupation. She said that Sukarno outlined the aims of his new government to them and gave her copies of the constitution of the new republic, which called for, among other principles, democracy, unity, and social justice for all the people.

Sukarno also informed his American friends that he was having difficulty holding back the Indonesian populace, which threatened to attack the Dutch who were trying to reclaim the country. He did not know how long he could handle the situation. Overseas, Dutch forces were not yet available for release from their own war-ravaged country to come recover their colony, and the British troops maintained an uneasy truce. However, using American arms and equipment that were just arriving, the Dutch colonials in Batavia began to kill Indonesians in open street warfare. At that point OSS headquarters ordered Foster evacuated. She came back to Washington by ship, at her own request, in order to properly prepare her assessment of the situation in Indonesia. Upon reaching headquarters she was instructed to brief Dean Acheson, undersecretary of state, on the situation as she saw it in Southeast Asia.

The anticommunist hysteria that swept the country in the early 1950s swept Jane Foster and her Russian-born husband into the vortex of the storm. In addition to personally presenting and briefing her report on Indonesia to Secretary Acheson, Foster also gave a copy of it to one Jack Sobel, who passed it to his Russian comrades at the United Nations. This led eventually to Senator Joseph McCarthy's witch-hunt against the Zladovskis, who by that time were working in Austria with the U.S. Information Service. They were indicted for espionage but never faced the charge in the United States. They were granted asylum in France and lived there until they both died. In her autobiography Jane quoted a passage from Aeschylus that perhaps summed up what must have been, at the end, a very sad life: "How easy for one who fares in pleasant ways to admonish those in adversity. With eyes open, with willing mind, I erred. I do not deny it. Mankind I helped, but could not help myself."

Many women who were posted to India ended their careers in OSS in the China theater. Julia McWilliams took over the Registry in K'un-ming. Elly Thiry went to Chungking, the capital of Free China and the Nationalist headquarters, again as secretary to Colonel Heppner. Marjorie Severyns switched to Secret Intelligence and later became a correspondent for *Life* magazine. Rosamond Frame compiled target studies for R&A. All of us, including myself, met our future husbands under the wide blue skies of western China.

Here too there was intrigue between Chiang Kai-shek's Kuomintang party and Mao Tse-tung's agents, who infiltrated communist women spies into Nationalist strongholds. There were intransigent Free French forces from Indochina who refused to serve under the Chinese military while an OSS recruit, Ho Chi Minh, worked with Americans in an early effort to unite his country. And when the war abruptly ended, there were the final heroic rescues of Allied prisoners from Japanese slave camps throughout Asia.

The China theater was the furthermost eastern outpost in Asia of Donovan's far-flung OSS empire. In many ways it was also the most challenging, requiring insight and tact in dealing with an alien culture and a country already torn apart by armed rivals with diametrically opposed political concepts.

CHAPTER 19

Over the Hump
to China

Agnes Davis Greene is one of the few OSS women today who can trace the effectiveness of OSS in China in the mid-1940s, when political positioning came first and the war against Japan was a secondary issue. Agnes Greene was there.

We were reliving those days of OSS in China, relaxing at the retirement home in Fort Myers, Florida, where she and her husband, George, live. Greene is a genuine old China hand, an authority on the political mirage that was China in World War II. "OSS started limited operations in the China theater in January 1943 under SACO, the acronym for Sino-American Cooperative Organization," Greene began her recollections, tracing the events that led up to her wartime experiences.

Agnes's parents were missionaries in Shanghai, where she was born and educated. She spent four years at Ohio Wesleyan College and then returned to China in 1933. There she met George Greene, a graduate of the University of Michigan and an officer with the Bank of Shanghai. Fluent in Chinese, he had a fine career ahead of him before the Japanese invasion of China changed their lives. On a business trip in early December 1941 George was captured and interned at Santo Tomas when the Japanese attacked the Philippines. He was eventually repatriated on the *Gripsholm*. Agnes and her parents had fled China earlier and returned to the United States.

Agnes Greene's memory flashed back over half a century, to a China in upheaval under Japanese rule. In the mid-1930s, Chinese communists led by Mao Tse-tung had made the long march north to the mountains of Yenan, where they had established an enclave. The Nationalists, under Generalissimo Chiang Kai-shek, set up their capital in Chungking, Szechuan Province, West China. The chief communist representatives in Chungking were cosmopolitan, charming Chou En-lai and his aide, intelligence chief Kang Sheng, the son of bourgeois parents who had opted to join the Communist Party and had been trained in intelligence work in Moscow. There were also embassy and military representatives from Britain, the United States, the Soviet Union, France, and the Netherlands, all with varied postwar goals.

Greene continued:

Under SACO, OSS worked with the Chinese Nationalists and also with a U.S. navy group under Capt. Milton Miles, which operated a coast watch reporting to the U.S. Pacific Fleet on weather and Japanese shipping. Head of Chiang's secret service was a tough little cop, Gen. Tai Li, who controlled some four hundred spy stations throughout China, focusing mainly on maverick warlords who were building up their own fiefdoms. Tai Li was loyal only to Chiang and resented OSS, a foreign intelligence service operating in his country.

There were two long years of intramural fighting before OSS became an autonomous agency, developing intelligence sources and programming sabotage and morale operations against the Japanese, all of which Tai Li claimed to have penetrated.

Greene also pointed out that even the early American command in China was not particularly open to OSS activities. Gen. Joseph Stilwell's primary concern was to develop a fighting force of American and Chinese to challenge the Japanese in Burma, where he came to depend a great deal on the support of OSS Detachment 101. Our American ambassador, Clarence Gauss, diplomatically chose to work with Chiang.

Greene noted that these two men had instituted a ban forbidding women from entering the China theater. Stilwell and Gauss both agreed that the presence of females in a war zone was unacceptable, especially since all essential materiel had to be flown over the Hump, a treacherous divide between jagged spurs of the Himalayas known as the Skyway to Hell. Pilots rated it the most dangerous, terrifying aerial transport run in the world, crossing five hundred miles of uncharted mountains and jungle at twenty thousand feet from upper Assam in India to the Yunnan plateau.

U.S. National Archives files corroborate Greene's point. In a cable sent from Col. Robert Hall, OSS headquarters, Washington, to Capt. Ray Cromley, OSS K'un-ming, the message was loud and clear: "You [Cromley] want a Miss La Donna Anderson assigned your office. Even General Chennault has been unable to bring in women secretaries. Women in China have been one of the hottest issues in the theater. Many men seeking to end this controversy have acquired badly burned fingers. Both Stilwell and Gauss bitterly oppose it. It is not a profitable issue upon which to stick out your neck."

Agnes Greene worked for months in the OSS New Delhi station with the Secret Intelligence Branch (SI) waiting for orders to proceed to China. She had been recruited by a former China friend, Margaret Griggs of Washington, who had also hired Agnes's father, Dr. Walter Davis, for a position with Research and Analysis (R&A). Her break came in late 1944 when

Gen. Albert C. Wedemeyer took over as chief of American forces in China, relieving Stilwell. General Wedemeyer's opposite number at the American embassy was a colorful, outspoken Oklahoman, Ambassador Patrick J. Hurley, who replaced China-wise Clarence Gauss. Colonel Heppner, a good friend of General Wedemeyer from SEAC days, became the chief of the OSS detachment in China.

In his book *Wedemeyer Reports* the general said that he had initially opposed assignment of women in advance battle areas, but while in New Delhi with the South East Asia Command (SEAC) he realized that "it would work out all right. The women proved to be invaluable, their conduct exemplary." This change regarding women in the China theater was also reflected in a wire that Colonel Heppner sent to OSS headquarters, New Delhi, from Chungking: "We can find very good use for girls now working in India. We are in dire need of secretaries and since living conditions are very good, I think they would be happy in their assignments."

Agnes Greene was one of the first OSS women to arrive in Chungking in late 1944, together with Rosamond Frame (an R&A officer) and secretaries Virginia Durand, Marthabelle Kirshaw, and Eleanor Thiry, who by now was also Colonel Heppner's office manager. "I was slated for China without knowing the eventual destination of my husband," Greene recalled.

"I was both surprised and delighted when he showed up in Chungking three months after me, posted to an assignment with R&A. We thought we were in real trouble then. Through some bureaucratic glitch, we were in the same theater, contrary to General Donovan's orders. Luckily Dick Heppner needed someone with George's potential, so he kept us both. Our conjugal relationship was never officially reported to headquarters."

During his tenure, George Greene, one-time banker and successful businessman in Shanghai, prepared important studies on economic conditions in occupied China and was able to establish contact with business sources in key Chinese cities then under Japanese control.

Eleanor Thiry, who arrived in Chungking with this first contingent of women, wrote of her arrival in a secret diary, which she kept, in shorthand, against security regulations: "It was a foggy evening when our plane touched down. Near one of the hangars we could see a few of Chennault's Flying Tiger aircraft, their engine cowlings overpainted with grotesque dragon faces. Chungking was built on hundreds of hills. Lights were flickering up and down like an army of fireflies. The Yangtze was a river of silver flowing through the center of town."[1]

Thiry was delighted with Green Gate, where the women were billeted: "It's a lovely rambling residence on a hilltop. We climb 150 steps to reach the green gate, which opens on a garden.

The living room is spacious, with a large fireplace at one end and French doors opening onto the gardens. Most of us have separate bedrooms. Mine has a small balcony that overlooks the city far below."

Green Gate was about five bumpy miles from the OSS office. The women were driven to work in jeeps. The office headquarters overlooked the Yangtze from a street noisy day and night with the high-pitched din of squeaky buses, riverboat whistles, the singsong dirges of coolies loading cargo, and squealing pigs being driven to market. Even the sky above this capital city of Free China was not exempt from the day-and-night buzzing of aircraft. There was none of the hush-hush atmosphere associated with clandestine operations. The OSS building, recently constructed, was bugged — not by devices hidden in the walls but by ingratiating Chinese employees reporting back to either the Nationalists or the communists, or both.

A comprehensive study — *OSS in China: Prelude to Cold War* — was recently written by a Chinese scholar, Dr. Maochun Yu, and published by Yale University Press. Dr. Yu had access to Chinese communist documents during the period he studied in Tientsin at Nankai University. He later emigrated to the United States, where he attended Swarthmore College and the University of California at Berkeley. He is now an instructor in Asian history at the U.S. Naval Academy, Annapolis. In

404

his study Dr. Yu reports that a massive intelligence buildup by Russians and communist Chinese from Yenan was aimed primarily at the Nationalist government, although OSS activities were also penetrated. Thousands of secret agents under Chou En-lai's direction gathered information on policy, personnel, and the activities of Chiang's people, specifically on Tai Li's Bureau of Investigation and Statistics (BIS). Chou even placed one of his best agents, Yan Bachang, as a military adviser in the Nationalist army, with the rank of lieutenant general.

In February 1942 Tai Li had uncovered a communist espionage ring in the heart of his telecommunications center. Penetration was organized by an attractive woman, eighteen-year-old Moscow-trained Zhang Luping. She supplied Yenan with personnel charts of BIS as well as the location of Tai Li's radio stations across the continent, their frequencies, and codes. All this information was systematically forwarded to 15 Zenjiayan Road, Chou En-lai's quarters. From there it was relayed by secret transmitters to Yenan. One of the code clerks was Yan Bachang's daughter, Yan Mingfu, who also had been trained in Moscow.

The Chou En-lai ring also penetrated OSS in Chungking. One of the most flagrant violations of OSS security involved a deputy chief of OSS stationed in K'un-ming who made weekly business (and also pleasure) trips to Chungking.

Dr. Yu notes that "through suave hobnobbing" Yan Bachang was able to "help in arranging a serene house on the river in the suburbs as a setting for hitherto furtive trysts the high-ranking officer had held with a beautiful OSS secretary in his Chungking office."

As a token of his gratitude, the deputy chief asked Yan how he could repay him. A seemingly harmless reciprocal arrangement was suggested. Yan had heard that OSS was training young Chinese soldiers at a parachute school at K'ai-yüan, Yunnan. Could the deputy chief arrange to admit some of his relatives and friends to this school? They wanted to serve their country and work with OSS. Recruits for the training program were still being accepted, and the OSS officer readily agreed. Chinese communist history records that a company of young Chinese communists from Yenan, loyal to Mao Tse-tung, were accepted and trained by OSS. A dramatic "mutiny" of one of three OSS-trained crack parachute teams occurred during the communist takeover by Mao in 1949, hastening the defeat of the Nationalist government.

Meanwhile, in Chungking, OSS agents also continued their undercover work. Both Greene and Frame spent their days at the office, analyzing reports from OSS teams scattered throughout China, interrogating agents, and writing reports on their findings. Greene, who eventually became head of SI, shared duties at first with SI chief Col. John Whittaker, a former *Chicago Daily News* correspondent, and with Maj. Quentin Roosevelt, grandson of Theodore Roosevelt and Donovan's personal representative to the Chiang government. Work for the two women spies did not end when they locked their safes and left the office for the day; Greene and Frame were always most welcome at parties and official functions in the Chinese capital, partially because there was an acute shortage of attractive female dinner partners, but also because both spoke excellent Chinese.

Frame and Greene depended a great deal on Colonel Whittaker, whose quick mind Frame once described to me as a "searchlight playing on the ill defined shadows of intrigue, confusion and doubt that beclouded so many issues in Chinese political circles." After the former reporter had channeled their thinking, suggested leading questions, and explained the situation, he would often end the friendly session with the typical newsman's admonition: "Pump 'em, girls, pump 'em!"

Frame's job with R&A focused on reports from OSS's fast-growing command post at Sian in Shensi Province, about a thousand miles north of Chungking. Frame's office charted eleven Chinese secret-society representatives in Sian, composed of moneyed groups who placed their own interests above the national welfare and frequently collaborated with the Japanese. A smuggling racket was also exposed when

OSS men captured the mistress of the leader of an espionage ring. She was transmitting information about the OSS detachment to the Japanese, writing with a millet-gruel ink that became visible when treated with iodine.

Like Greene, Frame was born in Shanghai of missionary parents. Her mother was Alice Browne Caldwell, president of Yenching University. Frame was graduated from Mount Holyoke College in 1937 and became a concert pianist. She was petite and energetic, with a cordial manner that won over friends and enemies alike. Her ear for language was as good as her talent for music. Frame understood eleven Chinese dialects. She began her work with OSS in New Delhi, working with my former roommate there, Joy Homer, a young liberal writer who had worked with our American-supported flood-relief committee in North China before the war. The two women were assigned the job of infiltrating suspect delegations from China to India during 1943–44. Some of these were known to be Japanese agents, and others were hired to spy on the British and Americans in New Delhi by the Chiang government.

Frame and Homer were instrumental in exposing two Chinese officials who were transmitting information to Japanese in Singapore. One night, when Homer was walking home to her billet along the dark streets in New Delhi, a mysterious accident occurred. Homer was run over by an automobile that veered off the street and sideswiped her on the sidewalk. She reported that the driver was Asiatic. Homer was so badly injured that she was sent home. Frame left shortly after that for assignment in Chungking, where she was already listed on Tai Li's roster as a "dangerous thinker."

At the same time that new OSS women were checking into Chungking's Green Gate, the OSS advance base in K'un-ming four hundred miles south of Chungking was also expanding. I flew over the Hump in a storm-tossed flight with imperturbable Julia McWilliams, who calmly read a book while all the rest of us were preparing to die. By war's end, thirty women had been stationed in this frontier country of western China.

The OSS compound was located on the outskirts of town, surrounded by high mud walls. Before the war K'un-ming had been a resort town, the end of the rail line from Indochina where French colonials spent their vacations enjoying this invigorating mountain retreat, the sparkling sunshine, and the medieval ambience of the walled city itself. To the north was a beautiful lake with a fleet of fishing sampans. Towering above the city was West Mountain, the landmark for Hump and combat pilots nearing that welcome safe haven, K'un-ming Airport. K'un-ming was also the end of the Burma Road, closed from 1942 to early 1945 while the Japanese controlled that country.

Vital military supplies were now arriving aboard lumbering trucks caked with red clay from Burma.

Most of the women at K'un-ming headquarters had special operational skills. Julia McWilliams continued the important job of organizing Registry material, as she had done in Ceylon. Reports were coming in constantly from OSS field missions that were gradually spreading out to China's coastal cities. One priority target was the pinpointing of prisoner-of-war camp sites. Later this specific intelligence data enabled OSS rescue teams to zero in on these camps accurately and liberate Allied prisoners held by the Japanese.

A reports officer recently arrived from the OSS Cairo station, Mary Livingston Eddy, worked closely with McWilliams. One of Eddy's first moves to energize a rather slow-moving Message Center was to saw a hole in the wooden floor of her office directly above the communications-center office downstairs. Through this hole she could pass a small wicker basket with bell attached, to expedite the flow of cable traffic.

Capt. Emily Shek of New York City was one of the few OSS WACs in K'un-ming. Earlier she had worked in Washington in Special Operations and had made an extensive study of Formosa as part of a strategic intelligence survey for the Fourteenth Air Force in China. She marked time in Ceylon waiting for a clearance to China. On the long flight from Assam to K'un-ming, waggish OSS colleagues aboard introduced Emily Shek as Chiang Kai-shek's sister.

Shek continued to work on target studies, focusing on Hong Kong, where her husband, young son, and parents were living. Immediately after the war Shek flew to Canton, where she was the first OSS woman to report on the transition to Chinese control. She then booked passage on a junk bound for Hong Kong with a cargo of goats, and most of the time was spent outmaneuvering pirates on the China Sea. When she arrived in Hong Kong, again the first OSS woman to reach the British colony, she learned that her husband and parents had been killed by a direct hit on the shipyard her father owned. By sheer luck Shek's thirteen-year-old son, Henry Leland Shek, had been impressed by the Japanese and sent to work in a labor camp in another part of the island. Four days later she was reunited with him through the help of family friends.

The OSS women, some twenty of us, were billeted in a newly opened subdivision in K'un-ming on a street that — unique in western China — was well paved. Here too lived high-ranking members of the American military as well as Chinese bankers and officials. Our building, protected by massive wooden walls, was a modernistic structure with tile roof and encircling balconies. Called Mei Yuan — beau-

411

tiful garden — it was landscaped with a reflecting pool, fragrant plum trees, and clusters
of bamboo. There was a large reception room
on the first floor. Carved-teak Chinese chairs
were arranged stiffly against the walls, and an
upright piano in an alcove served as an entertainment center after dinner. Curtains made
from white parachute silk billowed from full-
length windows. Upstairs was a dormitory
painted powder blue, with a few separate bedrooms and a single bath. Abutting this main
house was a long, motel-like building with
more individual bedrooms for the women who
continued to arrive until the end of the war.

We were a conglomerate group. Some came
from as far away as Alaska. Others had been
transferred from Cairo and London bases.
China-missionary daughters had signed up
hoping someday to return to their parents' par-
ishes. There were writers, artists, analysts, communications specialists, and secretaries filling
the crowded dormitories. We shared a somewhat dismal army mess, which usually featured
daily portions of Spam and powdered eggs. We
enjoyed occasional mixed parties on the large
balcony that encircled the top floor of Mei
Yuan. On a hand-cranked phonograph we
danced to scratchy USO-issued recordings of
such wartime favorites as "I'll Be Seeing You,"
"Lili Marlene," and "Don't Sit under the Apple
Tree."

The OSS women who spoke Chinese helped

run Mei Yuan smoothly. Mary Hutchinson was a linguist with native fluency, a former prisoner-of-war in Weihsien, where she had been secretary to American ambassador Leighton Stuart. Hutchinson hoped to return to her home where she had left relatives and friends interned in Japanese prisons. Meanwhile, she helped implement target studies for the Fourteenth and Tenth U.S. Air Forces and also interpreted requirements from women residents to the Chinese household staff.

Among the new arrivals in the early summer of 1945 was able, outspoken Marjorie Kennedy, trained at the Pentagon in order-of-battle analysis. Toward the end of the war Kennedy worked almost exclusively on Operation Carbonado, a huge Allied invasion planned to open up the port city of Canton. In addition to the Chinese Combat Command, American air force units in China and armies from Europe would be pouring eastward after V-E Day for a concerted drive to defeat the thousands of Japanese still under arms in Asia. After the A-bomb halted all planning and operations aimed at Canton, Kennedy was one of the OSS women who transferred to the Central Intelligence Agency, where she held an executive position until she met and married William A. Depuy, later a four-star army general whose career spanned World War II, Korea, and Vietnam.

Jeanne Taylor, an artist with the Visual Presentation Branch, was one of the women transferred from Ceylon with her boss, Paul Child. Taylor was credited with piecing together, from captured Japanese blueprints, specifications for the building of a Japanese "splinter" fleet in Hong Kong shipyards. These shipyards, pinpointed by Taylor, were targeted for successful Allied bombing missions.

I reported for duty from India at the K'unming Morale Operations (MO) shop the day after I arrived, still groggy from our Hump flight.[2] Headquarters was a tent pitched next to a mud-brick print shop abutting the OSS compound wall.

On my first day I was greeted by two friendly Chinese colleagues. Ma Kuo-liang was a young, liberal magazine editor from Shanghai; his partner, Ting Kong, nicknamed Shao Ting (Little Tack), later became a famous cartoonist. When I walked in, Ting was sketching a leaflet, a graphic explanation of how to sabotage Japanese vehicles by urinating in the gas tank. Roger Starr, who had done such fine MO work with Detachment 101 in Burma, was sitting behind a desk checking intelligence reports from Marjorie Severyns in Chungking. He introduced me to a talented New York artist, William Arthur Smith, busy at work just then sketching an empty rice bowl held by two thin hands, dramatically illustrating to the Chinese under Japanese rule just how well Japan's

Greater East Asia Co-prosperity Sphere was working.

I was given a hasty briefing by our MO chief, Roland E. Dulin, recently reassigned from Rome where he had participated in the Sauerkraut action. K'un-ming, he told me, was the center of long-range MO editorial production. Our field missions, dropped into critical OSS bases in China, waged spot psychological warfare using crude printing presses with hand-carved characters in a small type font. Most recently, field teams had been able to get light-weight aluminum offset presses developed especially by R&A in Washington. Black-radio programs were beamed to limited audiences on the coast from a Chungking base, and also from a studio in the outskirts of K'un-ming. The director was a New York media man, Gordon Auchincloss.

Once apprised of what Dulin called the overall picture, I was assigned to a project under way in Chungking run by Lt. Laird Ogle, involving MO operations against railroads west of the Yangtze River. "Ogle needs some leaflets for his Chinese and Korean agents explaining how to surreptitiously place pieces of OSS-developed coal where they will be shoveled into the engine's firebox and explode at the proper time," Dulin explained. "We are trying to disrupt Japanese troop movements in that area."

I had met Ogle during our training in Washington. His sister Carla was stationed with OSS

in London. Ogle was a charming noncon-
formist, educated in Switzerland, who had
come to China with Dulin from Rome. (On his
way to Korea at the end of the war he was with
an OSS team captured by a roving band of
Chinese communists. The communists murdered the leader of that team, Capt. John
Birch, the namesake of the conservative American political society of later years.)

On this first busy day at work, I ate lunch at
the base mess hall. En route back to the tent, I
was accosted by a friendly brown cocker
spaniel holding a tennis ball in his mouth. He
had no collar, and I assumed he was one of the
many dogs adopted as pets by the men and
women of the K'un-ming detachment. He followed me as I walked, demanding that I throw
the ball for him. Later, after a brisk romp, he
curled up under my desk and went to sleep.

I had almost forgotten he was there when I
felt his tail wagging against my leg. I looked up
to see a tall, handsome officer standing over
me, eagles gleaming on his shoulder, an
amused grin on his face. I recognized Colonel
Heppner. "So that's why my dog has defected!"
he said. "MO strikes again!"

I protested, "But he followed me! All I did
was throw the tennis ball for him!"

"That was all you had to do!" The colonel
smiled. "It's an addiction. He thinks he's a
Labrador Retriever!"

I was then introduced to Sammy. He had just

416

recently arrived over the Burma Road with a contingent of war dogs from Assam. I later learned why he was called Sammy: his pedigree papers listed him as My Assam Dragon.

Through Sammy there developed a warm friendship between Richard Heppner and me. I kept Sammy at Mei Yuan whenever the colonel was on one of his frequent field trips. The three of us walked along the banks of the canals that divided the rice paddies. We walked along mountain trails above the city. We drifted over the quiet waters of K'un-ming Lake on a sampan in the moonlight, when you could hear the haunting music from Chinese flutes softly floating across from the pagodas that arched above the trees. In those days there was a lonesome side to everyone's life, stationed so far from home in an alien country.

The war abruptly ended after Hiroshima and Nagasaki, just as General Donovan had predicted. He was at Sian on an inspection trip when it happened. Unwittingly, the MO black radio had also predicted that "a catastrophe would hit Japan the first week in August." It was part of a broadcast beamed to Nanking and based upon the prophecy of a Chinese seer known as the Hermit, who was versed in the pseudosciences of astrology, numerology, phrenology, and palmistry so popular with his Chinese audiences.

A short week before the top-secret atom bomb was dropped, Gordon Auchincloss confessed to me that the Hermit needed some new material, an attention-getting message to give his audience a jolt. I suggested that an earthquake of great magnitude would destroy Japan. Auchincloss disagreed, arguing that the Japanese were used to earthquakes. I persisted, "Then add a tidal wave." That too was vetoed. Auchincloss finally came up with his own solution, one that appealed to the Hermit. He explained, "After appropriate eerie background music, the Great Seer will give out an announcement, backed by the position of the stars, that a disaster of catastrophic proportions will take place in a Japanese city sometime during the first week of August."

Several days later I walked into the tent and found the entire staff gathered around Roger Starr. "It's awful," he said. "Simply awful. We just dropped an atomic bomb over Hiroshima and wiped the whole goddamned city off the map." Dulin added, "But it also means that this war will soon be over. There will be no more killing!"

At the compound that evening Americans and Chinese colleagues celebrated the occasion by setting off huge strands of firecrackers that stretched from rooftops to the ground. They exploded like huge zippers in bursts of flames. "Fireworks," Shao Ting reminded me, "were invented by us Chinese back in the seventh century. You might say we started the process that has led over the centuries to the production of an atomic bomb by you Americans."

Almost immediately General Wedemeyer gave Colonel Heppner the assignment of locating, contacting, and rescuing Allied prisoners. OSS "mercy missions" fanned out all over China and recovered prisoners who had been incarcerated by the Japanese since the beginning of the war in Asia. It was a proud day when OSS Team Cardinal reached Mukden and located Gen. Jonathan M. Wainwright, General MacArthur's commander at Corregidor when the Japanese captured the Philippines.

As the days went by and Japanese enclaves continued to surrender throughout Asia, peace brought a sudden vacuum to daily life in K'unming. Up until now there had been purpose, urgency, importance in the work we were doing. Now suddenly we had no direction, and the prospect of returning to a routine life was difficult to imagine. Many of the OSS men in uniform would soon be civilians. They would never again blow up a bridge, count Japanese convoys rolling along dusty roads in China, write false news stories, or intercept wireless messages.

Most OSS personnel went home by way of India and a long boat trip across several oceans. I remained for another month to help assemble the history of the China detachment. My husband, by then Commander MacDonald, elected to remain in Bangkok, where he had taken the Japanese surrender. He established what was to become one of the most prestigious English-language newspapers in Asia, the *Bangkok Post*. We were amicably divorced later, and he took up a new life in Bangkok.

I saw Colonel Heppner and his staff off on a plane to Shanghai, where he established headquarters until OSS was dissolved by presidential order in September 1945. Until then, work continued on tracking down war criminals, reassessing the rapidly changing political situation, and arranging to leave friendly Chinese agents "in place" in key Chinese cities if the communists took over the government.

OSS in China received an impressive commendation from the War Department at the close of operations for outstanding performance of duty in vital missions against the common enemy. The department cited OSS for an "admirable record of heroism, resourcefulness, initiative and successful operations against a ruthless enemy."[3] The commendation further stated that the achievements of OSS constituted a "chapter beyond parallel in China." During the period from 1 January to 2 September 1945, the unit numbered fewer than two thousand personnel but was directly responsible for killing over twelve thousand Japanese. In addition, OSS captured, destroyed, or rendered inoperative more than one hundred vessels of every category as well as vast quantities of ordnance material, rolling stock, and pack animals.

Tribute was paid to the Special Operations and Operational Group teams:

These highly aggressive and efficient gue-rilla teams, by parachuting or infiltrating behind enemy lines, maintained a constantly mounting sabotage campaign against Japanese radio, railroad and transport facilities. Other teams trained and dispatched native operatives, formed intelligence networks and guaranteed a constant flow of information which was radioed to Headquarters and aided in the rescue of downed American airmen.

In the closing days of the war, the Office of Strategic Services was given the vital humanitarian and military assignment of locating, contacting and protecting Allied prisoners of war and civilian internees at camps scattered throughout China, Manchuria, Korea and French Indochina. The highly efficient manner in which simultaneous airborne landings were carried out after the aerial distribution of psychological surrender leaflets prepared and printed in China by OSS personnel was a glowing tribute to careful planning, excellent teamwork and unremitting devotion to duty of all personnel.

I was never cited in any glowing commendation for the last subversive act I performed before leaving China for an unknown future in New York City: I arranged passage for Sammy back to Scarsdale, New York, where Colonel Heppner's mother awaited him. I wrote up a set of false orders ensuring that Sammy would be flown home as an outstanding member of the ferocious Dogs for Defense, which had guarded our compound against petty thieves and enemy infiltration. He was listed as an airplane spotter.

With the departure of American forces from K'un-ming, the little town was reverting to prewar peace and quiet. Many of the women with whom I had worked in China either went home to family or former jobs, elected to join the new central intelligence service, or married the men who had shared their lives in wartime and with whom they had fallen in love.

Elly Thiry became the bride of Basil Summers, assistant military attaché to the British embassy in Chungking. They were married in London on 23 November 1946 and, as she last reported in her diary, "lived happily ever after."

Virginia Rathbun, who arrived on General Donovan's plane just before the end of the war, met an Australian soldier of fortune, Gilbert Stuart, at a victory celebration. In her diary she described him as the most handsome, fascinating man she had ever met: "Colonel Stuart was head of the twelve Chinese commando groups which he had helped to train for OSS.

He was an unusual man, an adventurer, a loner who confided in no one, and about whom there was much speculation and mystery."[4] Rathbun was assigned to OSS headquarters in Shanghai, where she and another K'un-ming colleague, Phoebe Hearst Brown, were in charge of Registry, retitled Document Control. Rathbun and Stuart were married in Shanghai in January 1946, at Holy Trinity Church.

Julia McWilliams and Paul Child went home to Washington, where they were married a year later. She found a second career as the now famous French Chef. She became interested in cooking in Paris, where her husband was stationed with the State Department.

Mary Eddy also met an intriguing suitor, an ornithologist with OSS, S. Dillon Ripley, who spent a great deal of his free time collecting rare birds before he became secretary of the Smithsonian Institution. He proposed to her the year after they returned home to Washington.

Marjorie Severyns married a handsome war correspondent with the United Press, Al Ravenholt, in a ceremony in Shanghai in 1948. General Wedemeyer gave the bride in marriage.

Rosamond Frame married OSS captain Thibaut de St. Phalle, whom she had met earlier on the long sea voyage to India. De St. Phalle had been slated for duty behind Japanese lines on the China coast; Frame spent the entire voyage teaching him Chinese for his hazardous assignment. After the war, while waiting for orders to return home, he invited Rosie to a "special celebration." He reserved a garden enclave at the Imperial Hotel in New Delhi, set up a table with flowers and champagne, presented her with a gardenia corsage, and proposed to her under a full moon.

I was discharged from OSS and went to work for *Glamour* magazine in New York City, where Dick Heppner and I resumed our friendship. We were married at my grandmother's home in Connecticut, and Sammy attended the reception. He became part of the happy life we enjoyed together until Dick's untimely death at the age of forty-nine. At that time he had taken a leave of absence from General Donovan's New York law firm where he was a partner and where a number of his OSS colleagues then worked. He was appointed deputy assistant secretary of defense for international security and had just completed a world tour of U.S. bases when he died of a burst aorta in Walter Reed Army Hospital in Washington in 1958.

Life for me had suddenly changed once again, and it was difficult to face the reality of this tragedy. Eventually I went back to work, with the help of old OSS comrades, to begin a second career in intelligence with the new Central Intelligence Agency.

EPILOGUE

Space-Age Spies: Women in CIA

In 1959 I rejoined the sisterhood of spies at the Central Intelligence Agency, where I was to spend fourteen years in Operations in Washington, in the Far East, and on other temporary duty assignments overseas. The agency had been established by Congress twelve years earlier. OSS veteran Allen Dulles was now the director, bringing something of the creativity, the élan, that General Donovan had inculcated into the wartime OSS that I had known.

The space age in espionage was just developing. The first CIA U-2 reconnaissance flight soared over Soviet airspace on 4 July 1956, cameras seventy thousand feet in the sky recording life below in what were then the Iron Curtain countries. With this flight came a new era in high spying, opening up uncharted dimensions to intelligence collection.

CIA headquarters was still located at Twenty-third and E Streets in Washington when I was ushered into the office of Allen

Dulles for a job interview. He greeted me with true OSS camaraderie, but he was also engrossed at that moment in inspecting an impressive model of the new agency complex then being built across the Potomac in Langley, Virginia.

"Look at our new campus," he grinned, touching the model gingerly, his hands gnarled with arthritis. "Our headquarters building has marble halls, two hundred acres of lawn, magnificent trees. Reminds me of Princeton. Far more impressive than my brother's concrete mausoleum here in Washington." (His brother, John Foster Dulles, was then secretary of state.)

When I reported for work at the agency later that month I recognized a few friends, women who had once been in OSS and had later signed on with CIA. Most of them were assigned to office work; there were a few who wrote reports, did research, or were employed in lower-level operations. Most of the women in the early days of CIA theorized that the intrigue and excitement were worth the occasional discrimination they encountered with the "old boy net." I remember one of these old boys, just back from chief-of-station-hood in Europe in the early 1960s, pontificating, "We had no female case officers in my station. Women were responsible for support operations such as research, analysis, and office management. I feel women are just not as stable as men in critical positions."

As the years went by I watched the career development of the younger women within the agency workforce. These were the bright, college-trained, computer-smart new breed of agents. At coffee breaks we heard that one exceptional woman was being considered for a chief-of-station slot in a small African post, an assignment considered a clear sign of upward mobility. Another was moving into counter-intelligence work as assistant to a branch chief. Someone else was actually running agents. Eventually I did, too. And more and more I noticed that people from many ethnic groups were being hired, Asians and Afro-Americans as well as many Europeans with linguistic talent.

By 1994, CIA professional employees were 59 percent male, 41 percent female. Today an operations officer, male or female, usually holds a bachelor's degree at the very least, often has worked from two to four years in industry, is fluent in a foreign language, and has had overseas experience.

The late William E. Colby, director of CIA from 1973 to 1976, was an outspoken supporter of equality for women in government. He cited Stella Rimington, the first woman director general of the British intelligence service, MI5. Rimington, a single mother, worked her way up through Britain's intelligence service for twenty-two years before she reached the top in 1991. Colby believed that as equal opportunities develop, a woman will one day be appointed director of CIA.

When it happens, this woman will be qualified to handle a much wider field of global challenges than General Donovan faced when he commanded OSS. This woman director will have to monitor economic issues across the board. Industrial espionage is a well-defined threat to national security. There is also a lawlessness that has enveloped new democracies to the point that terrorism, narcotics trafficking, and organized crime threaten not only our allies but our own safety. Spying is not localized today as it was during World War II, when information was dispatched surreptitiously over prescribed radio wavelengths. The orbiting spies in the sky require a whole new system of imagery and experts who can translate and evaluate the products.

Today, several stories in the second CIA building at Langley are filled with wall-to-wall machines receiving worldwide intelligence, protected from enemy bugging by specially constructed tinted-glass windows. A system now known as Intelink permits the intelligence community and the Department of Defense to share super-secret information on this technology cloned from the Internet.

The ladies of OSS wrote on manual typewriters, made carbon duplicates, and used cumbersome VariTypers to reproduce material. They learned Morse code for receiving and transmitting messages. For intelligence analyses, reports officers depended a great deal upon foreign publications, captured documents, and messages from in-place or stay-behind agents. Secret documents were filed in manila folders in bulky safes. There was no such thing as instant information recovery at the push of a computer button.

Eloise Randolph Page, one-time executive secretary to Donovan, is one of those women who successfully made the transition from the OSS era of manual typewriters to the cyberspace world of today's CIA. Page was graduated from the Peabody Conservatory of Music in Baltimore and learned typing and shorthand to qualify for an office job with OSS. Her memories of Donovan are mixed. "He was a most unreasonable man, with an Irish temper, but he could charm the birds right off the trees," she recalled. "I was in total awe of him and of all the men in authority in those early days, but I learned quickly. After about six months I was able to stand up to the general, and later to male colleagues in CIA."

Toward the end of the war, Donovan's executive assistant, James Murphy, asked Page to go to Brussels and run the X-2 office there. The war had ended when she assumed this job, but she stayed on to work with Belgian security, tracking down Nazi spies and collaborators.

When she finally came home, Page hoped to resume her music education. Instead she was asked to join the new CIA, where she rose to become one of the agency's top operations executives and the first woman chief of station in Athens.

Looking back over her career, Page reflected that women in CIA still face an uphill battle against older agency chiefs who "became feudal barons and could never consider women as their equals." But she added, "Our new career women are proving them wrong. Historically, I suppose you could say that the women of OSS prepared the groundwork for their sisters who came after them in CIA."

Elizabeth Swantek was one of the early CIA women assigned to Special Operations working abroad on an equal basis with male colleagues. She was still in high school in Davis, West Virginia, when Pearl Harbor was bombed. Swantek graduated in the spring of the following year, the valedictorian of her class, and applied for a job with the Army Signal Corps in Washington. She went to work in the still-unfinished Pentagon building.

Swantek's career over the next nine years prepared her for the many varied assignments she undertook with the agency. With the Signal Corps she learned radio transmission, and toward the end of the war she joined the navy WAVEs, went to boot camp, and took medical training at the Bethesda Naval Hospital. After the war she entered the University of California at Berkeley, majoring in political science and languages including Russian. Upon graduation she was recruited by CIA and was almost immediately dispatched to Germany with the Office of Special Operations in 1951.

It was the period of the Cold War. Two years earlier, on 5 September 1949, CIA had made its first agent drop by unmarked C-47 aircraft behind the Iron Curtain, the beginning of a penetration of the Soviet Union that lasted until 1954, well after the death of Stalin. Until this time the Soviet Union had been a denied area. Access was now achieved by recruitment or penetration, usually airborne.

Swantek became part of these operations under OSS veteran Harry Rositzke, at base headquarters in Munich. In his memoir, *The CIA Secret Operations*, Rositzke wrote, "I have never worked before or since with a group so highly motivated and totally committed. They knew the hazards their agents faced and they worked with zeal and camaraderie that I have never seen elsewhere in peacetime." Swantek too recalls this part of her long career as perhaps one of the most demanding:

I was dispatched to an isolated chalet on a lake in southern Bavaria. Here I joined two male colleagues with whom I worked for the next two years. Our job as a team was to assess, select, and train candidates to infiltrate the Soviet Union.

These volunteers were former Soviet citizens living in Western Europe, or refugees and defectors. Their mission, upon being infiltrated behind the Iron Curtain, was to establish and legalize themselves, serve as long-term assets, and exfiltrate at a future date.

Their training was intense, lasting for six months, and consisted of survival techniques, parachute jumps, drop-zone familiarization, and wireless transmission. I participated in every phase of this, including parachuting with the team.

Swantek recalls three young agents who were especially close to her:

Each was completely different in personality, but they were all willing to sacrifice their lives. The youngest was an idealistic student who opposed Soviet dictatorship because both his parents had died before a firing squad. The second, a Latvian, saw the Russians as conquerors of his country. And the third agent, an Armenian factory worker, was a street-wise, self-assured young man bored with life in a displaced-persons camp.

At a final farewell party for these men, they called me their little sister. We danced, ate a final full meal, and I listened to their last-minute thoughts on being dropped into darkness and possibly death. Our people had worked constantly to update their documentation. Their Russian-made clothes were authentic, their cover stories carefully memorized and tested over a long training period. Only the RS-1 transceiver they carried in their luggage would immediately destroy them if detected.

When Swantek said good-bye to them the next day when they were on their way to board the unmarked C-47 aircraft, the youngest turned to her wistfully and whispered, "I want so very much to live."

But he didn't. He was picked up almost immediately and executed. As for the others, the Armenian was able to reach his destination but was imprisoned several years later when he tried to leave the country near the southern border. The Latvian stayed on in Russia, continued to report spasmodically, and eventually married. Early radio signals, sent out at great risk by the two agents still surviving, confirmed that the Soviets were not planning an all-out attack on Europe, as was feared at that time.

Swantek came back to Washington after two years in the field to prepare for further special operations. "During my career," she told me years later in West Virginia, after her retirement, "I wore many faces. I was a tour director, a buyer, someone's girlfriend, a photographer, an art collector, even a young teenage boy. It helped to have an innocent-looking open face, a sense of humor, stamina, and the fearlessness of the very young."

At the end of her service she was presented with the CIA Career Intelligence Medal by Lt. Gen. Vernon A. Walters, then deputy director of the agency. At the ceremony at agency headquarters on 28 January 1975 the general commented, "Elizabeth Swantek's career has been a laudatory one. She came in twenty-three years ago at a relatively low grade and burst out and upward in a series of remarkable activities which included opening a station by herself. The memory of what she has done at CIA will inspire both men and women who come after."

Some women in CIA are action-oriented. There is excitement in meeting agents on dark street corners in Istanbul, recruiting dock workers in Japan to spy on North Korean shipping, or penetrating subversive labor unions in Rome. Then there are others who enjoy the challenge of working behind desks with computer data, developing over the years a sort of sixth sense about the shadowy careers of Soviet KGB or GRU agents. Jeanne Vertefeuille was one of those women who became an agency heroine for the detective work she did with the Counterintelligence staff. She helped to unmask CIA's most infamous penetration, the mole known as Aldrich Ames.[1]

Vertefeuille came to the agency in 1954, a young recruit from the University of Connecticut, where she had majored in French and German. She learned shorthand to qualify for a CIA job during Dulles's tenure. Throughout her career she maintained a quiet reserve that reflected competence and good sense. Plain in appearance, she lived alone and kept her own counsel.

During her early career Vertefeuille spent two tours in Africa and was then posted to Europe in the 1960s. Later, after completing a career training course, she found her niche in the agency in the field of counterintelligence as head of the Soviet Research Section. In this work Vertefeuille was responsible for converting incoming basic intelligence into carefully evaluated analyses. The raw material that came across her desk was often fragmentary or contradictory. Analysts such as Vertefeuille were expected to sift through the data and produce a finished report by evaluating, integrating, and interpreting the material. She became an expert in the shifting field of Soviet espionage.

Vertefeuille had been transferred to Libreville, the capital of Gabon, West Africa, as the first woman station chief there, when Aldrich Ames was assigned to her former office in the Counterintelligence Branch at Langley headquarters in 1985. Ames's appointment eventually became the major thrust in Vertefeuille's career. Instead of tracing foreign agents, she was asked to readapt her thinking to the possibility that there was a mole in the agency, a fellow worker sitting at the next desk, eating with her in the cafeteria.

In June 1985 Aldrich Ames began to pass quantities of secret material to his contact, Sergei Chuvakin, first secretary in the Soviet embassy, a man Ames told his colleagues he was trying to recruit to work for CIA. Instead, Ames was working within his own office as Moscow's master spy. He was paid close to $3 million over the course of nine years, and he betrayed dozens of CIA Soviet recruits, ten of whom are known to have been executed. He also revealed hundreds of CIA secret operations to the KGB.

Repercussions of these early betrayals were beginning to be felt by early 1986, when twenty CIA agents in the Soviet Union vanished. Back from her African tour, Vertefeuille was assigned a small task force to try to solve this serious breach in security. Two women were assigned to the team, together with two male retirees. There was a strange lack of determination at higher levels to attack the problem of a possible mole. The men at the top wanted to dismiss the embarrassing possibility that there was a traitor in their midst. CIA ethics could never spawn a traitor, they argued; the breach could have been the result of a compromise in the communications network; agents could have been "doubled." This rationalizing was frustrating to Vertefeuille's team, but they groped patiently over a period of four years, piecing together a jigsaw puzzle of facts and suspicions that eventually eliminated all suspects except Ames.

One of the first pieces in the puzzle was supplied by that sine qua non, woman's intuition. One member of the team, Sandy Grimes, had carpooled with Ames when they lived in Reston, Virginia. She said she had "bad vibes" about this rather obnoxious colleague who at that time was a newcomer to CIA. Ames's father had worked for CIA and had managed to get his son a job as a file clerk after he flunked out of the University of Chicago, where he had majored in drama. After a career training program and a degree from George Washington University, Ames and his first wife, Nancy Segebarth, also a CIA colleague, separated. He was then posted to Mexico City, where he met attractive twenty-nine-year-old Maria del Rosario Casas Dupuy, an employee at the Colombian embassy. They were married in 1985.

Slowly Vertefeuille began to put together parts of the puzzle. "Ames had always had bad teeth," she told me. "But suddenly he was sporting new and obviously expensive dentures. His usually messy hair was now carefully coiffed, and he wore costly Italian suits with British-made shoes. Explaining his sudden affluence, he told us that his wife's mother was very wealthy. However, another agency woman who worked for Ames in Mexico City as an intelligence assistant, Diana Worthen, knew the second Mrs. Ames as an underpaid staff member at the Colombian embassy in Mexico City with no financial support at all from her mother." Ames still dabbled in little theater, and Vertefeuille said she was never sure when he was acting. He also drank a great deal, brazenly flaunted a half-million-dollar home in Arlington that he had bought for cash, and drove to work in a flashy white Jaguar.

Vertefeuille said the case against Ames began to close in when she asked the agency to take legal steps to check his bank accounts and credit-card records. By August 1992 she had learned that hundreds of thousands of dollars had been systematically deposited into his account. Two months later Sandy Grimes hit pay dirt when she correlated the dates of Ames's meetings with his Soviet contact, Chuvakin. She learned that many deposits had been made shortly after lunches at the Georgetown restaurant where the pair regularly met.

By January 1993 Vertefeuille's team was convinced that they had their mole, and they now included Ames's wife Rosario as an accomplice. The FBI was asked to move in on the case. The bureau placed the suspects under surveillance, tapped their phone, bugged their house, and downloaded files from Ames's computer. As the evidence mounted, the FBI planned to arrest Ames on the day before he was scheduled to go on agency business to Moscow, where Chuvakin had promised him a *dacha* and $4 million when he "retired" from his traitorous activities.

After his arrest the FBI began the process of debriefing Ames about his Soviet contacts, with Vertefeuille as the only CIA representative at these meetings. "I knew he was uncomfortable when I took my seat opposite him at the table," Vertefeuille recalled. "We had shared the same office, we knew each other over the years, but I was not prepared for this final denouement."

Rick Ames testified that his Soviet contact had been worried about the sudden arrests of CIA agents in Moscow between 1985 and 1986. The contact felt that these arrests might lead the agency to look for a mole in their ranks and jeopardize Ames's position. The Soviets suggested that if Ames provided the name of another CIA officer, the KGB would plant clues to frame that innocent person. Vertefeuille recalled, "Rick looked straight at me across the table and said, 'I gave them your name, Jeanne, as a believable mole.' I must confess this really hurt, but from an analyst's point of view, he could really have framed me. As a woman, perhaps I was also particularly vulnerable."

Both Swantek and Vertefeuille worked for the Directorate of Operations (DO), the clandestine arm of CIA that collects foreign intelligence and conducts covert operations and counterintelligence work. Of all the directorates, DO offered the most excitement, action, and career rewards.

"Humint" — information collected by human agents — plays a major part in DO's coverage of intelligence. A veteran woman operator, Virginia O. Gavaghen, is chairman of the agency's National Humint Requirements Branch. Another colleague, Amy L. Tozzi, won the National Intelligence Medal of Achievement for the work she did in upgrading an intelligence system that had been in place since the founding of CIA. Tozzi has spent thirty-six years, fourteen overseas, in support of clandestine operations. Two generations of DO officers have been served by Tozzi's new system of covering the intelligence cycle, from planning and direction through collection and processing to analysis and dissemination.

In recent years, however, "elint" or electronic intelligence has become vital to modern intelligence. At CIA today, a Directorate of Science and Technology (S&T) conducts reconnaissance from outer space over vast areas in near-synoptic periods. The deputy director of S&T is a woman, Dr. Ruth A. David, who is science and technical adviser to the CIA director. She earned her doctorate from Stanford University in electrical engineering. Her job at the agency involves overseeing research and development and the application of technology to agency operations.

OSS analysts had to depend heavily on intelligence information provided by agents operating behind enemy lines or from within enemy-controlled borders. The radio communication required for the movement of timely and critical information also provided the weakest link in the security of the agents. Their battery-powered radio equipment could be a traitorous beacon, an invisible finger pointing to an agent's location when he was transmitting. Enemy direction finders could zero in and quickly eliminate this vital intelligence link. Being caught with the cumbersome equipment invariably meant torture and death.

Satellites in space have revolutionized the collection of intelligence data. Today the agency branch that handles certain phases of S&T is NIMA, the National Imagery and Map Agency (formerly the National Photographic Interpretation Center). Until 1997 the director was Nancy Bone, who has spent twenty-seven dedicated years in photo interpretation work, most recently at the administrative level.

Bone — slim and attractive, with a charm that belies her toughness in making decisions — came to Washington from Wichita, Kansas. She had graduated from Saint Louis University and taught English for two years before deciding on a career in government. "As an English major I knew much more about Shakespeare than I did about intelligence," she recalled. "I applied for a job with the CIA, took a polygraph test, and went to work on database compilation."

Database is to the modern craft of intelligence what miles of files and index cards were to the analysts of OSS days. It represents the systematic surveillance of aerospace, surface, or subsurface areas, persons, or things by visual, aural, electronic, or photographic means. For years one of the basic suppliers of database input to CIA has been the Foreign Broadcast Information Service, which monitors and records media output throughout the world. Women have always held important positions in this service.

The young English teacher from Kansas eventually mastered database requirements and worked her way up until she was assigned to the photo interpretation center in September 1993. Most of the women working in this field are university graduates, many with science degrees and computer-trained, sharing a fascination with this new imagery intelligence. They work on an equal basis with the men in this department, many of whom are military personnel on detached service to CIA.

Since much of the information NIMA obtains from satellites is open to interpretation, the final analysis of the material depends largely on prior knowledge, technical training, and ability to understand the imagery. As Bone explained the concept:

> What we work from is a factual base of information obtained through the neutral eye of a satellite soaring above Bosnia, the Iraqi marshes of Al 'Amarah, or the Lop Nor missile site in Western China.
>
> Our eyes in the skies sent back the first proof of the mass graves and bombed-out villages that were part of the Serb ethnic cleansing in Bosnia-Herzegovina. We watched the systematic destruction of Iraq's southern wetlands by Saddam Hussein's forces, who built up strategic dams and caused the evaporation of wetlands near the confluence of the Tigris and Euphrates Rivers. This sanctuary had been a marshy refuge for insurgents opposing Saddam. On the basis of satellite photography we determined that the previously suspected facility at Lop Nor was indeed a Chinese nuclear test site.

These resources have also been utilized within the United States in assisting relief agencies such as the Federal Emergency Management Agency to make a speedy assessment of natural disasters. "During the hurricane season of 1995, for example, we were able to assess damage done by Hurricane Marilyn when it struck the Virgin Islands," Bone explained, pointing out that CIA intervened upon request since it operates within the United

States only with top governmental clearance. "We took the detailed images provided by satellites, added data from other sources such as police reporting, media coverage, and even Internet input. Color coordination was important. The map of Saint Thomas showed areas of devastation in bright red, heavy structural damage in violet. We also looked for debris fields, similar to bomb damage, beach erosion, or submerged roads and airfields. Computer-generated maps, superimposed, showed a vivid picture of the devastation."

Nancy Bone is an excellent example of what the women in CIA have done in the ever-expanding field of satellite intelligence, where properly trained analysts make intelligence reports happen by combining a skilled reading of imagery with computerized database input and a knowledge of the political or military problems involved. It is also important to select qualified personnel for these specialized operations. Hythia D. Young, deputy director of NIMA's human resources, is in charge of hiring the right people with the right skills to handle NIMA's worldwide coverage. Young, who holds a master's degree from Texas Southern University and has been with the agency for nearly twenty-five years, is among the first Afro-American women assigned to executive positions.

A CIA recruitment brochure designed to lure

potential lady spies into the shadowy world of espionage points out that "advancement of women comes with experience, skill and education, combined with a sense of mission. Performance is consistently rewarded."[2] But in the mid-1990s there was growing bitterness among the agency's women employees, who felt that they were not receiving "career enhancing" assignments and were immobilized within the grade 11–12 levels. Some two hundred mid-career women agents in Operations filed a class-action lawsuit against the agency charging that they had been blocked from posts as covert operatives, case officers, and station chiefs. That suit was eventually settled within the confines of the agency, and a CIA woman attorney helped to bring negotiations to a successful conclusion. She was Elizabeth Rindskopf, the eighth counsel general of CIA and the first woman appointed to that post. It was ironic that she should represent the agency in a suit claiming that women in CIA were denied upward mobility.

Rindskopf came to the General Counsel's Office eminently qualified, with a law degree from the University of Michigan. She had worked as a civil-rights lawyer in Atlanta and tried cases before the Supreme Court when she came to Washington, a widow with a young daughter. She was general counsel for the National Security Agency and later a legal adviser for the State Department. At CIA she supervised some sixty lawyers who operated at posts around the world, steering a tricky legal course between foreign and domestic law enforcement.

There are increasingly more women in CIA who hold executive posts. Joyce Pratt, comptroller of the agency, reports directly to the director. It is her job to assess priorities and then approve the finances that support CIA programs. She explained, "Take the problem of intercontinental ballistic missiles. Do they constitute a threat if launched by rogue nations against the United States? The intelligence community, addressing that problem, determined that there would be no immediate threat for the next decade. Therefore: funds for ballistic missile research would be curtailed in favor of more imminent issues such as terrorism, drugs, and peacekeeping. And I assigned these funds."

In the earlier days of CIA, the thought of a woman being named to the elite Intelligence Directorate would have been shrugged off by some of the so-called feudal barons. But in August 1995, then–CIA director John Deutch named Sandra Kruzman to serve as the associate deputy director for intelligence, the first woman to ever serve in that post. "I am confident that the directorate will benefit from her broad and deep experience and her unassailable integrity," Deutch stated at an annual CIA promotion ceremony that year. She joined the team of the agency's elite intelligence officers tasked with crafting strategic planning targeted at expanding global problems. Kruzman was cited as "smart on substance and organization issues." She started her job with CIA in 1966 as an economic analyst and worked her way up through a series of senior assignments. Her analytical and managerial talents won her the agency's Meritorious Officer Award in 1981 and 1989.

Another CIA officer who exemplifies the growing trend toward female leadership in the agency is Joanne Isham, who started her career after graduating from the University of Notre Dame with a degree in government and international studies. She started in 1977 in the Office of Security. Within a few years her networking skills and ability to deal with outsiders led to the position of director of congressional affairs, which had just been established by the agency. She is currently an associate deputy director for science and technology with the Resource Management staff.

Yet another woman, Sharon Basso, now heads the agency's Information staff. She is also the CIA ombudsman. Basso started as a secretary in 1964 and rose to the post of political analyst in the Directorate of Intelligence. Here she analyzed political trends in international organizations. She shifted to the Public Affairs Office, where she was deputy chief of media relations. Basso has received several government awards including the agency's Career Intelligence Medal.

One of the agency's largest directorates — Administration — encompasses a huge infrastructure that supports most CIA operations. This directorate is responsible for security of personnel and files, communications, finance and payroll, medical services, training, even printing and photography. The associate deputy director for administration is Elaine A. Gifford, who has also served with S&T, Research and Development, and Engineering. Diane Rankin is chief of printing and photography, an operation spawned during World War II, when film director John Ford headed what was then known as the Field Photographic Unit. Today Rankin's unit not only encompasses round-the-clock photo and printing support for CIA activities, the White House, and other government agencies but has also branched out into the developing art of digital electronic printing. Also in this field of automation, Terry S. Kees holds the job of director of information technology. She was awarded the National Medal of Intelligence Achievement for her development of major systems in support of the imagery needs of the intelligence community.

Another vital agency directorate handles the training in management, career fields, and languages that most interns undergo before reporting for their assignments. This key Directorate of Training and Education is headed by a talented Afro-American, Janice W. Fitzgerald, who studied at Harvard's John F. Kennedy School of Government.

In an attempt to address problems of sexual discrimination as well as racial and ethnic harassment, the agency established an Office of Equal Employment Opportunity (EEO), which today is headed by a lawyer, Dawn Renee Eilenberger. Young and energetic, she came to work in 1970 after graduating from the University of Virginia. She started in the General Counsel's Office and has headed EEO since 1994. Under her guidance, EEO has set up a series of intra-agency "employment" programs. "We have published a sexual-harassment handbook and have established a four-hour mandatory training course in this important area for senior managers," she explains. "We have tours of places like the Holocaust Museum in Washington, to better understand racial and religious pogroms."

Eilenberger's deputy, Ana Mercedes McCollim, is one of the first Hispanic women to hold a senior post in EEO. McCollim is a lawyer, a member of the Washington, D.C., bar who came to the agency from Congress, where she was legislative consul to Puerto Rico's congressman, Baltasar Corrada, and later staff assistant to Senator Edward Kennedy. Among her many duties at EEO is utilization of her language skills — Portuguese, Spanish, French, and English — in analyzing foreign laws as they apply to CIA clandestine operations.

In 1995 a woman was appointed to the agency's third highest office. She was Nora Slatkin, named executive director by John M. Deutch, the sixteenth director of CIA. Slatkin's duties in this position encompassed all four CIA directorates and all independent offices. She was, in effect, empowered by Deutch to run the agency.

Blonde and petite, with blue-gray eyes and a ready smile, Slatkin had been an outstanding assistant secretary of the navy for research, development, and acquisition, a position in which some of her chauvinist colleagues referred to her as Tora Tora Nora. Her ability as a quietly authoritative administrator was noted early and often critically during her tenure at CIA. A native of Glen Cove, New York, Slatkin is a Lehigh Phi Beta Kappa graduate with a degree in international relations. She also holds a master's degree in foreign service from Georgetown University and attended the Harvard University seminar for senior executives in national and international security.

In discussing goals for CIA, Slatkin told me that the number one objective was to make sure "that the workplace at CIA was a place where discrimination of any kind was not acceptable, where people were judged upon their capabilities, and where performance counted, regardless of race or gender." In 1996 roughly a third of the people appointed to the top sixty-four command positions in CIA were women, including Slatkin's assistant, Joan M. Biehler, who directs the CIA Human Resources Oversight Council.

Slatkin, who resigned after Deutch left in 1997, is still remembered for the position she took in support of women. "We have had problems at CIA, and some women have left the agency in frustration," she recalled. "But for every woman who left, there were hundreds more who stayed, excelled, and changed the agency in the process. These are women who have traveled the world, dined with ambassadors, briefed princes and presidents, run clandestine operations, and pioneered new technologies."

In a speech delivered to the Chicago Council on Foreign Relations on 15 May 1996, Slatkin noted the demands posed by the expanding fields of intelligence missions:

> We cannot afford to waste the talents of women or minorities now, any more than we could in the days of Donovan and the OSS. We still need the breadth of view that only a diverse work force can provide. In the post–Cold War world the CIA has limited resources and a mission that is compelling, perhaps more difficult than it was in the days when we had one primary adversary. The Soviet Union was a slow-moving, rela-

tively predictable target compared to the challenges we face today: stemming the proliferation of weapons of mass destruction; foiling the plans of terrorists, drug traffickers, and international organized-crime groups; discovering the intentions of rogue states like North Korea, Iran, Iraq, the Sudan, and Libya; and monitoring the progress of great powers such as Russia and China, who are in the process of transition. For this task we need to make full use of the talents of all of our men and women.

It was over half a century ago that General Donovan made his farewell address to some two thousand men and women on the Potomac Flats below the OSS headquarters building. President Truman had just abolished that wartime spy agency, and it was not until 1947 that Congress established America's new central intelligence service. General Donovan's proud words spoken in 1945 pertain as well to those men and women today who face the challenge of space-age espionage in the millennium ahead.

"We have come to the end of an experiment," Donovan told his audience.

This experiment was to determine whether a group of Americans constituting a cross section of racial origins, of abilities, of temperaments and talents could meet and risk an encounter with a long-established and well-trained enemy.

This could not have been done if you had not been willing to fuse yourselves into a team — a team that was made up not only of scholars and research experts and active units in operations and intelligence who engaged the enemy in direct encounter, but also of the great numbers of our organization who drove our motor vehicles, carried our mail, kept our records and documents and performed those innumerable duties of administrative services without which no organization can succeed. You have made a beginning in showing the people of America that only by decisions based upon accurate information can we have the chance of a peace that will endure.[3]

Notes

Prologue. "Wild Bill" Donovan and the Origins of OSS

1. David Donovan interview, 20 July 1995.
2. Discussions with McFadden, 1947–80. The author worked with McFadden in OSS, he later assisted her on her first book, *Undercover Girl*, and he was a close friend over the years. McFadden held many papers/clippings pertaining to the Donovan family, including material used in the Prologue. A Donovan law partner from 1934, McFadden died in 1984.
3. Directive no. 67, dated 13 June 1942, authorization by President Roosevelt; also National Archives and Records Administration (NARA) Microfilm M1642.
4. Heppner papers in the possession of the author.
5. "Diplomacy: It's Donovan," *Newsweek*, 26 July 1954.

Chapter 1. Invisible Apron Strings

1. Donovan's introduction to MacDonald, *Undercover Girl*.

2. Griggs quoted from MacDonald, *Under-cover Girl*, 21–22.
3. Ibid.

Chapter 2. Code-Room Mata Hari

1. Pack diary, "Cynthia" papers, Churchill College archives.
2. Downes, *Scarlet Thread*.
3. Putzell interview, 20 Mar. 1993, in which he recalled his own reactions to the Cynthia project, together with those of Buxton and Downes.
4. Hyde, *Cynthia*, 190–91.
5. "Cynthia" papers, Churchill College archives.
6. State Department papers, RG 59: 701-5111.
7. FBI file 116-7648.
8. State Department papers, RG 59.

Chapter 3. The Girls of R&A

1. NARA RG 226 Entry 146 Box 81 Folder 1149.
2. Hanson, *Distaff Side*, 39.
3. Infield, *Skorzeny*; also letter to author from C. G. Sweeting, Smithsonian aviation historian, 4 July 1997.
4. Peet interview, 10 Jan. 1957.

Chapter 4. Coordinating Secret Intelligence

1. Investiture of Mrs. John Murray Begg, Sept. 1948, with Order of Orange-Nassau, Degree of Knight. In the possession of the recipient. Copy to Chancellor of Netherlands, Order of Knighthood.

Chapter 5. Black Propaganda, Coast to Coast

1. Collingwood project: NARA RG 226 Entry 139 MO Wash. Box 120 Folders 1631–37.
2. Joint Chiefs of Staff 155/4D, dated 23 Dec. 1942.
3. NARA RG 226 Entry 139 MO Wash. Box 161 Folders 2150–51.
4. NARA RG 226 Entry 139 Box 169 Folder 2258.
5. Musac project: NARA RG 226 Entry 139 MO Wash. Box 132 Folders 2282–87.
6. Steinbeck quoted in Bancroft, *Autobiography of a Spy*, 176.
7. Donovan papers, U.S. Military History Institute, Carlisle, Pa.
8. Halle memo to Donovan: NARA RG 226 Entry 139 MO Wash. Box 136 Folder 2087.

Chapter 6. Operation Sauerkraut

1. Documents pertaining to Operation Sauerkraut, including Lauwers's citation written up and illustrated: NARA RG 226 Entry 154 Box 51 Folders 844–68.
2. "Free Love Offered Nazis on Furlough," *Washington Post*, 10 Oct. 1944.

Chapter 7. Underground in New York City

1. Foreign Nationalities Branch: NARA RG 226 OSS Entry 100 Box 131 Folder 14.
2. Quoted in Moseley, *Dulles*, 114.
3. Weis to author, 17 Aug. 1993.
4. Fowler interview, 17 Oct. 1992.
5. Project NET: Secretariat Office Project 0008, NARA RG 226 Entry 139 Box 242 Folder 3577.
6. Quoted in Rubin, *Istanbul Intrigues*, 117.
7. Quoted in ibid., 116–17.
8. Carp material contained in letter from Allen Dulles, New York HQ, to David Bruce, London Station, 2 Mar. 1942: NARA RG 226 Entry 106 Box 13-21 Folders 100–166.
9. Spartacus Restaurant: memo from Carp to Allen Dulles, 28 Mar. 1942, NARA RG 226 Entry 092 Box 004 Folder 09.
10. NARA RG 226 Row 24 Compartment 15 Shelf C Entry 92 Box 60 Stack 16W4.

11. Rado reports: NARA RG 226 Entry 99 Box 72 Folder 10.
12. NARA RG 226 Entry 106 Box 0013 Folders 103–5.
13. Karlo interview, 5 Sept. 1993.

Chapter 8. London Station

1. London station: NARA Microfilm M1623 Roll 10, London war diaries, X-2.
2. Phillips, *Ventures in Diplomacy*.
3. Thomas interview, 27 Feb. 1993 ("for millionaires"); Phillips interview, 6 Sept. 1994 ("box of Kleenex").
4. Bruce, *OSS against the Reich*, 183.
5. Ibid.
6. Phillips, *Ventures in Diplomacy*.
7. Philby, *My Silent War*.
8. In-depth report on London WACs from Keene to author, 13 Feb. 1993.
9. Hornaday to author, 25 Mar. 1993.
10. NARA RG 226 Entry 190 Box 326 Folder 541.
11. Hannifin interview, 10 Mar. 1993.
12. MacPherson to author, 6 Jan. 1994.
13. Corsini to author, 8 June 1993.

Chapter 9. From Royal Suites to Back-Street London

1. This chapter draws on Ellery Huntington's Yugoslavia papers, in the possession of his widow, Catherine Huntington.
2. Shepherd project: NARA Microfilm Roll 38 Frame 340–42.
3. NARA RG 226 Entry 190 Box 587 Folder 463.
4. Yarrow papers, Eisenhower Library, Abilene, Kans.

Chapter 10. Cover and Documentation

1. Howe interview, 24 Jan. 1995. Howe set up the London message center, one of the first to be organized in the European theater of operations. He later left the London station to participate in SEAC operations against Sumatra. After the war he was deputy director of State Department Intelligence, 1948–56; executive secretary of State Department, 1956–58. He later joined the School of Advanced Studies, Johns Hopkins University.
2. Bruce, *OSS against the Reich.*
3. Igor Cassini, "Charlie Knickerbocker" gossip column, *New York Journal American*, 10 Nov. 1942.

1. Fayol, *Chambon-sur-Lignon sous l'occupation;* Foot, *SOE in France.*

2. DSC award: General Orders No. 44, War Department, Washington, D.C., 13 May 1946. Medal on permanent display at the CIA Exhibit Center, Langley, Va.

3. "Reporter Finds Capital Crowded," *New York Post,* 4 Sept. 1941.

4. "Vichy Bars Jews," *New York Post,* 24 Nov. 1941; "People Are Cold and Hungry," *New York Post,* 22 Jan. 1942.

5. Fayol, *Chambon-sur-Lignon sous l'occupation,* 118. See also Foot, *SOE in France.*

6. Foot, *SOE in France.*

7. Hall activity report, 30 Sept. 1944: NARA RG 226 Entry 92 Box 296 Folder 18494/32 Wash. REG Ad-7.

8. NARA RG 226 Entry 190 Box 347 Folder 240.

9. Donovan memo to President Truman, 12 May 1945: NARA Microfilm M1642 Roll 25 Frame 902. Also Gamble (Paris) to Donovan, 13 June 1945: NARA Microfilm M1642 Roll 25 Frame 902.

10. "Virginia Goillot of French Resistance Dies," *Baltimore Sun,* 13 Jan. 1982.

Chapter 12. The Agent Who Lived Her Cover

1. Legendre interview, 20 Apr. 1993.
2. Putzell interview, 20 Mar. 1993.
3. Report for Washington HQ record, dictated 28 Mar. 1945 to Allen Dulles's secretary in Bern: NARA RG 226 Entry 190 Box 626 Folder 772 Wash. Dir. Ops.
4. Legendre, *Sands Ceased to Run*, 242.
5. Dulles cable to Donovan: NARA RG 226 Entry 190 Box 626 Folder 772; Donovan cable to Honolulu: NARA RG 226 Entry 190 Box 4 Folder 1.

Chapter 13. Turning a Nazi Agent

1. Boyd to author, 2 Jan. 1993; see also Willets, *Sting of Glory*.
2. Guyot DSC citation: HQ ETO USA, 8 May 1945. Suitland Federal Records Comm. NNRR RG 332 ETOL US ET ADJ Sec. Awards from U.S. to foreigners, 1944–45. Box 3 (G–L) Doc.8:78/52.
3. Geoffrey M. T. Jones, report, "OSS Champagne Campaign," Veterans of Strategic Services headquarters files, Rockefeller Center, New York. See also Adleman and Walton, *Champagne Campaign*.

Chapter 14. Through Enemy Lines

1. Gulovich citation: HQ U.S. Military Academy, West Point, N.Y., 14 May 1946, General Orders No. 26, Section 3; also NARA RG 226 Entry 8-15 Box 133 Folders 570, 590. Notes on procedure at review presentation of decorations, 22 May 1946: S-3 Office, HQ Corps of Cadets, West Point, N.Y. Reports on presentation: "Czech Heroine Decorated at West Point," *New York Herald Tribune*, 26 May 1946; "Czechoslovak Girl Honored by Cadets," *New York Times*, 25 May 1946.
2. NARA RG 226 Entry 108B84F691 Box 84 Folder 691.
3. This account draws on Gulovich interviews, 30 May 1993, 27 Aug. 1994; also Gulovich to author, 3 April 1993.
4. Gulovich report to OSS headquarters, Bari, Italy, 17 July 1945: NARA RG 226 Entry 108 Box 64 Folder 507.

Chapter 15. Espionage in the Twilight Zones

1. Butch file: NARA RG 226 Entry 127 Box 22 Folder 155.
2. Casey, tribute written for dust jacket of Romanones, *Spy Wore Red*.
3. Rathbun diary in her possession.

4. Tuckerman interview, 3 June 1995.
5. Larson interview, 12 Feb. 1993.
6. Orr interview, 7 May 1994.
7. Smiley interview, 3 June 1993.
8. Yeager to author, 22 Feb. 1996.
9. Bancroft, *Autobiography of a Spy.*
10. *New York Times*, 19 Jan. 1997.

Chapter 16. Through the Transom into India

1. This chapter draws on correspondence with Bondurant, 11 Aug. 1995, and Patterson, 20 June 1995. Both OSS veterans later became authorities on India, Patterson on the political aspects, Bondurant on Gandhi's theories of nonviolence.
2. NARA RE165 ABC 385 India (8 Apr. 1943); also personal papers in possession of author.
3. NARA RG 226 Entry 110 Box B52 Folder 14.
4. DuBois to Fahs, 21 Apr. 1945: NARA RG 226 Entry 53 Box 2. File incoming received Dec. 1944–Apr. 1945.

Chapter 17. Black Mail

1. NARA RG 226 Entry 108 Box 83 Folder 691.

2. Ibid.
3. Ibid.

Chapter 18. Kandy Was Dandy

1. Thiry diary in her possession.
2. Letters (SEAC impressions) in possession of Virginia Webbert.
3. Foster, *Unamerican Lady*, 123–26.
4. McWilliams, letters in her possession. See also Fitch, *Appetite for Life*.
5. DuBois to Fahs, 22 Aug. 1944: NARA RG 226 Entry 1 Box 29 Folder 11; DuBois to Heppner: NARA RG 226 Entry 110 Box 51 Folder 510.
6. NARA RG 226 Entry 110 Box 52 Folder 16.
7. Hanson interview, 12 Mar. 1994.
8. Caldwell, *Secret War*; Taylor quoted in memo from Edwin Putzell to Colonel Roberts, OSS Washington Director's Office, 12 Sept. 1944.
9. Cannon interview, 2 Feb. 1995.
10. Roland Emblem of Meritorious Civilian Service, HQ SSO, APO 432, 5 Nov. 1945, signed Capt. Herbert J. Bluchell, chief, SI.
11. This and other McWilliams reports quoted from copies in her possession.
12. McWilliams citation in her possession.
13. DuBois to Fahs, 22 Aug. 1944: NARA

SEAC file Box 20.

14. MacDonald to author, 21 July 1989.
15. Foster, *Unamerican Lady*, 120.
16. Ibid., 160–62.

Chapter 19. Over the Hump to China

1. Thiry diary in her possession.
2. Report on China MO/Roland Dulin: NARA RG 226 Entry 110 Box 51 Folder 506; samples of MO material: NARA RG 226 Entry 139 Box 135 Folders 1815–17.
3. OSS unit commendation: General Orders No. 27, 1 Feb. 1946, Shanghai, China, by command of Lt. Gen. Albert Wedemeyer.
4. Rathbun diary in her possession.

Epilogue. Space-Age Spies

1. For a detailed account of this case, see Early, *Confessions of a Spy: The Real Story of Aldrich Ames.*
2. Procurement bulletin published by CIA Employment and Recruitment Center, P.O. Box 72727, Arlington, VA 22204.
3. Donovan's farewell address in Veterans of Strategic Services headquarters files, Rockefeller Center, New York. See also Dunlop, *Donovan, American Master Spy*, 473–74, and Ford, *Donovan of OSS*, 344.

Bibliography

Books

Aaron, David. *Crossing by Night.* New York: William Morrow, 1993.

Acheson, Dean. *The Struggle for a Free Europe.* New York: W. W. Norton, 1971.

Adleman, Robert, and George Walton. *The Champagne Campaign.* Boston: Little, Brown, 1969.

Alsop, Stewart, and Thomas Braden. *Sub Rosa: The OSS and American Espionage.* New York: Reynal and Hitchcock, 1946.

Bancroft, Mary. *Autobiography of a Spy.* New York: William Morrow, 1983.

Barzini, Luigi. *The Italians.* New York: Bantam/Atheneum, 1964.

Bennett, Ralph. *Ultra in the West.* New York: Charles Scribner's Sons, 1979.

Bondurant, Joan. *Conquest of Violence.* Princeton: Princeton University Press, 1988.

Brinkley, David. *Washington Goes to War.* New York: Alfred A. Knopf, 1988.

Brown, Anthony Cave. *Bodyguard of Lies.* New York: Harper and Row, 1975.

———. *The Last Hero: Wild Bill Donovan.* New York: Times Books, 1982.

Bruce, David. *OSS against the Reich: The World War II Diaries of Colonel David Bruce.* Edited by Nelson Langford. Kent, Ohio: Kent State University Press, 1991.

Brugioni, Dino A. *From Balloons to Blackbirds.* McLean, Va.: Association of Former Intelligence Officers, 1993.

Caldwell, Oliver. *A Secret War: American in China.* Carbondale: Southern Illinois University Press, 1972.

Casey, William J. *Scouting the Future: The Public Speeches of Casey.* Compiled by William R. Corson and Robert T. Crowley. Washington, D.C.: Regnery Gateway, 1989.

———. *The Secret War against Hitler.* Washington D.C.: Regnery Gateway, 1988.

Chalou, George C. *The Secrets War: The Office of Strategic Services in WWII.* Washington, D.C.: National Archives and Records Administration, 1992.

Churchill, Peter. *Missions secrètes en France.* Paris: Presses de la Cité, 1967.

CIA History Staff. *CORONA: America's First Satellite Program.* Washington, D.C.: Center for the Study of Intelligence, CIA, 1995.

Corson, William R., and Robert T. Crowley. *The New KGB, Engine of Soviet Power.* New York: William Morrow, 1985.

Cruickshank, Charles. *SOE in the Far East.* New York: Oxford University Press, 1983.

Davis, Kenneth S. *Experience of War.* Garden City, N.Y.: Doubleday, 1965.

Dawidoff, Nicholas. *The Catcher Was a Spy: The Mysterious Life of Moe Berg.* New York: Vintage Books, 1995.

Deschamps, Hélène. *Spyglass.* New York: Henry Holt, 1995.

Downes, Donald C. *The Scarlet Thread: Adventures in Wartime Espionage.* London: Derek Verschoyle, 1953.

Dulles, Allen, ed. *Great True Spy Stories.* Secaucus, N.J.: Castle, 1968.

————. *Operation Sunrise.* New York: Basic Books, 1979.

————. *The Secret Surrender.* New York: Harper and Row, 1966.

Dunlop, Richard. *Behind Japanese Lines with the OSS in Burma.* Chicago: Rand McNally, 1979.

————. *Donovan, American Master Spy.* Chicago: Rand McNally, 1982.

Early, Pete. *Confessions of a Spy: The Real Story of Aldrich Ames.* New York: Putnam, 1997.

Eisenhower, Dwight D. *Crusade in Europe.* Garden City, N.Y.: Doubleday, 1948.

Fabrizio, Calvi, and Olivier Schmidt. *OSS: La guerre secrète en France.* Paris: Hachette, 1990.

Fayol, Pierre. *Le Chambon-sur-Lignon sous l'occupation (1940–1944).* Paris: Edition L'Harmattan, 1990.

Fenn, Charles. *Ho Chi Minh.* New York: Scribner and Sons, 1973.

Fitch, Noel Riley. *Appetite for Life: The Biography of Julia Child.* Garden City, N.Y.: Doubleday, 1997.

Fleming, Peter. *Operation Sea Lion.* New York: Simon and Schuster, 1957.

Foot, M. R. D. *SOE in France.* London: HMSO, 1966.

Ford, Corey. *Donovan of OSS.* Boston: Little, Brown, 1970.

Foster, Jane. *An Unamerican Lady.* London: Sidgwick and Jackson, 1980.

Fussell, Paul. *In Wartime: Understanding and Behavior in the Second World War.* New York: Oxford University Press, 1989.

Gisevius, Hans. *To the Bitter End.* Boston: Houghton Mifflin, 1947.

Giskes, H. J. *London Calling North Pole.* London: William Kimber, 1953.

Grose, Peter. *Gentleman Spy: The Life of Allen Dulles.* Boston: Houghton Mifflin, 1994.

Hall, Roger. *You're Stepping on My Cloak and Dagger.* New York: W. W. Norton, 1957.

Hanson, Bernice. *From the Distaff Side.* Bethel, Conn.: Rutledge Books, 1996.

Henderson, W. *From China Burma India to the Kwai.* Leon Junction, Tex.: O&B Publishers, 1992.

Hochman, Sandra, with Sybil Wong. *Satellite Spies.* New York: Bobbs-Merrill, 1976.

Hoehling, A. A. *Women Who Spied.* New York: Dodd, Mead, 1967.

Hood, William. *The Mole.* New York: W. W. Norton, 1982.

Hunt, E. Howard. *Undercover: Memoirs of an American Secret Agent.* New York: Berkeley

Publishing Co., 1974.

Hutton, J. Bernard. *Women in Espionage*. New York: Macmillan, 1971.

Hyde, H. Montgomery. *Cynthia*. New York: Farrar Straus, 1965.

————. *Room 3603*. New York: Dell, 1964.

Hymoff, Edward. *The OSS in World War II*. New York: Ballantine Books, 1972.

Infield, Glenn B. *Skorzeny: Hitler's Commando*. New York: St. Martin's, 1981.

Irving, David. *The War between the Generals*. New York: Congdon and Lattes, 1981.

Kahn, David. *Seizing the Enigma*. Boston: Houghton Mifflin, 1991.

Katz, Barry M. *Foreign Intelligence: Research and Analysis in the Office of Strategic Services, 1942–1945*. Cambridge, Mass.: Harvard University Press, 1989.

Koke, Louise G. *Our Hotel in Bali*. Wellington, N.Z.: January Books, 1987.

Kramer, Rita. *Flames in the Field*. London: Michael Joseph, 1995.

Kurzman, Dan. *The Race for Rome*. New York: Pinnacle Books, 1977.

Kutler, Stanley I. *The American Inquisition: Justice and Injustice in the Cold War*. New York: Hill and Wang, 1982.

Legendre, Gertrude S. *The Sands Ceased to Run*. New York: William-Frederick, 1947.

Lewis, Flora. *Red Pawn: The Story of Noel Field*. Garden City, N.Y.: Doubleday, 1965.

Linebarger, Paul M. A. *Psychological War-*

fare. Washington, D.C.: Infantry Journal Press, 1948.

Lochner, Louis P., ed. and trans. *The Goebbels Diaries, 1942–1943.* New York: Garden City, N.Y.: Doubleday, 1948.

Lovell, Mary S. *Cast No Shadow.* New York: Random House, 1992.

MacDonald, Alexander. *Bangkok Editor.* New York: Macmillan, 1950.

MacDonald, Elizabeth P. *Undercover Girl.* New York: Macmillan, 1947. Reprint, Binghamton, N.Y.: Time Life Wartime Classics, 1995.

McIntosh, Elizabeth P. *The Role of Women in Intelligence.* McLean, Va.: Association of Former Intelligence Officers, 1989.

Maclean, Fitzroy. *Disputed Barricade.* London: Jonathan Cape, 1957.

Mangold, Tom. *Cold Warrior: James Jesus Angleton, the CIA's Master Spy Hunter.* New York: Simon and Schuster, 1991.

Mannes, Marya. *Out of My Times.* New York: Doubleday, 1971.

Martin, David C. *Wilderness of Mirrors.* New York: Harper and Row, 1980.

Mauch, Christof, and Jurgen Heideking. *American Intelligence and the German Resistance to Hitler.* Boulder, Colo.: Westview Press, 1996.

Melton, H. Keith. *The Ultimate Spy Book.* New York: DK Publishing Co., 1996.

Merrick, Gordon. *The Strumpet Wind.* New York: William Morrow, 1947.

Montagu, Ewen. *The Man Who Never Was*. New York: Bantam Books, 1953.

Morgan, William J. *The OSS and I*. New York: W. W. Norton, 1957.

Moseley, Leonard. *Dulles: A Biography of Eleanor, Allen, and John Foster Dulles and Their Family Network*. New York: Dial Press, 1978.

Moyzisch, L. C. *Operation Cicero*. New York: Coward-McCann, 1950.

Murrow, Edward R. *This Is London*. New York: Schocken Books, 1985.

Patti, Archimedes L. A. *Why Vietnam: Prelude to America's Albatross*. Berkeley: University of California Press, 1980.

Persico, Joseph E. *Piercing the Reich*. New York: Viking Press, 1978.

Philby, Eleanor. *Kim Philby, the Spy I Married*. New York: Ballantine Books, 1968.

Philby, Kim. *My Silent War*. New York: Ballantine Books, 1968.

Philips, David Atlee. *Secret War Diary*. Bethesda, Md.: Stone Trail Press, 1988.

―――. *The Night Watch*. New York: Atheneum, 1977.

Phillips, William. *Ventures in Diplomacy*. Boston: Beacon Publishing Co., 1953.

Powers, Thomas. *The Man Who Kept the Secrets*. New York: Alfred A. Knopf, 1979.

Ranelagh, John. *CIA: A History*. London: BBC Books, 1992.

Reischauer, Edwin O. *The United States and Japan*. Cambridge, Mass.: Harvard University Press, 1957.

Romanones, Aline, Countess of. *The Spy Wore Red.* New York: Random House, 1987.

Rositzke, Harry. *The CIA Secret Operations.* Boulder, Colo.: Westview Press, 1977.

Rossiter, Margaret L. *Women in the Resistance.* New York: Praeger Scientific, 1986.

Rubin, Barry. *Istanbul Intrigues.* New York: McGraw-Hill, 1989.

Sender, Toni. *The Autobiography of a German Rebel.* New York: Vanguard, 1940.

Shulman, Milton. *Defeat in the West.* New York: E. P. Dutton, 1948.

Singlaub, John K. *Hazardous Duty.* New York: Summit, 1991.

Smith, Bradley F. *Reaching Judgment at Nuremburg.* New York: Basic Books, 1977.

———. *The Shadow Warriors.* New York: Basic Books, 1988.

Smith, Bradley F., and Elena Agarossi. *Operation Sunrise: The Secret Surrender.* New York: Basic Books, 1979.

Smith, Laurence Dwight. *Cryptography.* London: George Allen and Unwin, 1944.

Smith, R. Harris. *OSS: The Secret History.* Berkeley: University of California Press, 1972.

Spencer, Otha C. *Flying the Hump.* College Station: Texas A&M University Press, 1992.

Spoto, Donald. *Blue Angel: The Life of Marlene Dietrich.* Garden City, N.Y.: Doubleday, 1992.

Stephenson, Jill. *The Nazi Organisation of*

Women. London: Croom Helm, 1981.

Steven, Roy Stewart. *Operation Splinter Factor.* Philadelphia: Lippincott, 1974.

Stevenson, William. *A Man Called Intrepid.* New York: Harcourt Brace Jovanovich, 1976.

Stuart, Gilbert, with Alan Levy. *Kind-Hearted Tiger.* Boston: Little, Brown, 1964.

Taylor, Edmond. *Awakening from History.* Boston: Gambit, 1969.

———. *Richer by Asia.* Boston: Houghton Mifflin, 1947.

Tompkins, Peter. *A Spy in Rome.* New York: Simon and Schuster, 1962.

Tuchman, Barbara. *Stilwell and the American Experience in China.* New York: Bantam Books, 1971.

U.S. War Department. *The Overseas Targets: War Report of the OSS.* Vols. 1 and 2. New York: Walker, 1976.

Wallach, Erica. *Light at Midnight.* Garden City, N.Y.: Doubleday, 1947.

Waller, John. *The Unseen War in Europe.* New York: Random House, 1996.

Wedemeyer, Albert C. *Wedemeyer Reports.* New York: Devin-Adair, 1958.

West, Nigel. *Secret War: The Story of SOE.* London: Hodder and Stoughton, 1992.

White, Lewis, ed. *On All Fronts: Czechs and Slovaks in World War II.* Boulder, Colo.: East European Monographs; distributed by Columbia University Press, 1991–95.

White, Theodore H., and Annalee Jacoby.

Thunder out of China. New York: William Sloane Associates, 1946.

Wilhelm, William, and Maria de Blasio. *The Other Italy.* New York: W. W. Norton, 1988.

Willets, Ann. *The Sting of Glory.* New York: Random House, 1954.

Willis, James F. *Prologue to Nuremburg.* Westport, Conn.: Greenwood Press, 1982.

Winks, Robin W. *Cloak and Gown.* New York: William Morrow, 1987.

Winterbotham, F. W. *The Ultra Secret.* London: Weidenfeld and Nicolson, 1974.

Wise, David, and Thomas B. Ross. *The Espionage Establishment.* New York: Random House, 1967.

Woodward, Bob. *Veil: The Secret Wars of the CIA, 1981–1987.* New York: Simon and Schuster, 1987.

Wright, Peter. *Spy Catcher.* New York: Viking Penguin 1987.

Yeager, Chuck, and Leo Janus. *Yeager: An Autobiography.* New York: Bantam Books, 1985.

Yu, Maochun. *OSS in China: Prelude to Cold War.* New Haven, Conn.: Yale University Press, 1996.

Articles

Cassini, Igor. "Charlie Knickerbocker" gossip column. *New York Journal American,* 10 Nov. 1942.

"Czech Heroine Decorated at West Point." *New York Herald Tribune*, 26 May 1946.

"Czechoslovak Girl Honored by Cadets." *New York Times*, 25 May 1946.

"Diplomacy: It's Donovan." *Newsweek*, 26 July 1954.

"Free Love Offered Nazis on Furlough." *Washington Post*, 10 Oct. 1944.

Hall, Virginia. "People Are Cold and Hungry." *New York Post*, 22 Jan. 1942.

———. "Reporter Finds Capital Crowded," *New York Post*, 4 Sept. 1941.

———. "Vichy Bars Jews." *New York Post*, 24 Nov. 1941.

Obituary of Mary Bancroft. *New York Times*, 19 Jan. 1997.

Obituary of William J. Donovan. *New York Times*, 10 Feb. 1959.

"Virginia Goillot of French Resistance Dies." *Baltimore Sun*, 13 Jan. 1982.

Archival Sources

Donovan, Gen. W. J. Papers. Manuscript Dept., U.S. Military History Institute, Carlisle, Pa.

Pack, Elizabeth. "Cynthia" papers and her diaries. Archives Center, Churchill College, Cambridge, England.

Yarrow, Bernard. Papers. Eisenhower Library, Abilene, Kans.

Amstutz, Millicent (Mrs. Robert Garrison). Letters in her possession, Indian Harbor Beach, Fla.

Coolidge, Joseph R. Papers on OSS/India/ Vietnam in his possession, Squam Lake, N.H.

Hall, Virginia. Papers in the possession of her niece, Lorna Lee Catling, Baltimore, Md.

Heppner, Richard P. Papers in the possession of the author.

Huntington, Ellery. Papers in the possession of his widow, Catherine DuBois Huntington, Alexandria, Va.

Jones, Geoffrey M. T. Report, "OSS Champagne Campaign." Copy sent to author, 12 Jan. 1996, of original in Veterans of Strategic Services headquarters files, Rockefeller Center, New York.

Keene, Katherine. Papers in her possession, Seattle, Wash.

McWilliams, Julia (Mrs. Paul Child). Letters and OSS reports in her possession, Cambridge, Mass.

Painter, Mary (Mrs. George Garin). Letters in the possession of her sister, Mrs. Charles Morse, Northfield, Minn.

Podoski, Barbara Lauwers. Sauerkraut papers (reproductions) in her possession, Washington, D.C.

Rathbun, Virginia (Mrs. E. H. Howard). Diaries and OSS reports in her possession, Providence, R.I.

Smith-Hutton, Jane. MO source material in her possession, Hendersonville, N.C.

Thiry, Eleanor (Mrs. Basil Sommers). Diary in her possession, Atlanta, Ga.

Webbert, Virginia. Memoirs and letters in her possession, Arlington, Va.

Interviews

Amstutz, Millicent (Mrs. Robert Garrison). Indian Harbor, Fla., 1 Feb. 1993.

Barnett, Patricia. Washington, D.C., 21 Jan. 1994.

Begg, Jeanne (Mrs. Harold H. Claggett Jr.). Washington, D.C., 12 May 1994.

Bell, Evangeline (Mrs. David Bruce). Washington, D.C., 23 Oct. 1993.

Bone, Nancy. CIA headquarters, Langley, Va., 24 Jan. 1997.

Boyle, Ann Gallagher. Alexandria, Va., 15 May 1993.

Bushnell, Louise. OSS symposium, Washington, D.C., 1990.

Cairns, Anne Mary (Mrs. William Ingraham). Alexandria, Va., 12 Mar. 1996.

Cannon, James W. Washington, D.C., 2 Feb. 1995.

Catling, Lorna Lee (Virginia Hall's niece). Baltimore, Md., 4 Aug. 1994.

Clark, Jane (Mrs. Eric Erickson). Warrenton, Va., 10 July 1990.

Colbert, Evelyn. Washington, D.C., 5 Apr. 1993.

Coolidge, Joseph R. Squam Lake, N.H., 12 Oct. 1996.

Corvo, Max. OSS assembly, Cambridge, Mass., 17 Oct. 1992.

Cuniberti, Julia. Washington, D.C., 3 May 1993.

Defourneaux, Rene Julian. CIA headquarters, Langley, Va., 27 Mar. 1996.

De Heller, Madeleine W. Warrenton, Va., 6 Feb. 1944.

Deschamps, Hélène, Washington, D.C., 18 July 1995.

Di Giacomo, Wanda. Kensington, Md., 20 June 1993.

Dodson, Cordelia (Mrs. William Hood). Silver Spring, Md., 16 Feb. 1993.

Donovan, David. Berryville, Va., 20 July 1995.

Donovan, Mary (Mrs. Max Corvo). Middletown, Conn., 1 Nov. 1992.

Douglas, Jean Wallace (Mrs. Leslie Douglas). Washington, D.C., 21 June 1993.

DuBois, Catherine (Mrs. Ellery Huntington). Alexandria, Va., 3 May 1994.

Dunlop, David. Interview regarding Kay Halle, Washington, D.C., 6 Feb. 1991.

Eilenberger, Dawn Renee. CIA headquarters, Langley, Va., 24 Jan. 1997.

Fowler, Patricia Warner. OSS assembly, Cambridge, Mass., 17 Oct. 1992.

Frame, Rosamond. Naples, Fla., Jan. 1950.

Glaser, Erica (Mrs. Robert Wallach). Warrenton, Va., 21 May 1994.

Goiran, Roger. Dunedin, Fla., 10 June 1993.

Greene, Agnes (Mrs. George Greene). Fort Meyers, Fla., 18 Mar. 1993.

Gulovich, Maria (Mrs. Hans Liu). OSS conference, Washington, D.C., 30 May 1993; OSS commemorative mission, Baňská Bystrica, Slovakia, 27 Aug. 1994.

Hannifin, Sue. Coco Beach, Fla., 10 Mar. 1993.

Hans, Barbara (Mrs. John Waller). McLean, Va., 1 May 1993.

Hanson, Bernice. Aldie, Va., 12 Mar. 1994.

Howe, Fisher. Washington, D.C., 24 Jan. 1995.

Karlo, Peter. OSS Donovan award dinner, Dallas, Tex., 5 Sept. 1993.

Larson, Florence. Alexandria, Va., 12 Feb. 1993.

Legendre, Gertrude. Goose Creek, S.C., 20 Apr. 1993.

Levenson, Marjorie. Bethesda, Md., 2 Nov. 1995.

Lussier, Betty. New York, 8 Mar. 1993.

McFadden, Thomas J. New York, 1947–80.

Mattison, Alma. Bethesda, Md., 4 June 1994.

Moore, Alice. Washington, D.C., 15 Jan. 1993.

Nelson, Irene. McLean, Va., 6 May 1993.

Orr, Irene Gurney. Mahopac, N.Y., 7 May 1994.

Page, Eloise Randolph. Washington, D.C., 13 Oct. 1993; CIA headquarters, Langley, Va., 28 Jan. 1997.

Patterson, Maureen. Hadley, Mass., 20 June 1995.

Peet, Knox. Utica, N.Y., 10 Jan. 1957.

Phillips, Beatrice (Mrs. Ellery Strauss). Washington, D.C., 6 Sept. 1994.

Podoski, Barbara Lauwers. Washington, D.C., 1992–97.

Pratt, Joyce. CIA headquarters, Langley, Va., 5 Mar. 1997.

Putzell, Edwin. Naples, Fla., 20 Mar. 1993.

Severyns, Marjorie (Mrs. Arthur Ravenholt). Bangkok, Thailand, 1 Nov. 1987.

Shek, Emily. New York, 4 Feb. 1993.

Sipe, Elizabeth (Mrs. David Morris). Sewickley, Pa., 19 May 1994.

Slatkin, Nora. McLean, Va., 27 Mar. 1997.

Smiley, Jane (Mrs. Parker Hart). Washington, D.C., 3 June 1993.

Smith-Hutton, Jane. Washington, D.C., 18 Oct. 1995.

Swantek, Elizabeth. Davis, W.Va., 19 Mar. 1996.

Symington, Mary Norris. Washington, D.C., 4 Aug. 1996.

Thomas, Ruth Ellen (Mrs. Matthew McCullough). Vero Beach, Fla., 27 Feb. 1993.

Tuckerman, Laura W. (Mrs. William G. Trieste). Annapolis, Md., 3 June 1995.

Vertefeuille, Jeanne. CIA headquarters, Langley, Va., 24 Jan. 1997.

Williams, Will. Leesburg, Va., 5 May 1994.

Yarrow, Sylvia Tim. New York, 11 July 1992.

Correspondence with Author

Baker, Russell. New York, 20 Mar. 1990.

Bland, Caroline Copeland. Southern Pines, N.C., 4 Aug. 1993.

Bondurant, Joan. Tucson, Ariz., 11 Aug. 1995.

Boyd, Ann Willets. Sewickley, Pa., 2 Jan. 1993.

Corsini, Aimee Russell. Grosseto, Italy, 8 June 1993.

Dodson, Cordelia (Mrs. William Hood). New Harbor, Me., 20 June 1993.

Gulovich, Maria (Mrs. Hans Liu). Oxnard, Calif., 1993–95.

Hornaday, William. Bonita Springs, Fla., 25 Mar. 1993.

Houston, Lawrence. Washington, D.C., 12 May 1994.

Keene, Katherine. Seattle, Wash., 13 Feb. 1993.

MacDonald, Alexander. Brewster, Mass., 21 July 1989.

MacPherson, Frances Perdita (Mrs. John Schaffner). East Hampton, N.Y., 6 Jan. 1994.

McWilliams, Julia (Mrs. Paul Child). Cambridge, Mass., 1996–97.

Moore, Dan (friend of Kay Halle). Washington,

D.C., 19 July 1991.

Patterson, Maureen. Hadley, Mass., 20 June 1993.

Sweeting, C. G. Clinton, Md., 4 July 1997.

Wallach, Robert J. Burke, Va., 12 Feb. 1994.

Weis, Elinore Grecey. Valley Stream, N.Y., 17 Aug. 1993.

Windmiller, Marshall. Alameda, Calif., 11 and 27 Jan. 1995.

Yeager, Charles (Chuck). Cedar Ridge, Calif., 22 Feb. 1996.

The employees of G.K. Hall hope you have enjoyed this Large Print book. All our Large Print titles are designed for easy reading, and all our books are made to last. Other G.K. Hall books are available at your library, through selected bookstores, or directly from us.

For information about titles, please call:

(800) 223-1244
(800) 223-6121

To share your comments, please write:

Publisher
G.K. Hall & Co.
P.O. Box 159
Thorndike, ME 04986